# TERTIARY LEVEL BIOLOGY

TERTIARY LEVEL BIOLOGY

# Avian Ecology

C. M. PERRINS, B.Sc., M.A., D. Phil.

Director
Edward Grey Institute of Field Ornithology
University of Oxford

T. R. BIRKHEAD, B.Sc., D.Phil.

Lecturer in Zoology
University of Sheffield

**Blackie**

Glasgow and London
Distributed in the USA by
Chapman and Hall
New York

Blackie & Son Limited
Bishopbriggs, Glasgow G64 2NZ

Furnival House, 14–18 High Holborn, London WC1V 6BX

Distributed in the USA by
Chapman and Hall
in association with Methuen, Inc.
733 Third Avenue, New York, N.Y. 10017

598.25
P42a
130242
nov. 1984

© 1983 Blackie & Son Ltd
First published 1983

**British Library Cataloguing in Publication Data**

Perrins, C. M.
 Avian ecology.—(Tertiary level biology)
 1. Birds—Ecology
 I. Title  II. Birkhead, T. R.
 III. Series
 598.2'5  QL673

 ISBN 0–216–91478–7
 ISBN 0–216–91477–9 Pbk

**Library of Congress Cataloging in Publication Data**

Perrins, Christopher M.
 Avian ecology.

 (Tertiary level biology)
 Includes index.
 1. Birds—Ecology. I. Birkhead, T. R.
 II. Title. III. Series.
 QL673.P46 1984   598.25   83–7875
 ISBN 0–412–00411–9 (Chapman and Hall)
 ISBN 0–412–00421–6 (Chapman and Hall: pbk.)

Filmset by Thomson Press (India) Limited, New Delhi,
and printed in Great Britain by Bell & Bain Ltd., Glasgow

# Preface

Somewhere in the region of fifty bird books a year are published in Britain alone. With such an embarrassment of riches, is there any need for another one? We feel that there is a gap at the level at which this book is aimed—that of the advanced undergraduate and the serious amateur wishing to know more about the ways of birds, and perhaps about the ways of professional ornithologists! There is a fairly substantial 'niche' between the popular bird books and the very detailed texts which cover specialized subjects. Moreover, there is a great deal of information in scientific journals which is not easily accessible to the average reader.

We have restricted our work to the ecology of birds for a number of reasons, not the least of which is that it is our own area of greatest knowledge. Many other aspects of birds, such as their general biology, are better treated in the literature, especially in comparison with other animal groups. Furthermore, to cover all aspects of the biology of birds would need a volume much larger than this. It still remains a problem to know what should be included and what should be left out. Almost all aspects of ecology are linked with other areas of biology. For example, breeding seasons run into hormonal and endocrinological aspects, and overlap with internal, circannual clocks. Similarly, many aspects of food and feeding are related to energetics and nutrition. It is difficult to separate the study of ecology from that of behaviour, and it has become more so in recent years, as many students of behaviour have directed their approach in terms of the fitness (i.e. the reproductive success and survival) of individual animals. Within the space available we have tried to present an overview of several important aspects of avian ecology and behaviour and we have included a bibliography which will allow particular points to be followed up in detail. A few general references are also given to fields beyond those covered here.

A number of people have helped us in the preparation of this book. We are especially grateful to our colleagues Drs N.B. Davies, E.K. Dunn and P. Boag for their constructive comments on the text. We also wish to thank Jayne Pellatt for preparing the figures, and Mary Perrins and Miss E. Gray for typing the manuscript.

C.M.P.<br>
T.R.B.

# Contents

# CHAPTER ONE

# INTRODUCTION

There are around 9 000 species of bird living in the world today, with a tremendous diversity of life-styles. They breed in regions ranging from the tropics to near the poles, and vary in size from humming-birds, weighing only a few grams, to the ostrich, weighing 90 kg. Our knowledge of the biology of birds exceeds that of all other groups of vertebrates. This is because, compared with other vertebrates, birds are relatively easy to study. Most are diurnal and can be readily observed. Moreover, the study of birds has not been confined to professional biologists. Much of our current knowledge has come from studies of amateurs. In the past, those who collected birds and their eggs provided a foundation for modern knowledge. In recent years, the detailed observations and ringing (banding) studies made by amateurs have greatly increased our understanding of bird biology.

More important than our knowledge of birds themselves is the fact that many fundamental biological principles and theories have resulted from studies of birds. This is true in a wide range of fields. For example, research on birds played a central role in the isolation and structure of prolactin (Riddle and Bates, 1939), while Darwin's studies of the Galapagos finches played an integral role in the development of his ideas about natural selection. More recently, contributions made by the study of birds in the areas of behaviour and ecology have been striking, such as in the evolution and function of animal signals (Huxley, Lorenz and Tinbergen), and the evolution of reproductive rates (Lack).

Our aim here is to present a synthesis of some of the major aspects of bird ecology and behaviour. In writing this book we have adopted an evolutionary approach—that is, we have discussed the various aspects of bird biology in terms of their function or adaptive significance (see

1

section 1.2). We have provided an outline of some of the major theoretical aspects of ecology and behaviour, together with appropriate examples. In recent years, there has been an increase in the use of mathematical models in ecology. These can sometimes appear daunting, especially to the non-mathematician, but they are important in that they help to provide a theoretical framework within which field and laboratory observations can be assembled. Where we have presented models (e.g. in Chapters 4 and 8), we have done so in such a way that they require virtually no mathematical knowledge.

The book is arranged as follows. The first two chapters are concerned with several aspects of bird behaviour, and provide a background to subsequent chapters. In Chapter 2 we consider two types of behaviour which are closely linked with ecology, territoriality and coloniality. Chapter 3 then examines behavioural aspects of breeding: mating systems, brood parasitism and co-operative breeding. Chapters 4 and 5 cover the ecology of reproduction, the timing of breeding, and reproductive rates. Chapter 6 follows on from this subject by looking at how reproductive rates, together with mortality rates, determine the way in which bird numbers are regulated. Ecological interactions between bird species, and species-specific differences in feeding ecology are considered in Chapter 7. Chapter 8 then examines individual differences in foraging behaviour. In the final chapter, migration is considered from an ecological and evolutionary standpoint.

Since our overall approach is an evolutionary one, the rest of this chapter considers the way in which natural selection has operated on the life-styles of birds, and the techniques which have been used to study the evolutionary aspects of their ecology and behaviour.

## 1.1  Natural selection

The lives of all animals have been shaped by natural selection. Indeed, a suitable definition of 'ecology' would be 'evolution in action'. In adopting an evolutionary approach, we must bear in mind that some basic features of birds, which first evolved some 150 million years ago, have restricted what natural selection has been able to act upon. The enormous energetic and aerodynamic demands of flight impose many restrictions on design. Birds could not fly as well as they do if they had lungs like mammals. The design of the avian lung enables birds to achieve a remarkably efficient uptake of oxygen and loss of carbon dioxide. One of the differences between bird and mammal lungs is that in birds the alveoli are very much smaller than in mammals, and, if they become collapsed, they cannot be reflated. It has been suggested that this, seemingly small, structural feature is of fundamental importance not only in avian respiration, but has also prevented birds from giving birth to live young. In birds the act of giving birth would irreversibly compress the structure of the young bird's lung, whereas the lung of the young mammal can be collapsed and reflated during birth (Duncker, 1978). If this is true, then most of the features of avian reproduction (such as their nesting habits, their nests, their eggs) have evolved because of one small but invaluable respiratory adaptation.

Animals can seldom become perfectly designed for a particular task, because several, conflicting evolutionary demands usually operate simultaneously. The outcome is an evolutionary compromise. For example, the females of many birds are less brightly coloured than the males. It has been suggested that dull coloration is advantageous because it makes birds less visible and therefore less vulnerable to predators. If this is so, then why are males not also dull-coloured? Presumably the answer is that males have to compete with other males for mates, and a dull-coloured male might be less able to attract a mate (see chapter 3). In other words, predation favours dull plumage, whereas mate attraction favours bright plumage. This argument is supported by the situation in ducks. In many species of duck, males acquire a dull, 'eclipse' plumage and resemble females during the time that they are moulting. At this time they are flightless and especially vulnerable to predators. Since they are not competing for mates while moulting, males do not require their bright colours, and a dull plumage provides safety from predators. This strategy appears to be a very sound one, but it carries a cost, since the birds have to undergo an extra moult and must therefore find the extra food to grow two sets of feathers each year. Natural selection does not favour individuals which use energy unnecessarily, and so the benefits of moulting twice a year must exceed the costs.

Such evolutionary compromises need not be morphological: they may just as easily be behavioural. The spacing of nests within a colony of gulls or terns provides a good example. An advantage of close neighbours is that birds from adjacent nests can join together to mob predators, such as crows and foxes, and by their combined efforts can often drive them away. However, some species of gulls are cannibalistic and will eat their neighbour's eggs or chicks. From that point of view, it is important for each pair of gulls to keep their neighbours at a distance. The gulls are therefore faced with a 'decision' about the optimum distance between adjacent nests. Natural selection will favour a compromise distance at which the greatest breeding success is achieved.

Discussions about adaptations or evolutionary advantages tend to degenerate into rather anthropomorphic language. For example, we talk about 'reproductive strategies', or about birds having to make 'decisions' about the spacing of nests. It is important to stress that such terms do not imply any conscious thought process by animals, and simply represent a straightforward way of saying that 'natural selection has, over the course of time, favoured individuals with a certain set of breeding characteristics, at the expense of individuals with different characteristics'. It is clearly simpler to refer to the latter as 'reproductive strategies', provided that it is understood to be a form of shorthand. Evolutionary discussions also carry the assumption that characteristics are inherited and can therefore be acted upon by natural selection. In only a few cases is this actually known (see Chapter 5).

## 1.2   The extent of knowledge

The types of knowledge that can be gained about ecology, behaviour and, indeed, all biology, can be divided into three types: the 'whats', the 'hows' and the 'whys'. An example will make the distinction clearer. We know the breeding seasons of many species of birds in some detail. We know *what* they are. We know rather less about *why* birds time their breeding as they do, although we can make some guesses as to the reasons for these timings—selective forces favouring those birds which breed at the best time have led to the breeding seasons which we observe today. We know very little about *how* the birds respond to the environment in such a way as to get their timing right.

It is important to understand the difference between 'how' and 'why' questions about biological phenomena. It is also important to see how these types of question are related to *causation* and *function*, and to *proximate* and *ultimate* factors, terms which occur frequently in the literature. Continuing the breeding season example, we can see how these terms are used:

*How* do birds time their breeding? The answer is that certain endocrine and physiological processes are the *causal* mechanisms, i.e. they cause the bird to breed at a certain time, stimulated by *proximate* factors, such as daylength.
*Why* do birds breed at specific times? The *function* of breeding at a particular time is that it results in the maximum production of young. The best time to breed is determined by *ultimate* factors, such as food availability for the young.

In this book we are concerned primarily with functional questions about the ecology and behaviour of birds. We are interested in the adaptive significance of particular features of their biology, rather than the underlying causes, which are normally the prerogative of physiologists. How do we determine the adaptive significance of features like breeding seasons, or clutch-size? The standard scientific approach is to observe the situation, formulate some hypotheses, make some predictions, and test those predictions by observations or experiment.

Experimentation is generally regarded as the most convincing way of testing predictions. Unfortunately, many ecological problems cannot be tested by experiment. For example, many species of sea-bird spend several years as immatures before they start to breed. One explanation for such deferred maturity is that their feeding skills take several years to develop and, as a result, any breeding attempt made before they can feed efficiently would be relatively unsuccessful. Moreover, by breeding at too young an age the birds may endanger their own lives. This is an interesting suggestion, but how does one test it? It may not be possible to experimentally induce a bird which normally breeds at five years old to start breeding at three. Biological ideas like this can, however, be tested using another method, referred to as the comparative approach.

Use of the comparative approach is like looking at the results of a long-term experiment done by natural selection over evolutionary time, and involves examining a group of species (or individuals, or families), to see if differences in their biology are correlated with differences in their ecology. The comparative approach is a powerful way of studying adaptation, as the following example shows. Some species of penguins and some albatrosses feed their young on krill, while others feed their young on squid. In both groups of birds the young of those fed on squid grow more slowly and take more years to reach maturity than those fed on krill. Are the differences in growth and maturity related to their diet? It is certainly odd that the same feature should occur in two quite unrelated groups of birds, but can one make more of it than that? As it happens, in this case the conclusions reached by the comparative approach have been verified by experiment. By switching the young of krill- and squid-eating albatrosses it has been shown that the growth rates of the young are related to their diet (Prince and Ricketts, 1981). The combination of all the evidence makes this seem a fairly convincing explanation.

The comparative approach does, however, have some limitations. The first concerns the inter-relationship between ecology and adaptation. It is quite possible that an albatross which feeds on squid will have evolved a different digestive system from one that eats krill. In other words the growth rate of a species may be genetically 'programmed' to match its diet.

If this was true, then in the example used above, the comparative observations would be unaffected, but the results of the chick-switching experiment would have been different.

Another problem with the comparative approach is that it is relatively easy to think up 'post hoc' adaptive explanations for differences between species. As Krebs and Davis (1981) point out, 'Many adaptive "explanations" are more a reflection of an observer's ingenuity rather than a description of what is going on in nature'. Clearly these limitations must be taken into account when employing the comparative method for testing predictions.

In the following chapters we have used examples which rely on both the experimental and comparative approach to test ideas about ecological and behavioural adaptions in birds.

CHAPTER TWO

# SOCIAL SYSTEMS: TERRITORIALITY AND COLONIALITY

## 2.1 Introduction

The diversity in dispersion pattern among birds is remarkable. Consider the Common Guillemot (Common Murre) which breeds in vast colonies of up to several hundred thousand, each pair defending a breeding area of only a few square centimetres, while other species, such as the Golden Eagle, occupy individual territories of up to ninety square kilometres! Why do some birds, such as the Grey Heron, breed in large, conspicuous

(a)

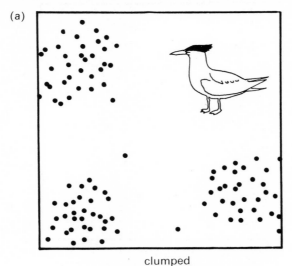

clumped
e.g. royal tern (Buckley and Buckley, 1977)

**Figure 2.1**  (For legend see over)

(b)

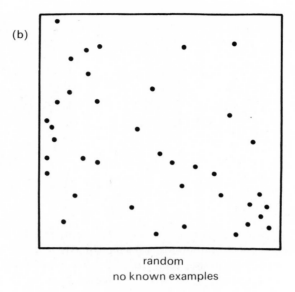

random
no known examples

(c)

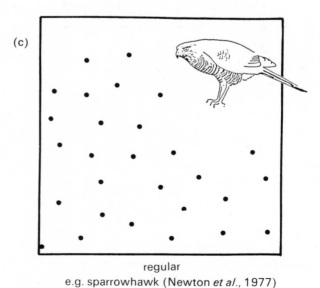

regular
e.g. sparrowhawk (Newton *et al.*, 1977)

**Figure 2.1**   Three main types of spatial distribution: birds may space themselves or their nests in a (*a*) clumped, (*b*) random or (*c*) regular manner.

**Figure 2.2** View of part of a King Penguin colony on Crozet Island, Antarctica, showing the remarkably regular spacing between nests. (Photograph, M.P. Harris).

colonies, while their close relatives, the bitterns, nest solitarily in dense cover? The aim of this chapter is to examine the main types of dispersion patterns shown by birds, and to look at the factors determining why species defend territories of different sizes, and why some birds breed alone and others as part of a colony.

We can recognize three main types of spatial distribution: birds may space themselves or their nests in a regular, random or clumped manner (Fig. 2.1). We will refer to clumped spacing as coloniality, and a regular distribution indicates territoriality, although the scale on which we record spacing is important since many species are both colonial and territorial. For example, the King Penguin shows a highly clumped breeding distribution, with a total of less than 50 known colonies, but pairs within each colony defend territories, which gives rise to a remarkably regular spacing pattern (Fig. 2.2).

## 2.2 Territoriality

'Territory' has been defined in a number of different ways; as 'any defended area' (Noble, 1939), and as 'an exclusive area' (Schoener, 1968). In an extensive review of territorial behaviour, Davies (1978) defined the term more loosely, suggesting that individuals or groups can be classed as territorial whenever they are 'spaced out more than would be expected from a random occupation of suitable habitats' (see Fig. 2.1c).

The vast majority of bird species are probably territorial to some extent, and because of the conspicuousness and widespread nature of territorial behaviour it is one of the most extensively studied aspects of bird biology. Territoriality is therefore an enormous subject, but we can divide it into three main categories: (i) the evolution and functions of territoriality (2.2.1); (ii) the mechanism of territory maintenance—how spacing is maintained (2.2.2); and (iii) the consequences of territoriality for populations (2.2.3).

As we have already said, territory size and type varies enormously between bird species, but six major types of territory have been recognized; these are described in Table 2.1. Here we will be concerned primarily with types A and C.

### 2.2.1   *The evolution and functions of territoriality*

When we talk about the evolution of territorial behaviour we are interested in the effect which territoriality has on the owner's survival and reproductive output. If owning a territory confers some overall advantage, then such individuals will tend to leave more offspring than those which do not defend territories.

A regular spacing pattern (Fig. 2.1c) implies that individuals or groups are defending space, and usually the space contains some resource(s) necessary for either successful breeding or survival. If all resources were superabundant then there would be little point in birds defending them. This means that *competition* for scarce resources is a crucial factor in the evolution of territoriality. The benefit of territoriality is that it results in owners having either more of a particular resource, or better quality resource, than they would otherwise have. The main resources which birds may defend in territories include food (type A territories; Table 2.1), breeding sites (type C) and mates (type D). In some species the resource could be space itself, since an increased distance between neighbours may reduce interference, cannibalism, or predation.

Although we have referred to the potential benefits of territoriality, we should bear in mind that there are also costs to territorial defence. Threatening and fighting intruders is time-consuming, energetically expensive and involves the risk of injury or even death. Clearly, there must be

**Table 2.1**   A functional classification of avian territories (based on Hinde, 1956).

| | |
|---|---|
| **Type A** | A large defended area within which all activities, such as roosting, courtship, mating, nesting and feeding occur. This is the classic 'all -purpose' territory which is especially frequent among song-birds like the European Blackbird (Snow, 1958), American Robin, and many corvids (crows, jays etc.). This type of territory may be occupied by a pair or a group of birds (e.g. Florida Scrub Jay—see Chapter 3). The importance of food in such territories is illustrated by the marked relationship between territory size and bird size: this is exactly what we would expect if food was an important determinant of territory size, since larger birds need more food in absolute terms (see Fig. 2.4). |
| **Type B** | A large defended area within which all breeding activities occur but which is not the primary source of food. This is a relatively rare type of territory, found in the European Nightjar and Reed Warbler. |
| **Type C** | A small defended area around the nest. Some hole nesting and many colonial species utilize this restricted form of territory. Examples: Starling, Pied Flycatcher, Tree Swallow, most sea-birds, herons, ibises, flamingos and some weaver finches. |
| **Type D** | A small defended pairing or mating territory. Examples include those on leks, of species like Ruffed Grouse, Black Grouse, Ruff. |
| **Type E** | Defended roosting positions and shelters. Many socially roosting birds defend sleeping positions, e.g. starlings and feral pigeons. |
| **Type F** | Non-breeding territories. Some species defend feeding areas either in winter or during the breeding season away from the breeding area. Gulls may defend areas of shore-line for just a few hours while they forage there, both outside and during the breeding season. Permanent winter feeding territories occur in some shrikes, the Pied Wagtail and European Robin. |

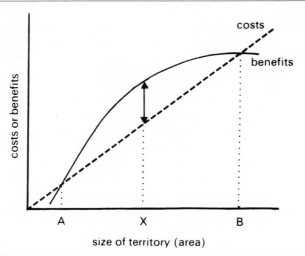

**Figure 2.3**   Brown's (1969) economic defendability model. As territory size increases, both the costs and benefits increase. The benefits (e.g. amount of food) increase initially but then level off once it exceeds the bird's needs. The costs (e.g. energetic) would continue to increase. The territory should only be defended between *A* and *B* and the optimum territory size is at *X* where the difference between the costs and benefits is greatest. (From Davies, 1978).

some sort of balance between the costs and benefits of territory defence, and we would therefore expect birds to defend territories only when the benefits exceed the costs, that is when it is worthwhile either in terms of survival or reproduction. The idea of 'economic defendability', proposed by Brown (1964), is summarized in Fig. 2.3, and this provides us with a theoretical framework, within which we can examine how territoriality affects fitness. There are two ways we can do this (Davies, 1978); we can either adopt a comparative approach and look at spacing behaviour in different species living under different ecological conditions, or we can compare some measure of fitness for individuals of the same species behaving in different ways (e.g. defending large versus small territories).

The comparative approach was pioneered by Crook (1965) in his study of weaverbirds (Ploceidae), where it was found that among species whose food sources (insects) were predictable in space and time, birds spaced out to breed and defended all-purpose, type A territories. In contrast, seed-eating weaverbirds, whose food supply has a patchy and unpredictable distribution, defended very small areas around their nest (type C territories) and bred in colonies. Crook's approach was extended by Lack (1968), who found the same trends in other families of birds.

In another comparative study, Schoener (1968) considered birds defending type A territories, and found that territory size was directly proportional to the bird's body weight; larger species defended larger areas (Fig. 2.4). A positive correlation between territory size and body weight (for species with similar diets) is exactly what we would expect if type A territories had evolved as a means of defending food sources, since large birds need more food than small ones.

The second type of approach, comparing individuals of the same species doing different things, also provides evidence to support this idea. It has been shown, for example, that in oven-birds, territory size is related to food abundance, and that when food abundance is high territory size is reduced (Stenger, 1958). This type of approach has been taken even further by trying to estimate the costs and benefits of territory defence in energetic terms, and the next section describes some of these studies.

(a)  *Territoriality and food.* Brown's  economic  defendability  model, shown in Fig. 2.3, predicts that the optimal territory size occurs where the difference between the costs and benefits is greatest ($X$ in Fig. 2.3). For no species have the shapes of the cost and benefit curves been worked out, but the general idea has been tested in terms of food resources and energy for several species. The testing of Brown's ideas has progressed in a number of

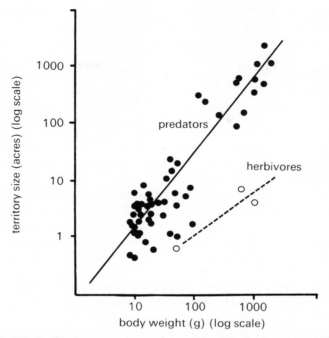

**Figure 2.4**  Relationship between mean territory size and body size among birds. Each point represents a different species. Note that a different relationship exists for predators and herbivores. (From Schoener, 1968).

stages, and the first stage has been to demonstrate that territories are, in fact, economically defendable. This has been done for some very different bird species, by comparing the energy *expended* each day by territorial birds with the metabolizable energy *intake* per day. If territories are economically defendable, then the energy available to the bird in its territory should not be less than the energy it expends in territory defence.

Golden-winged Sunbirds are the African equivalent of humming-birds; they defend individual territories outside the breeding season and feed mainly on nectar in *Leonotis* flowers. Gill and Wolf (1975) found that, because sunbirds chased off other sunbirds which might feed on nectar in their territory, territory owners had exclusive use of the *Leonotis* flowers, which resulted in much higher nectar levels than in undefended areas. The energy expended in maintaining a territory and the energy gained from the territory were estimated by (i) recording how much time the birds spent each day in activities such as sitting, foraging and territory defence, (ii) conducting laboratory experiments to calculate the energetic cost (in calories/hour) of each activity, and (iii) measuring the energy available in nectar. It was found that when individual flowers contained only 1 $\mu$l of nectar birds would take about eight hours per day to obtain their energy requirements. With 2 $\mu$l/flower they would take 4h/day, and with 3 $\mu$l/flower a bird need spend only 2.7h/day foraging. Territory defence ensured that no other sunbird took nectar, and if defence increased the average nectar level from 2 $\mu$l to 3 $\mu$l/flower, the bird would save 1.3h/day foraging time, an energetic saving of 780 calories/day. We must compare this with the energetic cost of territorial defence, which works out to be 728 calories/day. In other words, by defending a territory, sunbirds make a small net energetic profit each day.

Davies (1980) made similar calculations for a small insectivorous bird, the Pied Wagtail, and found that, although this species had very different time-budgets and diet, the balance between energy intake and expenditure each day was very similar to that in Golden-winged Sunbirds.

These studies represent some of the first to make any measurements of the costs and benefits of territoriality. Estimating energy expenditure is extremely difficult and these authors admit that their figures are rather crude. Given the problems inherent in such studies, the agreement between intake and expenditure is remarkably good, and the results indicate (1) that territories *are* economically defendable, and (2) that outside the breeding season, birds defend territories of such a size that they break even energetically. If birds defended areas larger than they actually needed at this time, then they would incur additional defence costs for no extra benefit. However, in the breeding season they will often have to defend areas larger than they themselves need so that there is sufficient food available to cover the additional energetic costs of breeding (i.e. the additional food needed for egg formation and for feeding a brood of growing young: see Chapter 5).

The second stage in these studies was to predict the range of resource levels over which territory defence would be worthwhile. At one extreme, if resources are very scarce, competition for them may be so intense that the costs of territory defence may exceed the benefits. At the other extreme, if resources are superabundant, a territory owner may gain relatively little from territory defence. In their sunbird study, Gill and Wolf (1975) calculated that if nectar levels were generally high, and territory defence increased nectar levels from 4 $\mu$l to 6 $\mu$l/flower, this would result in a saving of only half an hour's foraging time a day, whereas earlier we said that an increase from 1 $\mu$l to 2 $\mu$l/flower would save 4 hours foraging per day.

Therefore, when nectar levels are generally high, the costs of territory defence exceed the benefits.

Probably the most useful development in this whole approach to territoriality has been to predict the optimal amount of resource which an individual should defend, rather than simply the size of territory. In Golden-winged Sunbirds, territory size varied 300-fold, whereas the number of *Leonotis* flowers that were defended was approximately the same, 1600, in each territory. Pyke (1979) used Gill and Wolf's data to determine why sunbirds defended 1600 flowers, and not more or less, and constructed a model to see which of the following options sunbirds satisfied by defending 1600 flowers:

(i) Maximizing the daily net energy gain (equivalent to point $X$ in Fig. 2.3).
(ii) Maximizing the time spent resting.
(iii) Minimizing the daily energy expenditure (equivalent to point $A$ in Fig. 2.3).
(iv) Maximizing the ratio of gain to expenditure.

Pyke's calculations showed that, of these alternatives, (iii), minimizing the costs, predicted both the number of flowers defended *and* the type of energy budget, which most closely agreed with what the birds actually did.

(b) *Territories and mates.* Birds of some species defend territories only during the breeding season in order to acquire mates. The idea of economic defendability has been applied to the acquisition of mates and, just as with food resources, the spatial and temporal distribution of mates determines whether these can be defended economically. Territoriality and mating systems are discussed in the next chapter (3.3).

(c) *Territory and breeding sites.* For most birds which occupy type C territories (Table 2.1), territory is synonymous with breeding site. The tiny breeding sites of some colonial seabirds may differ in their quality, either in terms of their physical characteristics, or their position in the colony relative to other birds, but they are still defended in a way similar to that of larger territories.

Male shags compete vigorously for breeding sites and the best ones are those on broad ledges, protected from high seas and rain but with direct access to the sea. A long-term study with individually marked birds showed that nest-site quality accounted for more than 80% of the variation in breeding success between pairs (Table 2.2). This was clearly demonstrated by a natural 'experiment' in which a 'red tide' (a bloom of dinoflagellates which produce a toxic substance) killed off a substantial number of shags. After this reduction in population density some shags were able to move to

**Table 2.2** The effect of territory location and quality
on survival and reproductive success.

(a) Territory/nest site location: kittiwake (from Coulson,
1968).

|  | Location | |
|---|---|---|
|  | Centre | Edge of colony |
| Adult male annual survival | 88.4% | 81.4% |
| Young fledged/pair | 1.48 | 1.32 |

(b) Territory/nest site quality: shags (from Potts *et al.*,
1980)

|  | Territory/Nest site quality | | | | |
|---|---|---|---|---|---|
|  | Poor | | | | Good* |
|  | 0 | 1 | 2 | 3 | 4 |
| Mean number of chicks fledged/pair | 0.61 | 0.69 | 1.03 | 1.03 | 1.55 |

* Nest site quality was assessed independently of breeding
success.
*Note*: in both these examples territories are Type C, and
are therefore equivalent to nest sites.

better sites, because the owners had died, thereby increasing their own
breeding success (Potts *et al.*, 1980).

The position in a colony may also be important; Kittiwakes with
centrally located territories produced more offspring and lived longer than
those at the edge of the colony (Table 2.2).

(d) *Interspecific territoriality.* As we pointed out earlier, competition for
resources has been an important factor in the evolution of territorial
behaviour, and because their requirements are so similar most competition
occurs between members of the same species. However, some birds also
defend their territories against other species. The most likely explanation is
that territory owners exclude individuals of other species which are
sufficiently similar ecologically to themselves that they are likely to
compete with them for resources.

Interspecific territoriality has been clearly demonstrated in an experimental field study of Great Tits and Chaffinches, species in separate
families but ecologically similar in feeding areas and feeding methods.
Reed (1982) compared the distribution of Great Tit and Chaffinch

territories in two areas, one on the mainland of Scotland and the other 9 km away on the island of Eigg. On the mainland the territories of the two species showed considerable overlap, while on the island there was no overlap and the two species behaved aggressively towards each other. To determine whether the spacing of territories on the island was due to interspecific aggression two experiments were conducted. In the first, the responses of each species to tape-recordings of the song of the other and its own species were recorded. On the mainland both species responded aggressively only to conspecific song, whereas on the island both species responded aggressively to the songs of their own *and* the other species. The second experiment showed that when Chaffinches were removed from part of the island, the Great Tits expanded their territories and moved into the areas from which the Chaffinches had been removed. This suggests that before they were removed the Chaffinches had excluded Great Tits from some areas. These two experiments clearly showed the existence of interspecific territoriality between Great Tits and Chaffinches in the island environment. The reason for interspecific territoriality on the island and not on the mainland is probably because islands tend to be ecologically simpler than adjacent areas of mainland of similar size (see Chapter 7). Consequently when two ecologically similar species like the Great Tit and Chaffinch occur in the same area, one of them (usually the larger one—in this case the Chaffinch), excludes the other from certain habitats.

Interspecific territoriality may also occur between birds and other animals; for example, both humming-birds and several species of insect (e.g. bees and butterflies) feed on nectar, and both types of animal have been recorded evicting the other from their respective territories (Primack and Howe, 1975; Boyden, 1978).

(e) *Non-breeding territories.* Relatively few species defend individual winter feeding territories. The European Robin and Pied Wagtail may maintain such territories throughout the winter in Britain. Similarly, some sunbirds also defend territories outside the breeding season. In fact, the studies described in section (a) above were conducted in just such territories, mainly because the situation in non-breeding territories is relatively simple compared with breeding territories. This is because non-breeding territories are occupied usually by only a single bird, and since the territory is defended solely for this individual's benefit, the complications of additional food requirements necessary for breeding are avoided.

Some species defend territories for just a few days while on migration. The Pied Flycatcher provides a particularly good example of this type of territoriality. During the breeding season Pied Flycatchers defend only their nest-hole (type C territory, Table 2.1), but while on migration may defend a feeding territory (type F, Table 2.1). Bibby and Green (1980) found that Scandinavian Pied Flycatchers en route to Africa made a 1–9 day stop-over in Portugal where they maintained feeding territories against other Pied Flycatchers. These territories were maintained only until the birds had accumulated sufficient reserves to make a non-stop flight across the Sahara Desert (see also Chapter 9).

### 2.2.2.  *How is spacing maintained?*

Everything we have said about territoriality so far has been concerned with the function of territorial behaviour. We will conclude this section by saying something about the way in which spacing arises and is maintained.

Most of the social signals which birds use are visual and/or auditory, and their function is either the attraction of partners or the defence of resources. It is thought that most birds use a multi-tier territory defence system, with long range, intermediate and short-range signals. Among passerines the most frequent long-range signals are auditory, i.e. songs and calls. In non-passerines and birds which live in open areas, long-range signals are often visual. Not surprisingly, a few species combine visual and auditory signals, as in the Skylark, which performs a song flight to advertise territory ownership. Among passerines, intermediate-range signals may consist of chasing and attack.

In some cases the specific signals which birds use to defend their territories have been identified experimentally. Red-winged Blackbirds, for example, use song and a visual display which emphasizes their red shoulder patches, to deter territory intruders. Red-winged Blackbirds which have been muted (by cutting the nerves supplying the syrinx) were less successful in maintaining their territory than were sham-operated control birds. In a separate experiment, birds which had had their red epaulets painted black were also less efficient in territory defence than control birds (Peek, 1972). Thus, in this species, both vocal and visual signals were important in territory defence.

This type of experimental approach was taken one stage further by Krebs (1977); he removed Great Tits from their territories and replaced them with loudspeakers broadcasting Great Tit song. Intruding Great Tits took longer to occupy these territories than others in which no sound or a control sound was broadcast. In Peek's experiment with Red-winged Blackbirds it was impossible to tell whether song or other calls were

**Figure 2.5**  Sandwich Terns (standing) around plaster models of terns (sitting) (see text, section 2.2.2). (Photograph, J. Veen).

important in territory defence, but in Krebs' experiment it was clear that song was the territorial signal.

In colonial species, spacing results from two opposing factors; mutual attraction and mutual repulsion. The spacing we observe is a compromise between these two factors, and Veen's (1977) study of Sandwich Terns provides a nice example of how spacing comes about. Sandwich Terns show a high degree of mutual attraction and breed colonially, but within a colony aggression (mutual repulsion) spaces the birds out. When Veen placed plaster models of terns on a sandy beach early in the season, terns were attracted to them and formed a colony among them (Fig. 2.5). However, the terns tended to breed much closer (28.3 cm on average) to the plaster models than they did to real terns (38.4 cm) because the models could not behave aggressively, and so mutual repulsion was minimal (Fig. 2.6).

Considering all types of territories (Table 2.1), owners are usually dominant over and able to evict all conspecific intruders. This is probably because owners have already invested a considerable amount of time and effort in territory maintenance, consequently have more to lose than an

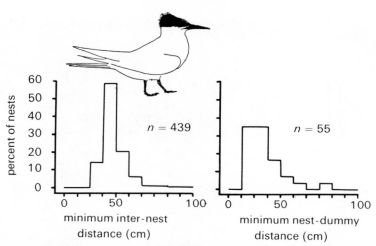

**Figure 2.6** Distribution of distances between (*a*) Sandwich Tern nests and other Sandwich Tern nests, mean value = 38.42 cm; (*b*) Sandwich Tern nests and plaster models of Sandwich Terns; mean value = 28.27 cm ($t = 12.17$, $P \leq 0.01$). (From Veen, 1977).

intruder, and may therefore be prepared to fight harder to hold onto their territory.

Among monogamous bird species occupying type A territories, defence is carried out mainly by the male. In type C territories, both members of the pair participate more evenly in defence. Among co-operatively breeding species (see Chapter 3), all group members may help in territory defence.

### 2.2.3.   *Consequences of territoriality for populations*

Huxley (1934) likened birds' territories to rubber discs: as population density increased the discs were compressed, up to a point beyond which they could not be compressed further. In real terms this means that as the density of a population increases territory size gets smaller, but there is a minimum size, beyond which a territory would be too small to support a bird (see Fig. 6.7). Numerous studies have shown that if birds are removed from their territory, their places are filled by conspecifics, often within a matter of hours (e.g. Orians, 1961; Harris, 1970; Krebs, 1971), suggesting that potential settlers had been excluded by the territorial individuals. This indicates that territorial behaviour may indeed limit population density.

In Chapter 6 we discuss how population density is regulated, and one theory, postulated by Wynne-Edwards (1962) is that density is regulated by

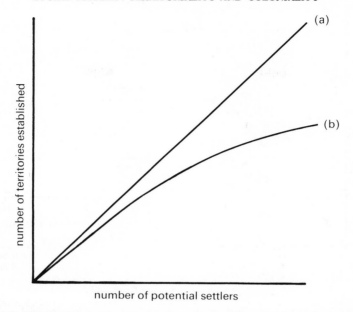

**Figure 2.7**  Relationship between the number of potential settlers in territories and the number of territories established, (*a*) where no birds are excluded, and (*b*) where the total number of territories is limited and some birds are excluded. (From Davies, 1978).

social behaviour such as territoriality. However, Wynne-Edwards suggested that the *function* of territorial behaviour was to regulate population density, whereas in fact all the available evidence suggests that any effect which territorial behaviour might have on population density is merely a *consequence*. The reasons why Wynne-Edwards' view is incorrect are discussed in section 6.3.4.

Figure 2.7 shows two consequences of territorial behaviour; in (*a*) all potential settlers obtain territories, while in (*b*) there is a minimum territory size and so some individuals are excluded. Brown (1969) proposed a graphical model, which is an extension of situation (*b*) in Figure 2.7, to explain how territoriality might limit density. His model comprised three population levels and three categories of habitat quality (Figure 2.8). Habitat A has the best quality, B has poorer quality, and habitat C is so poor it is not suitable for breeding. When the population density is low (level 1) all individuals can settle in habitat A, but once this habitat is full, that is when population level 2 is reached, birds must settle in habitat B.

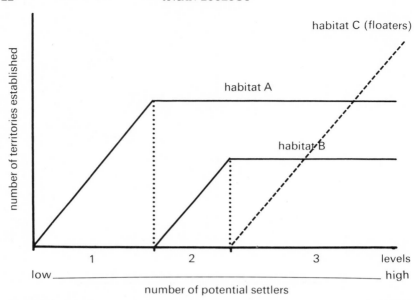

**Figure 2.8** A graphical model of how territoriality may limit population density. At low population density (level 1) no birds are prevented from setting in the best habitat (habitat *A*). At population level 2 some individuals are excluded from habitat *A* and must settle in habitat *B*. At the highest population density (level 3) some birds are prevented from establishing territories at all and must occupy the poorest habitat (habitat *C*) as a floating population. (From Brown, 1969).

Once habitat B is full birds would have to settle in habitat C and be non-breeders or 'floaters'.

This model can be tested by removal experiments; if territory owners are removed and their places are taken by others this then demonstrates that territoriality does exclude some individuals from particular habitats. In Red Grouse, territorial vacancies created experimentally were taken up by individuals from flocks of non-territorial birds (floaters) which otherwise would not have bred (Watson, 1967). This example fits Brown's model in that (*a*) the territorial individuals clearly have an advantage in terms of fitness (because they could breed whereas the non-territorial birds or floaters could not), and (*b*) that territoriality limits population density.

Fretwell's (1972) alternative model is an extension of situation (*a*) in Fig. 2.7. He suggested that if individuals were not excluded by others they should simply settle in the habitat which, at that moment would be of

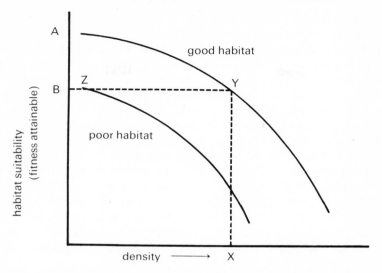

**Figure 2.9** A graphical model of how territoriality may serve as a means of population density assessment.Territorial behaviour does not limit density in either the good or the poor habitat. In both habitats habitat suitability decreases with increasing population density. Initially birds will settle only in the good habitat, but as the density there increases there will be a point ($X$) where a bird can do equally well by settling in the good habitat at density $Y$ or the poor habitat at density $Z$. (From Fretwell, 1972).

greatest advantage (in terms of fitness) (Fig. 2.9). In his model there are two habitat types, 'good' and 'poor', and in both cases the model assumes that the suitability of the habitat decreases with increasing density of birds in them. This is what we would expect, because the more birds which have to share a resource the less there will be for each individual. 'Suitability' here refers to the fitness which a bird could attain in each habitat. Initially birds would do best by settling in the good habitat, but once the population density in that habitat reached a certain level (point $X$ in Fig. 2.9), then a bird could attain the same fitness either by settling in the good habitat at a fairly high density (point $Y$ in Fig. 2.9) or by settling in the poorer habitat at a lower density (point $Z$ in Fig. 2.9). The basic difference between Brown's model and Fretwell's is that in the former territorial behaviour results in the exclusion of some individuals from certain areas, while in Fretwell's model there is no exclusion and birds simply assess the quality of the habitats and the density of birds there and then settle where they will attain the greatest fitness. This concept is referred to as an 'ideal free distribution': the birds are 'ideal' in that they can settle where they will achieve the highest fitness, and 'free' in that they can move where they like and are not excluded from the habitat type.

The results of a study of Great Tits in Holland (Kluijver, 1951; Kluijver and Tinbergen, 1953) appear to fit Fretwell's model quite closely. In this study there were two habitat types, deciduous woodland and coniferous woodland, and of the two, the deciduous woodland was the better habitat in that it was occupied at a higher density. In both habitats breeding success was inversely related to population density, which, as we said above, was one of the model's assumptions. In the coniferous woodland Great Tit numbers fluctuated much more widely than in the deciduous woodland, indicating that the birds settled there in preference to the coniferous woodland. Fretwell's model predicts that the average breeding success should be similar in each habitat and in fact there was no difference in the reproductive success of Great Tits in deciduous and coniferous woodland. This suggests that in this case the birds settled where they could achieve the greatest reproductive success and that territorial behaviour had no effect on population density.

In conclusion it is clear that in some, but not all, species, territorial behaviour can regulate population density, but it is important to emphasize that the regulation is a consequence and not a function of territoriality.

## 2.3  Coloniality

Most colonial species are territorial and most defend type C territories (Table 2.1), which contain no resource other than the breeding site. Overall, about 13% of all bird species breed in colonies, but this type of breeding dispersion is particularly frequent among birds whose food supplies are patchily distributed and unpredictable in space and time. Shoaling fish and plankton represent patchily distributed prey, and virtually all sea-birds which exploit such prey breed colonially. The factors which favour colonial breeding (see below) are sometimes the same as those favouring social groups like feeding flocks and communal roosts, and in many instances birds which feed in flocks also breed in colonies (see Chapter 8).

Just as in section 2.2 in which we discussed territoriality, we can consider coloniality in terms of costs and benefits, although in contrast to studies of feeding territories (section 2.2.1), where costs and benefits can be estimated simply in energetic terms, in breeding colonies we have to measure costs and benefits in terms of reproductive output and survival, which are more complex to quantify. The functions of colonial breeding in birds are still being actively investigated and in the following sections we will outline the main ideas and the results of a number of studies.

The advantages of colonial breeding can be divided into two major categories, those concerned with avoiding predation and those associated with obtaining food.

### 2.3.1   Anti-predator advantages

(i)   *Vigilance and mobbing.* The idea here is that many pairs of eyes are better than a single pair, so a group of birds are more likely to detect an approaching predator sooner than a solitary individual. Early warning allows birds to prepare for the predator's attack, either by covering their eggs and young (e.g. some auks and penguins), or by mobbing the predator (gulls and terns). In Sand Martins, potential predators were detected sooner in large colonies than in small ones (Hoogland and Sherman, 1976), and in Black-headed Gulls, mobbing is sometimes successful in driving off predators such as crows (Kruuk, 1964).

(ii)   *Position in the colony.* Individuals at the centre of a breeding group are less vulnerable to predation than those at the edge. This effect is well documented, and reduced reproductive success among individuals at the edge of a colony has been reported in Adélie Penguins (Penny, 1968; Tenaza, 1971), Sooty Terns (Feare, 1976), and Pinyon Jays (Balda and Bateman, 1971).

(iii)   *Predator swamping.* By breeding colonially and synchronously (i.e. spatial and temporal clumping), birds may swamp the predators' food needs so that a reduced proportion of nests suffer predation. As long as predation does not increase proportionately with colony size, individuals will, on average, be safer in larger colonies.

The advantage of synchronous breeding can be seen by comparing two hypothetical colonies (Fig. 2.10); one in which breeding occurs fairly synchronously and the other in which breeding is less synchronous: the losses through predation are highest in the second colony. The same type of effect occurs among early and late breeders within each colony, and predators take a greater proportion of eggs or young from birds breeding out of phase with the rest of the colony.

The advantage of colonial breeding in terms of predator swamping is well documented for sea-birds and for some colonial passerines such as Red-

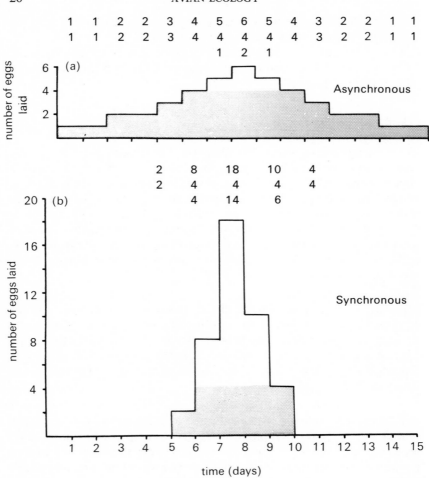

**Figure 2.10** Two hypothetical examples of breeding, (*a*) asynchronous, and (*b*) synch-ronous. Assume that predators can eat only a certain number of eggs each day, in this case four (represented by the shaded part of each histogram). The shaded part of the histograms is that which is vulnerable to predation, the white areas are the safe section of the population. The asynchronous colonies lay over 15 days, while the synchronous colonies lay over 5 days. The three rows of numbers above each histogram refer to (top) the number of eggs laid, (middle) the numbers taken by predators, and (bottom) numbers left. In (*a*) predators are able to take all but 4 out of 42 eggs (i.e. about 90%), but in (*b*) they take only 18 (i.e. about 43%). In other words, the greater the number of prey available each day the smaller *proportion* the predator can take; clearly success will be greatest in (*b*). Note also that within each colony (*a* and *b*) early and late birds are more vulnerable to predation than those laying at the peak.

**Table 2.3**  Some studies in which a predator-swamping effect has been shown to occur.

| Prey species | Predator | Reference |
|---|---|---|
| Black-headed Gull | Carrion Crow | Patterson (1965) |
| Common Tern | Great Horned Owl | Nisbet (1975) |
| Sandwich Tern | Black-headed Gull | Veen (1977) |
| Sooty Tern | Feral cats | Ashmole (1963) |
| Common Guillemot | Great Black-backed Gull | Birkhead (1977) |
| Sand Martin | Various species | Hoogland and Sherman (1976) |

winged Blackbirds (Robertson, 1973). Some examples are given in Table 2.3.

### 2.3.2.  *Feeding advantages*

The association between diet and breeding dispersion, noted by Crook (1965) and Lack (1968), strongly suggests that colonial breeding may in some way be advantageous for birds feeding on particular types of food. Indeed, a number of workers have suggested at various times that sociality in birds, i.e. flocking, communal roosting and colonial breeding, has evolved as a strategy for exploiting food supplies which tend to be patchily distributed and therefore difficult to locate. These ideas have been formulated by Ward and Zahavi (1973) into the 'information centre hypothesis'. This idea was proposed originally to explain the function of the enormous communal roosts of Red-billed Quelea, an African weaver-bird. Ward (1965) noticed that when Red-billed Quelea left the roost in the morning, some flocks flew directly to feeding areas, but others delayed their departure and appeared to follow those birds which had flown off directly. Ward suggested that birds which hung back had been relatively unsuccessful in their foraging the previous day and were following successful birds which flew straight to feeding areas. Later, Ward and Zahavi (1973) extended this idea to suggest that breeding colonies, as well as communal roosts, served as information centres.

The most detailed attempt to test this idea in the field has been made by Krebs (1974), working with Great Blue Herons, on the west coast of North America. Krebs predicted that if colonies were acting as information centres then (1) birds must exploit a food supply which is patchily distributed and that foraging individuals should not leave the colony independently of each other; (2) individuals foraging in groups should have a higher food intake than solitary birds. It was found that at low tide herons fed on fish trapped in pools on extensive mudflats. The number of fish in these pools varied from day to day and herons fed in different parts of the mudflats on different days, suggesting that the food supply was indeed unevenly distributed. There was also a marked tendency for birds to leave the colony in small groups, indicating that they might have been following each other. In addition, by placing life-size models of herons in pools, Krebs found that herons were more attracted to large groups of models than small groups, which indicated that, as well as following each other, herons also looked for feeding aggregations. Finally, it was found that larger groups of herons, up to about 20 birds, had a higher rate of food intake than smaller groups. This was not because individuals gained by group feeding, but simply because numbers of herons tended to build up in areas with abundant food. In conclusion, Krebs' results support the information centre idea, although some of his results are open to alternative interpretations. In this study it was not possible to test whether unsuccessful birds followed successful ones, but more recently, some laboratory experiments with wild caught Red-billed Quelea have shown this effect (De Groot, 1980).

### 2.3.3. *Costs of coloniality*

The main disadvantages of increased proximity are increased competition for resources, risks of rearing young other than one's own, cannibalism,

**Table 2.4** Some costs of coloniality

| Costs | Examples |
|---|---|
| (1) Increased competition for resources such as: | |
|     (a) Breeding sites | North Atlantic Gannet (Nelson, 1978) |
|     (b) Nest material | Sand Martin (Hoogland and Sherman, 1976) |
|     (c) Mates and matings | Snow Goose (Mineau and Cooke, 1979) |
|     (d) Food around colony | Brünnich's Guillemot (Thick-billed Murre) (Gaston *et al.*, in prep.) |
| (2) Risks of misdirected parental care | Guillemots (murres) (Tschanz, 1959, 1968) |
| (3) Risks of cannibalism | Herring Gull and Lesser Black-backed Gull (Parsons, 1971; Hunt and Hunt, 1976) |
| (4) Increased transmission of ectoparasites and disease | Purple Martins (Camin and Moss, 1970) Several Peruvian sea-birds (Duffy, 1983). |

and increased transmission of ectoparasites and disease (Table 2.4). There is evidence that competition for food, breeding sites, nesting materials, mates and matings is more severe in colonial species compared with those which breed spaced out. For example, the fledging weight of Brünnich's Guillemot (Thick-billed Murre) chicks is inversely related to colony size; weights were lowest at the largest colonies. Gaston *et al.* (in prep.) suggested that this was because, at large colonies, competition for food was intense and the local food supply depleted. It is not difficult to imagine how such an effect might occur; the smallest guillemot (murre) colonies contain only a few thousand individuals, but the largest may hold over a million birds which may remove 200 tons of food a day from the surrounding waters!

Guillemots or murres also provide us with a nice example of the risks of

**Figure 2.11**  Part of a colony of Common Guillemots (Common Murres) showing the high density breeding characteristic of this species. (Photograph. T. R. Birkhead).

misdirected parental care; they make no nest and breed in very close proximity (Fig. 2.11) so there is a risk that eggs or chicks may get mixed up and parents may rear unrelated offspring. Since this would be individually disadvantageous, there has been strong selection for individual recognition of eggs and young in guillemots. Their eggs are extremely variable in colour and pattern and chicks have distinctive calls which the parents learn even before the chick hatches. Detailed experiments by Tschanz (1959, 1960) on Common Guillemots have shown that parents recognize and will brood only their own egg or chick.

A number of studies, reviewed by Wittenberger and Hunt (in press), indicate that colonial species show a higher incidence of ectoparasite infestation, such as fleas and ticks, than solitary species. However, we know very little about the effect which ectoparasites have on their hosts, except that very occasionally they can cause birds to desert a colony and abandon their breeding attempt (e.g. Duffy, 1983).

In conclusion, this section has summarized the main advantages and disadvantages of colonial breeding, but so far it has not been possible to combine these different measures, so as to predict an optimal colony size or optimal spacing within a colony.

## 2.4. Conclusions

Two main factors determine whether birds live socially or solitarily. These are (a) the spatial distribution of resources, such as food and nest-sites, and (b) vulnerability to predation. In general, if resources are spatially clumped, the bird species exploiting those resources will tend to feed and breed together, i.e. feed in flocks and breed in colonies. If, on the other hand, resources are evenly spaced the birds will tend to defend large territories and be regularly spaced. Comparative studies both within bird families (e.g. weaver-birds; Crook, 1965) and between bird families (Lack, 1968) provide convincing support for the link between resource distribution and sociality.

Predation can favour either clumping together or spacing, depending upon the ecological circumstances. If prey are camouflaged (e.g. an incubating Woodcock), then predation is probably minimized by spacing out. Alternatively, if joint defence against nest predators is effective, then predation may strongly favour colonial breeding (e.g. gulls and terns).

In fact both the distribution of resources and predation will operate together to effect spacing, the end result being compromise between these conflicting selection pressures. For example, many sea-birds exploit spatially clumped prey (shoals of fish) and breed colonially. However, within colonies different species show different degrees of clumping: guillemots (murres) breed very close together because by so doing they form a defensive barrier to predatory gulls. Other species, such as terns, may maintain a metre or more between adjacent nests within a colony. When a predator approaches a colony, the terns fly up into the air and start to mob it. Since tern eggs are camouflaged, spacing helps to minimize the risk of their detection by the predator. In other words, the spacing pattern we see in terns is a compromise—they breed colonially because of the clumped nature of their food supply, but within a colony space themselves out to minimize predation.

Exactly the same sort of compromise between predation and feeding selection pressures may occur within feeding flocks of birds. For waders (shore-birds) feeding on intertidal mudflats, all species may be safest from predators by being part of a dense flock. However, for those species which hunt visually for prey on or near the surface of the mud, the close proximity of other flock members may interfere with feeding and favour increased spacing within the flock (an example is the Ringed Plover). In contrast, in species like the knot which feed by touch on prey living deeper in the mud, dense flocking does not interfere with feeding, and they can feed in a compact flock (Goss-Custard 1970, 1976).

## 2.5.  Summary

The first part of this chapter is concerned with territoriality. The evolution and functions of territorial behaviour are discussed in terms of the acquisition and maintenance of resources such as food, mates and breeding sites. For territoriality to evolve, the benefits of obtaining these types of resources must outweigh the costs. Studies of feeding territories have most successfully measured the energetic costs and benefits of defending a territory. Territories are maintained by aggressive behaviour, such as visual and vocal displays. One consequence of territorial behaviour is that, in some cases, it may exclude some individuals from breeding and must therefore limit population density (see Chapter 6). This is *not*, however, a function of territoriality.

About 13% of all bird species breed in colonies, and there is a strong association between colonial breeding and the spatial distribution of resources such as food: most colonial birds utilize spatially clumped foods.

The main benefits of colonial breeding are associated with (a) feeding advantages, and (b) reduced risks of predation. The costs of coloniality are more difficult to measure, but include increased competition for resources, the risk of rearing unrelated young, and the risk of transmission of ectoparasites and disease. The spacing patterns adopted by birds will almost always be a compromise between conflicting selection pressures.

CHAPTER THREE

# BREEDING SYSTEMS

## 3.1 Mating systems

### 3.1.1 *Introduction*

There are four main mating systems found in birds, categorized in terms of the duration of the pair bond and the number of mates obtained by each sex.

(a) *Monogamy*: a male and female form a pair bond for part of, or an entire, breeding season, or for a lifetime, and share parental care.

(b) *Polygyny*: a male mates with several females, but each female mates with only one male. A male may associate with several females simultaneously (simultaneous polygyny) or in succession (successive polygyny). Parental care is usually by females.

(c) *Polyandry* (the reverse of polygyny): a female associates with several males, either simultaneously or in succession. The male usually provides most of the parental care.

(d) *Promiscuity*: males and females may mate with different individuals so there is a mixture of polygyny and polyandry. Either the male or female may provide parental care. Polygyny, polyandry and promiscuity are sometimes collectively referred to as polygamy, i.e. having more than one mate.

In a detailed analysis of avian mating systems, Lack (1968) showed that about 92% of all bird species were monogamous. Of the rest 6% were classified as promiscuous, 2% polygynous and 0.4% as polyandrous. Lack (1968) also noted that the proportion of monogamous species differed between those which produced altricial young (93%) (see Chapter 5), and those which produced precocial young (83%). Since the young of precocial species can feed themselves and therefore require less parental care than altricial species, Lack (1968) suggested that the distribution and abundance of food played an important role in the evolution of mating systems.

The ideas of Lack (1968) and other workers (e.g. Orians, 1969) have been extended by Emlen and Oring (1977) to produce a comprehensive theory for the evolution of mating systems. They suggest that although males have more to gain than females from mating as often as possible (see below), a male's access to females will be determined to some extent by ecological conditions. Theoretically a male could increase the number of females he mates with by defending them or the resources they require, from other males. The resources most likely to be needed by females are food and nest sites, and the ability of males to defend females or resources will depend upon how they are distributed in space and time. If, for example, the spatial distribution of food is fairly even the chances of one male being able to monopolize a disproportionately large amount are slight. Under these ecological conditions all males will have access to similar areas and similar numbers of females visiting those areas, consequently the potential for polygyny in this situation is low. If, on the other hand, the spatial distribution of food or other resources is clumped, or patchy, then it is much more likely that some males will obtain good patches and others will get poor ones. Males in good patches may attract more females, so the potential for polygyny under such conditions will be high. The *temporal* distribution of mates is also important in determining the type of mating system. The crucial factor here is the number of receptive females relative to the number of sexually active males at any one time. This is referred to as the operational sex ratio (OSR). If we imagine a population with a real sex ratio of 1:1, then if all females became receptive at exactly the same time, then the OSR would also be 1:1, and the opportunity for males to mate with more than one female would be slight. However, if the females in a population come into reproductive condition over several weeks, then at any one time there would be many more sexually active males than receptive females. This would result in competition between males for females, but it would also allow males to court and mate with females sequentially, as they became receptive. Thus, as the OSR deviates from 1:1, the potential for polygamy increases.

For males of most birds (and other animals) the energetic costs of insemination are relatively low, since sperm are small and cheap to produce. More importantly, insemination usually carries no further commitment for the male. In females, however, the converse is true; eggs are relatively large and energetically expensive to produce, and insemination can carry a long-term commitment. In humans, for example, a female must carry the developing foetus for nine months and care for the child for a further fifteen years or so, until it reaches independence.

What this means is that theoretically males will increase their reproductive success by mating with as many females as possible, whereas the only way a female can increase her reproductive output is by increasing the rate at which she produces eggs. Since animals have evolved through natural selection to maximize their fitness (i.e. their lifetime reproductive output), we have a situation where males can make more matings than females. The consequence of this is that males will often be in competition with each other for matings, whereas unless there is a great shortage of males, females will not. However, because females make fewer matings than some males, it is more important for them to be selective about who they mate with. Both males and females make equal genetic contributions to subsequent generations. However, the variance of the success of males may be very great compared with females. This comes about because certain males may be successful (whereas others may fail to mate at all) while the reproductive output of females is less variable (see section 3.3).

### 3.1.2  *Monogamy*

Because of the fundamental differences between males and females outlined above, the 'interests' of each sex overlap but are not identical. Monogamous mating systems occur in such a wide range of ecological conditions that it is unlikely that monogamy can be explained by a single hypothesis. In fact monogamy has probably evolved in three ways (Wittenburger and Tilson, 1980).

(a)  *Monogamy occurs when male parental care is essential for female reproductive success.* The young of altricial species require considerable parental care; brooding, feeding and protection from predators. Indeed, Lack (1968) suggested that the main advantage of monogamy is that both male and female leave, on average, more offspring if they both help to raise a brood. However, it is important for our understanding of how monogamy evolved, to realise that male assistance is not always essential for a female to produce *some* young. In only two situations is male assistance essential: (a) where continuous nest attendance is vital for successful reproduction (e.g. gulls in a colony where the chicks are eaten if left unguarded); (b) where species rear only a single chick at a time (e.g. some sea-birds and vultures)—a larger brood would have evolved if one parent could rear the chick alone (Chapter 5).

For species which do not feed their young (e.g. many precocial species), these arguments are less applicable, and as we might expect a higher proportion of these species are polygamous. Nevertheless in many precocial species the male and female still co-operate to rear the young even though they do not feed them. In geese and swans for example, the male guards the female while she incubates, and after the young hatch both parents protect them (Scott, 1980).

To summarize, male parental care *increases* female reproductive success, but in only a few species is it *essential*. Some other factor(s), which we will now consider, must explain monogamy.

(b) *Monogamy occurs in territorial species when pairing with an unmated male is always better than pairing with an already mated male.* Polygyny, as we will see later, probably evolves when the difference in the quality of males or territories is large. The converse of this is that monogamy occurs when resources such as food are evenly dispersed and the differences in territory quality are small, in other words, when the difference in territory quality does not merit pairing with an already paired male. Most cases of monogamy are probably explicable in terms of a combination of (a) (above) and this explanation. For example, even when the environmental potential for polygamy does exist (e.g. when territories differ in quality), the benefits of co-operating with a partner to rear young may outweigh any advantages of either partner being polygamous.

(c) *Monogamy occurs in non-territorial species when males can reproduce most successfully by defending one female.* This situation will occur when resources are indefensible and where the sex ratio is biased towards males. A few passerines and most ducks fall into this category. Female ducks tend to suffer higher mortality than males and the resulting skewed sex ratio means that male competition for females is intense. This probably causes males to pair with females several months before the breeding season, and to defend them from other males until egg-laying.

### 3.1.3 *Polygyny*

1. *Resource defence polygyny.* This is the first of two major types of polygyny found in birds, and comprises male defence of resources which females need. When these resources are spatially clumped, some males may

be able to defend areas containing better quality or a greater quantity of the resource than other males.

One of the best-studied polygynous species is the Red-winged Blackbird. This species breeds in marshy areas over much of North America. In spring, males arrive at breeding areas before females. They compete for territories, and when the females arrive some males may pair with as many as ten females. Why are some males so successful in attracting mates while others may have only a single female or remain unpaired? It seems rather surprising that a female should pair with an already paired male while there are still unmated males available. If a female joins a male who is already paired she will have to share his parental care and other resources in his territory with other females.

The explanation for polygyny here lies in the patchiness of the food supply, and the large differences in territory quality which exist as a consequence. A female may choose to mate with an already paired male if the difference in quality of territory was sufficiently large to mean that she could rear more young by joining a mated male in a good territory, than by pairing monogamously with a male in a poor territory. This idea has been summarized graphically in Orians' (1969) 'polygyny threshold' model (Fig. 3.1).

This model makes a number of predictions (Orians, 1969; Garson *et al.*, 1981). Firstly, *a male's territory quality will be correlated with his mating success*. The existence of a correlation between territory quality and the number of females a male attracts has been demonstrated in a number of bird species. In both the Dickcissel and Bobolink, territory quality is reflected by the amount of vegetation they contain. Unpaired males held territories with little cover while males with two or three females had territories with more vegetation (Zimmerman, 1966; Martin, 1974). The idea that males in good territories attract the most females has been tested experimentally by Pleszczynska (1978) with Lark Buntings *Calamospiza melanocorys*. This species is a summer visitor to the prairie regions of North America. Males arrive on the breeding grounds before females and compete among themselves for territories. Some males pair with only a single female, others pairs first with one (the primary female), and later with another (the secondary) female, but assist only the primary female in rearing young. Lark Buntings breed in alfalfa fields which provide little cover or shade and much of the nestling mortality is due to extremes of temperature. By placing plastic rosettes of leaves to provide extra shade over some nests, fledging success was increased by 50% compared with control nests without extra shade. Thus a good measure of territory quality

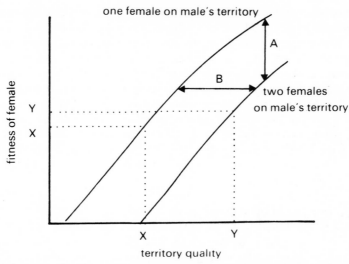

**Figure 3.1** Orian's (1969) polygyny threshold model. The main underlying assumption of the model is that the fitness of a female is correlated with the quality of territory she breeds in. A single female in a male's territory attains a greater fitness (upper line), than a female which has to share her male with another female (lower line). The difference between these two lines (*A*) is the decrease in fitness which a female experiences if she joins an already paired male rather than joining an unpaired male. However, if the difference in the quality of territories is large (*B* = the polygyny threshold), a female may do better by pairing with an already paired male. For example a female sharing a male on a good quality territory (*Y*) will do better than a female paired monogamously to a male on a poor territory (*X*).

in this species was the amount of cover in the territory. As predicted, the number of females in a male's territory was closely related to the amount of cover there. With increasing amounts of cover males were either unpaired, monogamous or bigamous. However, by adding extra cover to territories before females arrived Pleszczynska and Hansell (1981) were able to induce trigamy, which had never previously been recorded in this species.

Secondly, *if differences in territory quality affect polygyny then we would predict more polygyny in patchy environments.* This prediction was tested by Verner and Willson (1966) by comparing the habitats and mating systems of all North American passerines. They found that 277 out of 291 species (95%) were monogamous and that 14 (5%) were polygamous. Thirteen of these 14 species occurred in either marsh or grassland habitats where there are often marked differences in productivity (and therefore food abundance) in adjacent areas. Lack (1968) has pointed out that most of the polygynous species occur within a single family (the North American blackbirds, Icteridae) so the correlation between mating system and habitat may be coincidental. However, an examination of the breeding habits of Arctic Sandpipers shows a similar effect. Monogamous species tend to occur in areas where the food supply is evenly dispersed and predictable from year to year. In those regions of the tundra where food is patchily distributed and male territories vary greatly in quality, the sandpipers show varying degrees of polygamy (Pitelka *et al.*, 1974).

2. *Male dominance polygyny.* In this second main type of polygyny, males do not defend females, nor do they defend resources which females need. Instead they compete for status in communal displays, and females then choose males on the basis of their dominance. These communal displays are performed at traditional sites, called leks, where males congregate to attract and court females and where females come only to mate. This type of mating system has probably evolved when neither females nor the resources they need are economically defendable by males. In addition, the operational sex ratio is strongly skewed; with a preponderance of sexually active males. This occurs because females become receptive asynchronously, and as a consequence each male visits the lek over long periods (several weeks or months) while females visit the lek only briefly (for a few hours), to copulate. Females leave the lek after mating and rear their young unaided by the male. This is possible in species with precocial young (e.g. grouse, ruffs) or species inhabiting very rich environments so that the female can rear the young by herself (e.g. manakins; see Snow, 1976), or in species which do not rear their own young, such as brood parasites (see section 3.7). An outline of the lek behaviour of each of these types is given below to illustrate the similarities and some of the differences in behaviour between lekking species.

In *Sage Grouse*, which occur in the western U.S.A., each morning between February and May males congregate at traditional leks on sage-brush prairies. Each male occupies a small territory ($13–100m^2$ in area) and within this territory performs a remarkable, stereotyped display called 'the strut'. The display involves elaborate posturing and the filling of two oesophageal air sacs, then expelling the air to produce a popping sound. Females visit leks in April and congregate in dense groups near the most central territories. Each female spends very little time at the lek and copulates only once before going off (up to 4 km away) to produce her clutch of 4–6 eggs. Over 75% of all copulations are performed by just 10% of the males (Fig. 3.2.)

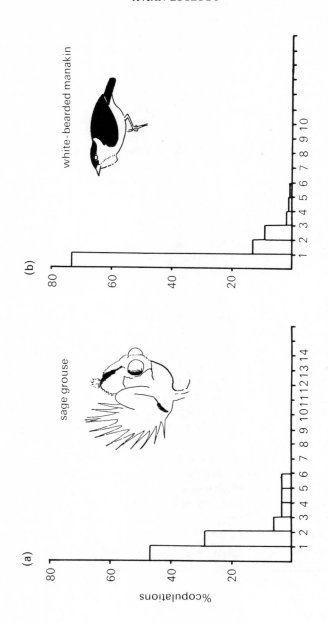

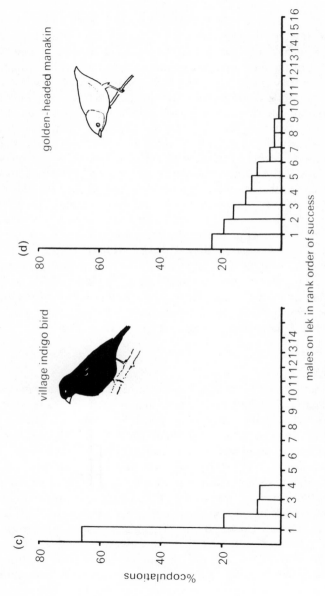

**Figure 3.2** Mating success (percentage copulations) of males in four bird species which display at leks. In each example males are ranked in descending order of the percentage copulations they performed during a breeding season. In each case a few males were responsible for most of the copulations. (*a*) Sage Grouse (from Wiley, 1973), (*b*) White-bearded Manakin (from Lill, 1974), (*c*) Village Indigobird (from Payne and Payne, 1977), and (*d*) Golden-Headed Manakin (Lill, 1976).

*White-bearded Manakins* (Pipridae) are small passerines inhabiting the tropical forests of South America. Leks occur in dense forest and may hold between 6 and 50 males. Each male defends a small territory or court (15–100 cm in diameter) on the forest floor, which he keeps clear of vegetation. Adjacent courts may be only a few cm apart. Males are present at the lek for most of the day and throughout much of the year, although most mating takes place between March and August.Males perform spectacular and elaborate courtship displays on their courts. Some males copulate with large numbers of females while others with few or none. At one lek one male accounted for 73% of all copulations seen. Females generally copulated several times with the same male over several days (a mating bout) prior to laying. The distribution of copulations was non-random (Fig. 3.2) and the number of copulations a male performed was correlated with the number of different females he mated with. A related species, the Golden-headed Manakin, has a similar lek system (Fig. 3.2).

The *Village Indigo-bird* is a small brood-parasitic (see section 3.7) African finch related to the weaver-birds. Males defend call-sites in trees throughout the breeding season (January–July). This species has a dispersed lek, with call sites generally several hundred members apart. Females appear to sample a number of males at their call sites, being courted by each male before returning to one male to copulate. In one population of 14 males, one male obtained more than 50% of all copulations, three males accounted for over 80%, while 8 males were never seen to copulate (Fig. 3.2).

### 3.1.4  *Polyandry*

In this form of mating system females mate with several males and males perform most parental care. Polyandry occurs in only a few species because it is usually males rather then females which benefit from repeated matings. Most cases of polyandry occur in the Rallidae and Charadriiformes (e.g. waders or shore-birds), most of which breed in marshy habitats. As we have seen, such habitats may be very productive, and females can readily replace clutches lost to predators. Among waders polyandry probably evolved from the habit of 'double-clutching' which occurs in some Arctic species: e.g. Temminck's Stint breeds in very productive areas of tundra and females can produce two clutches (fathered by one male) in rapid succession. The male cares for the first, and the female for the second clutch. Clearly this system could lead to polygamy if the female mated with another male for her second clutch. If feeding conditions are especially good and a female can produce several clutches, then she would increase her reproductive success by mating with several males in succession. The Spotted Sandpiper is sequentially polyandrous, producing clutches for up to four males in succession (Fig. 3.3).

The American Jacana is simultaneously polyandrous (Fig. 3.3) and here females defend 'super-territories' which encompass several male territories. Each male defends his territory against other males and the female will assist each male to defend his territory, even though she has access to all males' territories within her super-territory. A female may copulate with all her males on the same day so males are probably never certain that they fathered the clutch they care for!

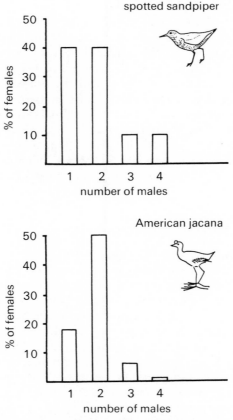

**Figure 3.3** Percentage of females mating with one, two, three or four males in the polyandrous Spotted Sandpiper (from Hays, 1972) and American Jacana (from Jenni, 1974).

The mating system of Greater Rheas appears to be a mixture of polygyny and successive polyandry. Males compete for small (2–15) flocks of females and only dominant males obtain such harems (polygyny). The male constructs the nest and each of his females contributes several eggs to the clutch. The average clutch size is about 28 eggs, but up to 62 have been recorded in one nest! After the females have produced eggs for one male they move on to another and lay more eggs (polyandry). All parental care is by the male; he incubates the eggs and guards the precocial young (Bruning, 1974).

### 3.1.5   *Flexibility of mating systems*

It is important to note that mating systems are not species specific, nor are they rigidly fixed. The males of many monogamous species (e.g. Magpie, Common Guillemot or Murre, and Lesser Snow Goose) adopt a 'mixed strategy' (Trivers, 1972), that is, they form a permanent pair bond with one female, but attempt to sneak copulations with other paired females. As a counter-measure, paired males attempt to guard their partners from males during the time when they can be fertilized (Birkhead, 1979, 1982). Also, some males of monogamous species may be facultative polygynists, forming pair bonds with two females if the opportunity arises (e.g. wheatear; Brooke, 1979). In the European Dunnock, monogamous, polygynous and polyandrous mating systems have all been recorded (Birkhead, 1981).

### 3.1.6   *Mating systems and sexual dimorphism*

In most monogamous birds the male and female are about the same size and generally have similar plumage. For example, virtually all sea-birds are monogamous and the sexes are indistinguishable in the field. In contrast, most polygamous birds are sexually dimorphic: in polygynous species males are usually larger and more brightly coloured than females, whereas in polyandrous species the reverse is true. The difference in the appearance between males and females in polygamous species is the result of natural selection operating differently on each sex (referred to as sexual selection). In polygamous species one sex assumes most of the parental duties: in polygynous species it is the female, while in polyandrous species it is the male. The sex performing most of the work in rearing the young constitutes a limiting resource and members of the other sex will compete for it. Thus in the polygynous Red-winged Blackbird, females take a disproportionate share of the chick-rearing, and males compete vigorously among themselves for females. In the polyandrous Jacana, the reverse is true. Among polygamous species bright plumage and large body size have evolved in the competing sex because these features have been advantageous in terms of mate attraction and in intra-sexual competition for mates, respectively. Hence in polygynous birds males are usually brighter and larger than females, while in polyandrous species the female is more brightly coloured, and in the Jacana, 75% larger than the male.

A particularly elegant experimental test of the adaptive significance of sexual dimorphism has been performed on Long-tailed Widow-birds. These are small (7 cm), polygynous members of the weaver-bird family, with marked sexual dimorphism. Females are dull brown with short tails while males are predominantly glossy black with an enormous (50 cm) tail. Andersson (1982) decreased or increased the length of males' tails and compared the number of females they obtained. Males whose tails were artificially increased by 25 cm (by glueing on extra feathers) obtained most females; an average of 1.89 per male. Control males (whose tails were either cut and glued back on, or were left untouched) acquired an average of 0.67 females. Males whose tails were reduced to 14 cm obtained the least females; 0.44 per male. This experiment indicates that in long-tailed Widow-birds sexual dimorphism is maintained because females prefer to mate with males possessing long tails.

## 3.2  Brood parasitism

### 3.2.1  *Introduction*

The brood parasites are birds which lay their eggs in the nests of other bird (host) species, which incubate and rear the young. Brood parasites are of special interest because of the extraordinary range of adaptations which they exhibit for their specialized way of life. About 80 species (approximately 1% of all birds) are brood parasites and this breeding system has evolved independently a number of times (Table 3.1). A brief description of the main groups is given below.

(a)  Honey-guides are sparrow-starling sized birds living in tropical Africa or Asia. They are unusual in that much of their diet consists of bee larvae and their wax cells, and they have symbiotic bacteria to digest the wax. Most honey-guides parasitize hole-nesting hosts such as barbets (Capitonidae) and woodpeckers (Picidae).

**Table 3.1**   Brood parasitic birds.

| Family | Common names | Breeding range | No. of species |
|--------|--------------|----------------|----------------|
| Cuculidae | Cuckoos | Old World and South America | About 50* |
| Ploceidae | Wydahs** and a weaver | Africa | 10 and 1 respectively |
| Icteridae | Cowbirds | N. and S. America | 5 species |
| Anatidae | Black-headed Duck | S. America | 1 species |
| Indicatoridae | Honey-guides | Africa/Asia | 11 species |

*Note*:  * Only about 40% of the 130 species of cuckoos are brood parasites.
** Also referred to as widow-birds (see section 3.6).

(b) The fifty or so species of Old World cuckoos occur mainly in Africa and Asia, with some in Australia and Europe. They are sparrow-crow sized birds, parasitizing insectivorous passerine species mostly smaller than themselves.

(c) The wydahs (Viduinae) occur in Africa. They are sparrow-sized birds usually with marked sexual dimorphism. Each wydah species parasitizes a particular estrildine finch species. Both host and parasites lay unmarked eggs, and host and parasite young are reared together.

(d) Cowbirds occur in Central and South America, with one species, the Brown-headed Cowbird, in North America. The latter parasitizes a greater range of host species (over 100 have been recorded) than perhaps any other brood-parasite.

### 3.2.2   *Effect of brood parasites on the host*

By duping another species into rearing its young, a brood parasite can increase its fitness at the expense of the host's. Natural selection will favour successful parasites but it will also favour host species which can avoid being parasitized or can discriminate against a parasite's eggs or young. The situation is similar to an arms race; adaptation for successful parasitism will be countered by adaptations to avoid parasitism by the hosts, which in turn will be countered by further parasitic adaptations, and so on.

As a result of parasitism the host's clutch-size may be reduced in a variety of ways. Female European Cuckoos usually remove one host egg before laying their own (Chance, 1940; Wyllie, 1981). However, if a female cuckoo finds a nest with a complete clutch she may eat or destroy the eggs, causing the host to re-nest and thereby giving herself another chance to parasitize the host. Several brood parasites, including the European Cuckoo and the Pied Crested Cuckoo, sometimes lay their eggs from a perch above the nest, with the result that the thick-shelled cuckoo egg damages one of the host's eggs. Cowbirds may puncture host eggs with their beak or claws so that they do not hatch. Once the young parasite hatches it may eject host eggs or young, as in the European Cuckoo and other cuckoo species. In species where the young parasite does not evict host eggs and young, the host and parasite young are reared together. Usually the parasite hatches before the host young and is better able to compete for food, with the result that host young either starve or fledge at reduced weight (see Chapter 5). Host young may be killed directly by the young parasite, as in the case of honey-guides; young honey-guides have sharp mandibular hooks with which they kill their host nest-mates. In addition to these effects, parasitism may increase the interval between successive nesting attempts, or may exhaust the host so that it is unable to re-nest. All these effects reduce the fitness of hosts.

### 3.2.3  *Adaptation of hosts and parasites: coevolutionary aspects*

Hosts can avoid or minimize the effects of parasites in a number of ways. Potential hosts may avoid being parasitized by attacking and driving off parasites, or by concealing their nests so the parasites cannot find them. They may reduce the effects of parasitism by discrimination and removal of parasite eggs and young, or by abandoning their nest if it is parasitized.

In many cases these adaptations of the host have been followed by counteradaptations by parasites. Most host species vigorously attack or mob parasites, but some parasites use subtle ploys to gain access to a host nest. In the Indian Koel (a cuckoo), the male approaches the nest of the host (the House Crow), calling loudly. The incubating crow leaves the nest to drive the noisy intruder away, and the female Koel slips into the nest to lay her egg. In the Pied Crested Cuckoo the male and female co-operate to drive hosts away from their nests. The European Cuckoo, usually much larger than its hosts, ignores the attacks by host species as it lays its egg in their nest.

Some brood parasites have a protrusible cloaca which enables them to place eggs in nests which are too small for the parasite itself to enter, such as tree-holes. Also, egg laying is often extremely rapid, minimizing the time that the parasite needs to be at the host's nest; in the European Cuckoo egg-laying takes only one or two seconds. The shells of brood parasite eggs are often thick or, or as in the Pied Crested Cuckoo, double-shelled, which means that they are unlikely to be damaged when dropped into a host's nest. Some brood parasites have the ability to retain eggs in their oviduct, enabling them to hold an egg until a suitable host is found. It may also allow embryonic development to proceed, which may partly explain why brood parasites usually have slightly shorter incubation periods than their hosts. Short incubation periods allow parasites to hatch before hosts so that parasite chicks can either eject host eggs or young or monopolize the food which parents bring to the nest.

Perhaps the best known adaptation of brood parasites concerns egg mimicry in the European cuckoo. Because some host species are able to discriminate between their own eggs and those of a parasite, and may either eject the parasite's egg or start another nesting attempt, there has been strong selection for some brood parasites to produce mimetic eggs. Parasite's eggs may mimic host eggs in colour and size. Since most parasites are larger than their hosts, this means that parasites which mimic the size of host eggs produce relatively small eggs. Mimicry of host egg-colour is particularly well developed in the European cuckoo. In any particular area cuckoo populations may comprise several types of 'gentes', each of the gens lays eggs of a constant type and parasitizes one main host species. Experiments have shown that cuckoo eggs placed in the nest of the 'wrong' host are more likely to be ejected or abandoned, than those in the 'correct' host nest. In cowbirds individual females parasitize a wide range of hosts; there is no mimicry and nothing comparable with the cuckoo's gens system.

Young parasites which eject host eggs and young do not resemble host young, and in only some of the species where host and parasite young are reared together is there any evidence that young parasites mimic host young. The most striking example of chick mimicry involves wydahs and their estrildine hosts. Nestling estrildine finches have complex species-specific gape patterns, and parents have innate recognition of their own species' pattern. Adults will not feed chicks of other estrildines placed experimentally in their nests (Nicolai, 1974). However, the gape patterns of young wydahs are identical to those of their host species' young. In addition, wydah chicks mimic the host chicks' very unusual feeding postures, their plumage and their begging calls (Nicolai, 1974).

### 3.2.4  *Reproductive strategies of brood parasites*

Most brood parasites tend to produce relatively small eggs compared with their non-parasitic relatives (Fig. 3.4). There are several advantages

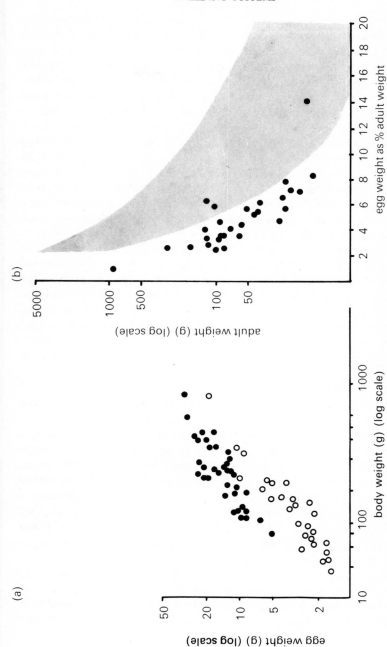

**Figure 3.4** (*a*) Relationship between egg weight and body weight in parasitic (open symbols) and nesting (i.e. non-parasitic) cuckoos (closed symbols). (Redrawn from Payne, 1974). (*b*) Egg weight as a percentage of body weight in all families of birds (stippled area) and for parasitic cuckoos; most points for cuckoos fall below those of other bird families. (Redrawn from data in Lack, 1968; Payne, 1974).

associated with this; first, small eggs may mimic the size of host eggs, second, smaller eggs require a shorter incubation period than large eggs, and third, it may allow parasitic females to allocate energy into a larger number of eggs. Since female cuckoos do not have to spend time and energy in incubation, this may explain why they are able to produce slightly more eggs than related, non-parasitic species. However, determining the number of eggs laid by brood parasites is extremely difficult. By very extensive observation and the ability to recognize the eggs of individual females, Chance (1940) found that the European Cuckoo produces at least 12 eggs per season. Payne (1977) used a different method for African cuckoos; he examined ovaries and found that females produced 16–25 eggs in a season in several series or 'clutches'. These data suggest that brood parasites lay more eggs than non-parasitic relatives, but since eggs are relatively small, the overall energetic input into reproduction is probably similar to birds with conventional breeding strategies.

Very little is known about the population dynamics of brood parasites, but we might expect them to be somewhat different from conventional breeders. Several life-history models (e.g. Fig. 5.8) suggest that there might be a trade-off between reproductive effort and adult survival. If this were so, then in brood parasites, which do not have to bear the costs of rearing young, we might expect survival rates to be higher than in non-parasitic relatives.

### 3.2.5 *The evolution of brood parasitism*

The evolutionary advantages of brood parasitism are potentially very great. Parental care is absent, and this may mean that theoretically females can allocate more energy into reproduction, or have a higher chance of survival to the next breeding season. Although it seems very likely that brood parasitism evolved from conventional breeding, its origins are difficult to determine. The most likely starting points are (a) the active take-over of the nest of one species by another, but where the species taking over the nest cares for its own young (this is exactly what happens in the Bay-winged cowbird, a species closely related to other cowbirds which are true brood-parasites). The next stage would be finding a nest and rapidly laying an egg or clutch in it, leaving the 'host' to rear the young. (b) Another possible precursor to brood parasitism is intra-specific brood parasitism. A few species, such as the European Starling, regularly dump eggs in the nest of their own species (Yom-Tov, 1980). The step between intra- and inter-specific brood parasitism is presumably small.

## 3.3 Co-operative breeding

### 3.3.1 *The problem*

Natural selection operates on individuals (rather than groups or species; see 6.3.4) and it follows from this that in order to gain genetic representation in subsequent generations, individuals might be expected to behave 'selfishly' (Dawkins, 1976). The converse of selfishness in this sense is altruism, and an altruistic act is one which increases the recipient's fitness but decreases the donor's fitness. As Darwin himself noted, the evolution of altruistic traits is problematical. The main interest in co-operatively breeding birds arises from the fact that some individuals ('helpers') appear to act altruistically, forgoing breeding in order to help a breeding pair to raise young. One explanation for such behaviour is that it evolved because helpers are genetically related to those they help, and the gain by helping to rear relatives more than offsets any reduction in individual fitness incurred by helping. The main reason for the dramatic upsurge in studies of co-operative breeders is that they provide an excellent opportunity to test theoretical ideas on the evolution of altruistic traits.

### 3.3.2 *Characteristics of co-operative breeding systems*

Co-operative breeding has been recorded for over 150 species in 10 diverse orders of birds (ostriches, geese, hawks, rails, terns, anis, swifts, kingfishers, woodpeckers, and, most commonly, song-birds). It occurs most frequently in the tropics and Australia and is rare in Europe and North America. Co-operative breeders share a number of features, mainly related to their population structure; most co-operative breeders have low breeding rates, high adult survival, low dispersal and deferred maturity (Chapter 6). Birds may not breed until they are at least two years old, spending the intervening period as helpers. Most co-operative breeders are sedentary and occupy stable environments in which the opportunities for breeding may be extremely limited. For example, the breeding habitat may be completely full, or 'saturated'. Sexual dimorphism is rare or slight and monogamy is the most frequent mating system.

Although there is considerable diversity in the types of co-operative breeding system, the following sketch is typical of several species. e.g. Florida Scrub Jay (Woolfenden, 1975; Emlen, 1978); babblers (*Turdoides* and *Pomatostomus* genera) (Gaston, 1978; Brown and Brown, 1981); and the Superb Blue Wren (Rowley, 1965). Co-operative breeders live in groups consisting of a breeding pair and a variable number of helpers (usually less than 10). They live in all-purpose (type A) territories (see Chapter 2), which all group members defend. Helpers are genetically related to the breeding pair and are usually offspring from a previous nesting attempt. Helpers are predominantly male, probably because males have more to gain from helping than females.

Other species may differ from this type of system in one or more respects. For example, in the Mexican Jay (Brown, 1963) and Acorn Woodpecker (Koenig, 1981), groups may contain at least two breeding pairs. In the Pied Kingfisher only one pair breeds, but in some areas helpers are genetically unrelated to the breeding pair.

### 3.3.3   *The evolution of co-operative breeding*

A number of hypotheses have attempted to explain the evolution of co-operative breeding in birds (Table 3.2). The one which has given studies of these birds so much impetus is (*a*), that helpers were behaving altruistically, that is, helping benefited breeders, but helpers gained nothing or incurred some disadvantage. Other possibilities are (*b*), that by helping helpers benefit themselves but breeders do not gain, and (*c*) that helping benefits both breeders and helpers. We will examine some of the evidence to see which of these explanations is most likely.

One of the main questions has been whether breeders benefit from having helpers, and this has been examined by comparing the breeding success of naturally occurring pairs with and without helpers. In most cases pairs with helpers produce more young than those without helpers (Emlen, 1978; Brown, 1978). Although this strongly suggests that helpers make a positive contribution, there are two problems. First, if large groups generally have larger or better territories than small groups, the greater reproductive success of large groups may simply reflect territory size or

**Table 3.2** Some hypotheses to explain the evolution of co-operative breeding in birds. Modified from Emlen (1978).

|  | *Costs or benefits to* | | *Explanation* |
|  | *Helper* | *Breeder* | |
| --- | --- | --- | --- |
| (*a*) | Decrease in fitness | Increase in fitness | Helper behaves 'altruistically' |
| (*b*) | Increase in fitness | Decrease in fitness | Helper behaves 'selfishly' |
| (*c*) | Increase in fitness | Increase in fitness | Both helpers and breeders benefit from helping |

quality. Second, as we shall see (Chapters 4, 5), breeding age may affect reproductive success: the presence of helpers in a group is good evidence that the breeding pair has bred successfully in the past and is experienced. On the other hand, small groups may consist of young, inexperienced birds. In other words, to demonstrate that helpers really do help, the effect of territory quality and breeding experience must be eliminated. Brown and Brown (1981) have done just this, working with Grey Crowned Babblers in Australia. They experimentally removed helpers from some groups, reducing group size to the smallest which occurred naturally. The breeding success of large groups (no helpers removed) experimentally reduced groups and natural small groups was compared. The experiment had three possible outcomes. (i) If helpers increase breeding success (hypotheses (*a*) and (*c*) in Table 3.2), then their removal would reduce breeding success to a level similar to that of natural small groups. (ii) If helpers are detrimental to breeders (hypothesis (*b*) in Table 3.2), then their removal should increase breeding success. (iii) If helpers have no

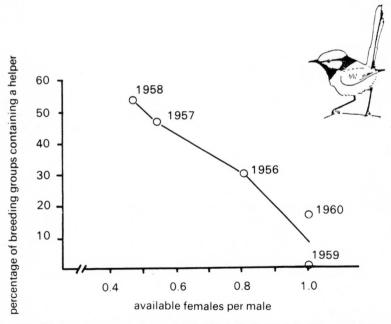

**Figure 3.5** The percentage occurrence of male helpers in Superb Blue Wrens in relation to the availability of female mates. When fewer females are available a greater percentage of groups contain helpers. (From Emlen, 1978).

influence, their removal will not affect breeding success. The results showed clearly that helpers do help (hypothesis (a)). Large groups produced over twice as many young (2.4/group) as the experimentally reduced groups (0.8/group). This effect occurred because larger groups started to breed earlier in the season and made a greater number of breeding attempts per season than smaller groups.

There may be a number of other benefits in having helpers (Table 3.3). For example, in Florida Scrub Jays, breeding birds with helpers had a significantly higher survival rate (87% per annum) than pairs without helpers (80% per annum). An advantage which arises is that larger groups are more efficient in detecting predators (Stallcup and Woolfenden, 1978) (see also 8.5).

Although larger groups produce more young than smaller groups, the number of young produced *per individual* is actually less in large groups. This means that the best way for an individual to make a genetic contribution to subsequent generations is to breed rather than to be a helper (Emlen, 1978; Woolfenden, 1981). If this is so, why do some individuals bother to remain as helpers? The answer seems to be that for most

**Table 3.3** Potential or actual costs and benefits of co-operative breeding.

|  | To breeder | To helper |
|---|---|---|
| Costs | 1. More birds in territory eat more food.<br>2. Activity of helpers draws predators' attention.<br>3. Helpers' incompetence may be detrimental.<br>4. Helpers may compete with breeders for the right to breed. | 1. Rearing parents' offspring demands time, energy and exposure to predators. |
| Benefits | 1. Assistance in rearing young.<br>2. If one parent dies, helpers ensure that some young survive.<br>3. Experience gained by helpers may result in them being good parents; so increases inclusive fitness of their parents.<br>4. Inter-group competition for territories favours large group size for territorial defence.<br>5. Other advantages of group living: increased foraging efficiency, detection of predators. (See Chapter 8 and 2). | 1. Experience in rearing young.<br>2. Access to resources in the group territory.<br>3. Advantages of group living.<br>4. Kin selected advantage in rearing relatives. |

co-operative breeders the opportunities for breeding are few and that helpers benefit themselves by helping.

In many species there exist non-breeding or floater populations (see Chapter 6). These birds generally occupy marginal habitats which are not suitable for breeding, while breeders occupy the optimal habitat. Some co-operative breeders occur in areas where the habitat is either suitable for breeding or not, i.e., there is no marginal habitat in which non-breeders can exist. Such birds have little choice but to remain in their natal territory until a breeding vacancy occurs. This situation exists for Acorn Woodpeckers (Koenig and Pitelka, 1981) and Florida Scrub Jays (Woolfenden, 1981). An analogous situation occurs in the Superb Blue Wren; in this species opportunities for breeding are few because females rather than territories are in short supply (see Fig. 3.5). By remaining in their natal territories as helpers, young birds may benefit themselves in several ways (Table 3.3), mainly by increasing their chances of breeding through increased survival and increased chances of obtaining a breeding space or a mate. In addition, by remaining as helpers, young birds increase the reproductive output of their parents and increase their own inclusive fitness.

In conclusion it seems that (i) helping benefits breeders, (ii) it occurs mainly when opportunities for breeding are few, and (iii) helpers do not suffer any decrease in fitness by helping; in fact there are several potential benefits from helping. Therefore co-operative breeding constitutes a form of co-operation (closest to hypothesis (c) in Table 3.1) in which both parties benefit.

## 3.4 Summary

This chapter has examined three behavioural aspects of reproduction; (a) mating systems, (b) brood parasitism and (c) co-operative breeding. The typical mating system of most birds is monogamy, but a few species are polygamous (i.e. they have more than one mate), either one male paired with several females (polygyny) or, more rarely, one female with several males (polyandry). The ways in which ecological factors such as the temporal and spatial distribution of resources have influenced the evolution of these different systems have been discussed. Brood parasitism is a breeding system peculiar to birds and social insects, and is of special interest because of the remarkable range of adaptions exhibited by brood parasitic birds. We have considered the types of effect which brood parasites have on their hosts; the adaptations and counter-adaptations of parasites and hosts, respectively; the strategies which brood parasites use;

and finally, we have speculated on how this particular breeding system might have evolved. Co-operative breeding was once considered to be an atypical breeding system, but in recent years more and more species have been found to be co-operative breeders, that is more than a single pair of birds working together to rear a brood of young. Co-operative breeding occurs in a wide diversity of bird families, but most of them have the following features in common: long life expectancy, low reproductive rates and 'helpers' which are close kin. The way in which co-operative breeding has evolved has fascinated behavioural ecologists for many years, because it involves some individuals ('helpers') behaving apparently against their own interests. Several long-term studies and a few experiments suggest that co-operative breeding benefits all parties concerned.

# CHAPTER FOUR

# REPRODUCTION I: BREEDING SEASONS

The act of leaving offspring to succeeding generations is the most important aspect of any animal's life. Natural selection will obviously favour those individuals which produce the largest number of offspring which themselves survive to breed. Two of the most important features of reproduction determining the success of an individual are the time at which it breeds and its rate of reproduction. Accordingly the breeding ecology of birds is usually divided into two sections: the timing of breeding (breeding seasons) and reproductive rates (clutch-size) and this is the division we use here. However, it is important to stress that although such a division is useful, it tends to mask the fact that both the timing of breeding and the clutch-size are closely linked and impose similar demands on parent birds. In order to reproduce, birds require a large amount of additional food. Let us suppose that a bird can maximize the number of offspring it can produce by breeding early in the season and by producing a large clutch of eggs. If it takes time to collect the necessary reserves for breeding, there may be a trade-off between the date at which it starts to breed and the number of eggs it lays. The earlier it lays, the fewer reserves it will have laid down, so the fewer eggs it can lay. As we have already emphasized (Chapter 1), birds do not make conscious decisions about such matters; natural selection simply favours those individuals with the optimum trade-off. In this chapter and the next, we consider the evolutionary (i.e. functional) aspects of breeding season and clutch-size.

## 4.1 Breeding seasons

### 4.1.1 *Introduction*

The breeding season of a species is defined as when it has eggs or young in the nest. More precisely, the timing of breeding of a species is usually based on the mean date on which each female laid the first egg of her clutch. Such a definition applies only to first clutches and excludes second or re-placement clutches (laid after the first one is lost).

### 4.1.2 *The timing of breeding: ultimate and proximate factors*

The time at which birds breed has evolved through natural selection, like other features of their biology, in order to maximize the number of young produced. Lack (1954) suggested that birds lay their eggs at a time of year which resulted in young in the nest when food was most abundant. Lack's idea has been supported by a number of studies (see below), but for some species his explanation is an over-simplification.

Since it is important for birds to breed at a time when food is sufficiently abundant to feed their growing young, natural selection will strongly favour individuals which time their breeding to coincide with the peak abundance of food. In this case we can say that the availability of food for the growing young is the *ultimate factor* affecting the timing of breeding. Ultimate factors are those which directly affect the evolution of a particular characteristic, in this case the timing of breeding.

However, for a bird to have young in the nest at the time of peak food availability, it must *start* breeding much earlier. For example, in species like the American Robin and European Blackbird, three weeks elapse from the start of egg-laying to having young in the nest; five days to form an egg, plus 3 or 4 days to lay a full clutch (one egg per day) plus 13 or 14 days for incubation. This interval does not take into account the time necessary for the development of the gonads from their winter resting state. A three-week interval between the start of egg formation and hatching is the shortest found in birds, most species take longer, some taking up to two months. The way in which birds time the onset of egg formation has been the subject of a number of detailed studies, beyond the scope of this book (for reviews see Murton and Westwood, 1977; Immelmann, 1971). It is sufficient here to say that birds use environmental cues such as daylength to time their breeding. Daylength is a *proximate factor* in the timing of breeding; it has no immediate value in terms of the birds' nutritional needs, but (and this is the important point) it provides a good indication of what is to come later in the season. Natural selection has favoured individuals which start egg formation when days reach a certain length, because this results in their having young in the nest when food is most abundant. Such individuals leave more surviving young than those breeding either earlier or later.

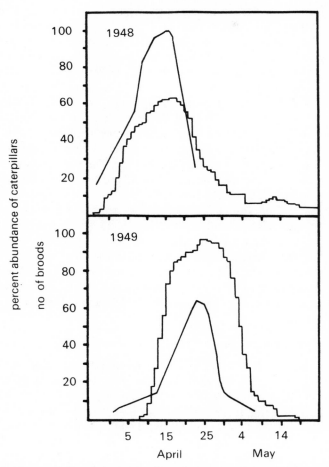

**Figure 4.1** The correlation between the time when young tits are in the nest and the abundance of caterpillars on the oak trees. Stepped graphs show daily combined total of Great and Blue Tit broods in nest boxes. Smoothed graphs show percentage abundance of caterpillars. Figures on vertical axis indicate percentage abundance of caterpillars and actual numbers of broods. (From Gibb, 1950).

Thus two sets of factors, ultimate and proximate, affect the timing of breeding in birds (and other organisms). We can think of ultimate factors as the evolutionary forces, while the proximate factors are the causes or mechanisms by which birds time their breeding.

There is now good evidence for a number of bird species that the time when they have young in the nest does indeed coincide with the peak availability of food. Figure 4.1 shows the situation for Blue and Great Tits, which feed their young on caterpillars. The timing of caterpillar abundance varies between years and over a period of 20 years the peak abundance varied by about one month. As expected, the tits' breeding season has also varied by about the same amount (Perrins, 1979).

In addition to quantitative studies of this sort, there is abundant circumstantial evidence for birds timing their breeding to coincide with peaks of food abundance. One of the most striking examples concerns small birds of prey in Europe. The Kestrel starts breeding relatively early (late April), feeding its young on small mammals which it apparently finds easier to catch before the grass has grown long. The Sparrowhawk feeds its young on the newly fledged young of woodland birds and starts breeding later, in early May. The Hobby breeds later still, mid-May, feeding its young on large insects and young swallows and martins which fledge even later than the young of woodland birds (Newton, 1979). In Southern Europe and North Africa there are two other small birds of prey which breed even later, laying their eggs in mid-summer. Both Eleonora's Falcon and the Sooty Falcon feed their young on small birds migrating to Africa from Europe. Many of these migrants get lost on their first journey and are an easy prey for the falcons (Vaughan, 1961; Clapham, 1964).

### 4.1.3 *Do birds get the timing right?*

Although the examples we have just described indicate a close association between the timing of breeding and the peak abundance of food, the situation is not quite as clearcut as it may first appear. There are two reasons for this. First, it is not known for many species precisely when the most critical time for finding food occurs: while the female is forming eggs (see below), while the young are in the nest, or just after the young have left the nest. In the latter case newly fledged young may need abundant food to maintain their body temperature. This is because although they are no longer growing very much they are more active and are not being brooded, nor are they keeping each other warm as they did in the nest. In addition, they may need abundant food while they learn to forage for themselves and to become independent of their parents. For many species there may be only a single peak of food abundance so that only one of these three stages can coincide with it.

The second difficulty concerns those cases where it is clear that some individuals do *not* breed at the best time. Several studies have shown that

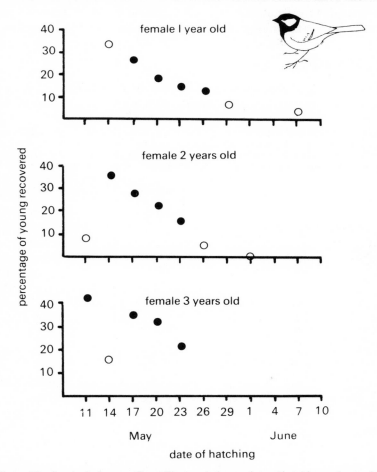

**Figure 4.2**   Survival of young Great Tits in relation to date of hatching and age of female. The term 'recovered' covers all those young birds which are known to have survived to at least three months after leaving the nest. The solid circles are based on more than five recoveries, the open circles are based on fewer than five and are hence less reliable. Note how the proportion of young which survive after fledging decreases with season regardless of the age of the female. (From Perrins, 1970).

birds breeding relatively early in the season produce a greater number of surviving young than those breeding later. An example is shown in Fig. 4.2 and it is clear from this that some birds are not breeding at the best time. If early breeders are the most successful then all individuals should breed early in the season. However, this may not always be possible because some females experience difficulty finding sufficient food to start egg formation. This constraint on the timing of breeding is discussed in the next section.

## 4.2 Food for the laying female

The amount of food that a female needs for the production of a clutch varies from species to species and depends upon two factors: the size of the

**Table 4.1** Egg weight and clutch weight as a proportion of female body weight in different species. Note: this table gives approximate figures. Since both individuals and eggs vary in size and clutch-size varies, it can only be used as a very rough guide. It does, however, give an indication of the great degree of variation. For further information see text.

| Species | Adult weight (g) | Egg weight (g) | Egg weight as % of body weight | Clutch-size | Clutch-size as % body weight |
|---|---|---|---|---|---|
| Ostrich | 90 000 | 1 600 | 1.8 | 6 | 10.8 |
| Emperor Penguin | 30 000 | 450 | 1.5 | 1 | 1.5 |
| Adélie Penguin | 5 000 | 124 | 2.5 | 2 | 5.0 |
| Manx Shearwater | 400 | 58 | 14.5 | 1 | 14.5 |
| Storm Petrel | 28 | 7 | 25.0 | 1 | 25.0 |
| Gannet | 3 300 | 106 | 3.0 | 1 | 3.0 |
| Mallard | 1 000 | 54 | 5.4 | 11 | 59.4 |
| Mute Swan | 9 000 | 340 | 3.8 | 6 | 22.8 |
| Osprey | 1 400 | 74 | 5.3 | 3 | 15.9 |
| Peregrine | 1 100 | 52 | 4.7 | 3 | 14.1 |
| Pheasant | 900 | 30 | 3.3 | 14 | 46.2 |
| Turkey | 3 500 | 75 | 2.1 | 12 | 25.2 |
| Ringed Plover | 60 | 10 | 16.7 | 4 | 66.8 |
| Herring Gull | 895 | 82 | 9.2 | 3 | 27.6 |
| Common Tern | 135 | 20 | 14.8 | 3 | 44.4 |
| Puffin | 500 | 65 | 13.0 | 1. | 13.0 |
| Wood Pigeon | 500 | 18 | 3.6 | 2 | 7.2 |
| Snowy owl | 2 000 | 83 | 4.1 | 5 | 20.5 |
| Vervain Humming-bird | 2 | 0.2 | 10.0 | 2 | 20.0 |
| Wren | 9.5 | 1.3 | 13.7 | 6 | 82.2 |
| Blackbird American Robin | 100 | 8 | 8.0 | 4 | 32.0 |
| Blue Tit | 11 | 1.3 | 11.8 | 11 | 130.0 |
| Red Cardinal | 40 | 3.2 | 8.0 | 4 | 32.0 |
| House (English) Sparrow | 30 | 3.0 | 10.0 | 5 | 50.0 |

bird and the size and number of eggs it lays. In general, small birds tend to produce both relatively large eggs (see section 3.5, Fig. 3.5) and large clutches, compared with large birds (Table 4.1). Consequently they require relatively larger amounts of energy for egg production than large birds. For example, the Blue Tit produces a clutch of 11 eggs each weighing 1.3 g, giving a total clutch weight of 14.3 g. This represents about 130% of the female's body weight. At the other extreme the Emperor Penguin produces only a single egg weighing 450 g, which constitutes only 1.5% of the female's weight. Table 4.1 emphasizes that for many species the

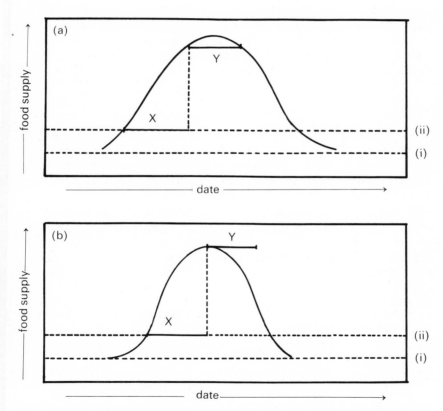

**Figure 4.3** Hypothetical relationship between food supply, date of laying and date of young becoming independent in two species (*a*) and (*b*). The curves show levels of food abundance against (i) the food required for general body maintenance and (ii) the food required for forming eggs. The straight line *X* represents the time required for forming and laying eggs and incubating these to the point of hatching. Line *Y* represents the time taken to raise the young to the point of independence. (From Perrins, 1970).

energetic demands of egg production can be considerable. In addition, these demands occur at a time when food is not at its most abundant.

The situation can be explained diagrammatically (Fig. 4.3). In these two diagrams, the lower dotted line denotes the level of food necessary for the bird to be able to maintain itself, and the upper line the level necessary for egg formation. The two horizontal bars show (1) the length of time between the start of incubation and the hatching of the young and (2) the nestling period. The only thing which is different in the two diagrams is the curve, the pattern of food abundance. In the upper diagram food is available in plenty for long enough for the birds to be able to raise their young before it starts to get scarcer, while in the lower one this is not the case. It seems likely that the lower diagram may apply to a number of species (Perrins, 1970).

The idea that the timing of breeding may be constrained by the female's ability to obtain sufficient food has been tested experimentally; this is discussed in the following section.

### 4.2.1  *Feeding experiments*

Several experimental studies have been conducted in which part of a study population has been provided with extra food in the weeks preceding egg-laying. In most of these, females receiving extra food have laid significantly earlier than the unfed control birds. In most cases the difference in timing of breeding is not large (Table 4.2), but in the Red-winged Blackbird, Ewald and Rohwer (1982) found that extra food advanced egg-laying by as much as three weeks, and in the Kestrel Drent and Daan (1980) found an advance of about a month. In all the studies listed in Table 4.2, laying date was advanced by the provision of additional food, but in most cases clutch-size remained unchanged.

**Table 4.2**  The effect of artificial feeding on the advancement of laying date. In each study the figures given show the advancement of laying of a number of individuals compared with controls in the same area.

| Species | Advance of laying date by provision of food | Reference |
|---|---|---|
| Kestrel | One month | Drent and Daan (1980) |
| Carrion Crow | 5 days | Yom-Tov (1974) |
| Red-winged Blackbird | 12–26 days | Ewald and Rohwer (1982) |
| Song Sparrow | 25 days | Smith *et al.* (1980) |
| Great Tit | 6 days | Källander (1974) |
| Willow Tit | 5–8 days | Bronssen and Jansson (1980) |
| Crested Tit | 2–5 days | ,,          ,,          ,, |

The results of these experiments support the idea that food availability at the time of egg formation can affect the timing of breeding. In the next two sections we consider ways in which some birds have minimized the problem of food shortage at the time of egg-laying.

## 4.2.2 *Food reserves*

Birds may be able to overcome the problem of food shortage by using food reserves laid down earlier. However, in practice it does not seem possible for many species to do this. There are probably two reasons for this. First, as Table 4.1 indicates, some birds, particularly the small ones, would need to build up impossibly large reserves to produce a clutch. Second, in the case of resident species, reserves would have to be laid down in the late winter or early spring, the time when food is most scarce. Migrant species may be living in areas where food is more abundant, but they need their food reserves for migration.

This is especially true for small migrants, such as warblers (see Chapter 9), but some larger species are able to migrate long distances while carrying reserves for breeding. The most striking example of this use of food reserves is found in the arctic breeding geese. The Lesser Snow Goose for example spends the winter in the southern United States, but breeds in the arctic regions of North America. Females accumulate reserves on the wintering grounds and migrate northwards to arrive at their snow-covered breeding areas still about 20% above their normal weight. Females are almost totally dependent on these body reserves for producing and incubating their eggs. Moreover, the weight of birds on their arrival is closely correlated with the number of eggs they lay. The heaviest females produce the largest clutches. By the time the goslings hatch, females have used all their food reserves, but by this stage the snow is rapidly thawing and the vegetation which the adults and young eat is growing rapidly (Ankey and McInnes, 1978). The use of food reserves in arctic geese enables them to start egg-laying very soon after their arrival at the breeding grounds. Their large body size enables them to carry sufficient reserves for both migration and breeding. Smaller long-distance migrants would need to carry relatively larger reserves if they were to do the same, and this does not appear to be an option open to them.

There is however, one species, an African weaver finch, the Red-billed Quelea, which does migrate with some of its reserves for breeding. Jones and Ward (1974) found that the Quelea stored protein in its flight muscles, and metabolized it during egg formation. The Red-billed Quelea is unusual (as far as current knowledge goes) in that it breeds several times a year, each time in a different place. It breeds just after the rains, and follows the rain belts as they move up and down central Africa (Jones and Ward, 1974). Like arctic geese, Quelea need to start breeding rapidly once they find a suitable area and the reserves they carry in their flight muscle help them to do this. However, they do not migrate long distances so they do not need large reserves for migration.

### 4.2.3  *Food hoarding*

Food hoarding is a special case of the use of food reserves for breeding. Most bird species which hoard food recover and eat it within a few days, but two species, Clark's Nutcracker and the European Jay, hoard large quantities of pine seeds and acorns respectively in the autumn for use in the following year (Tombach, 1977; Bossema, 1979). Clark's Nutcracker depends almost entirely on stored food, both for egg formation and for feeding its young.

### 4.2.4  *Courtship feeding*

Another way in which the problems of food shortage at the time of egg formation may be alleviated is by males providing some of the food which their partners need. This behaviour is called courtship feeding, but the term is misleading since in most species it occurs long after courtship. In fact it occurs most frequently while females are forming eggs and during laying and incubation (Royama, 1966). Courtship feeding is widespread in passerine birds, sea-birds and birds of prey (Newton, 1979). In some species the male may provide a large proportion of the female's food requirements. In the Blue Tit for example, the male provides up to 40% of the female's total food requirements during the period prior to laying (Krebs, 1970b). The male's contribution is even more marked in the Common Tern, and just prior to egg-laying the male may provide almost all the female's food. Nisbet (1973, 1977) found that the more food the male tern brought their mates, the earlier egg-laying occurred, and the larger the eggs and clutch.

### 4.3  Length of breeding season: number of broods

So far we have been concerned only with the onset of breeding, but in an evolutionary sense it is just as important for birds to 'know' when to stop breeding. Most species rear only a single brood in a year, while others may produce two or more. In this section we will examine the factors which determine the number of broods that different species rear each season.

Most large birds and almost all non-passerines raise only a single brood in a season. This is because the incubation period and duration of parental care are generally longer in larger birds, so they have less time in which to rear a second brood (Lack, 1968). Most small passerines also produce only a single brood, but some, such as the American Robin and European Blackbird, regularly rear more than one brood in a season. The House (= English) Sparrow often rears three broods in a season and the Barn Swallow usually rears two, but sometimes three broods.

Several factors are important in determining the number of broods reared in a season. These include breeding location, availability of food, duration of parental care, and costs to the parents.

*Breeding location.* Multiple broods occur more frequently among birds breeding at low latitudes because the summer is longer (see Fig. 4.4).

*Availability of food.* Birds may rear additional broods when food is unusually abundant. For example, the European Blackbird feeds its young on earthworms which are more easily collected when the soil is moist than when it is dry. Accordingly, they have more broods in wet seasons than in dry ones (Snow, 1958). Similarly, Barn Owls and Short-eared Owls may exceptionally rear two broods in those years when their main prey, small rodents, is especially abundant (Bunn *et al.*, 1982; Witherby *et al.*, 1952).

*Duration of parental care.* This differs markedly between bird species. Small passerines care for their young for about 12–14 days while they are in the nest and then for a further week or so once they have fledged. In contrast, species like the Tawny Owl spend about one month feeding the young in the nest followed by three months of care after fledging (Southern, 1954). Such a long period of parental care precludes a second brood, but such a strategy is presumably more successful in terms of the number of young produced. An even more extreme situation exists in some of the large albatrosses, such as the Wandering Albatross, where the combined incubation and fledging periods take about a year. As a result the adults are able to breed only every second year.

*Cost to the parents.* In many species late breeding attempts are relatively unsuccessful and produce few surviving young (see Fig. 4.2). In such cases the advantage of late breeding may be outweighed by the costs to the parent. If the chances of rearing young are low, then it will not be worthwhile making a breeding attempt. Although this is likely to be an important factor influencing a bird's 'decision' (in an evolutionary sense) to stop breeding, there are relatively few data to substantiate it. The costs to the parents include increased risk of predation, reduced time to lay down fat reserves for the winter or migration, and insufficient time to complete the moult. Most birds replace their feathers after breeding (Voitkevitch, 1966). This takes up to six weeks in small birds and longer in large birds. Moult is not usually undertaken at the same time as breeding because birds require extra food supplies to grow a new set of feathers. A delay in moult may put birds at a disadvantage compared with those individuals which stopped breeding earlier.

## 4.4    Variations in breeding season

In the preceding sections we have shown that the most important ultimate factor affecting the timing of birds' breeding season is the food supply, either for the young or for the laying female. The breeding seasons of

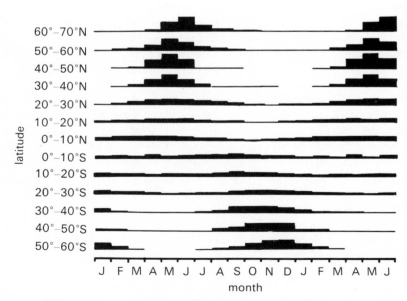

**Figure 4.4**  The breeding season of birds in relation to latitude. For further information see text. (From Baker, 1938).

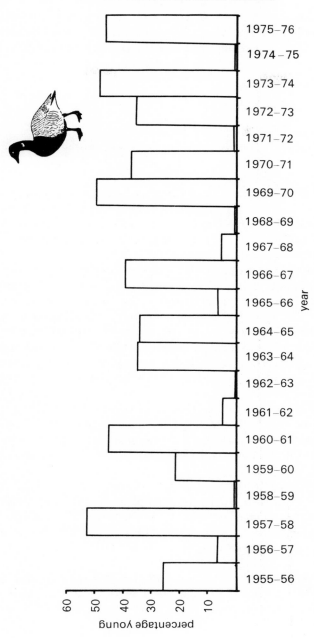

**Figure 4.5** The percentage of young birds in winter flocks of Brent Geese. (From Ogilvie and St. Joseph, 1976)

different species and of birds in different areas vary markedly and in this section we will consider some factors which influence food availability and hence the timing of breeding: geographical position, temperature, habitat and age.

### 4.4.1 *Geographical position*

There are three aspects of geographical position which have been shown to affect the timing of birds' breeding seasons: latitude, longitude and altitude.

*Latitude*. The effect of latitude on the timing of breeding seasons is marked (Fig. 4.4) and not unexpected. Spring arrives later at higher latitudes. In North America the onset of spring occurs about 4 or 5 days later for each northward shift of 1° of latitude (Hopkins, 1938) and the timing of birds' breeding season follows the same trend.

An additional effect of latitude is the spread of breeding as one moves from the equator towards the poles. As Fig. 4.4 shows, birds breed throughout much of the year in the tropics, but at high latitudes breeding is restricted to the short summer season. For birds breeding in the Arctic and Antarctic the timing of egg-laying is particularly important since the season is so short. Any delay in the onset may mean that birds have not completed their breeding cycle before the autumn freeze-up starts. For some arctic species such as waders, geese and sea-birds, late thaws are not unusual and in some years almost entire populations may fail to rear young (Fig. 4.5).

Although Fig. 4.4 indicates that birds can be found breeding in all months of the year in the tropics (especially in tropical rain forests), it is important to note that even within these areas most species have clearly defined breeding seasons (Miller, 1955).

*Longitude*. The central areas of large land masses such as North America and Europe experience lower winter temperatures than coastal areas and consequently take longer to warm up in the spring. The timing of birds' breeding seasons reflect this pattern, with those species in central areas breeding later than those in coastal regions.

*Altitude*. Hopkins (1938) calculated that spring arrived 4 or 5 days later for each 125 m increase in altitude. The breeding seasons of birds show similar delays with altitude (Table 4.3).

**Table 4.3** The laying date of the Meadow Pipit in northern England in relation to the altitude (from Coulson, 1956).

| Altitude (feet) | 0–50 | 50–250 | 250–750 | 750–1000 | more than 1000 |
|---|---|---|---|---|---|
| Mean date of laying (May) | 5.9 | 8.0 | 14.6 | 13.4 | 20.8 |

### 4.4.2 *Temperature*

Temperature varies according to the geographical factors discussed above, but annual differences in temperature within a single area may also affect the timing of birds' breeding seasons.

In most temperate and arctic areas the temperature at any given time of year is not predictable and at any locality the start of breeding may vary in different years. Generally, breeding occurs early when spring temperatures are high and later in cold or 'late' springs (Fig.4.6). Spring temperatures

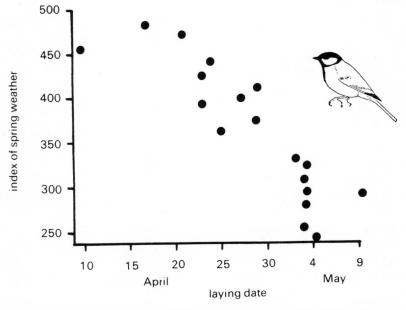

**Figure 4.6** Average date of breeding of Great Tit in relation to spring weather. The index of spring weather was obtained by adding the average for the maximum and minimum temperatures for each day from March 1st to April 20th. The date of laying is the average of the dates on which each female laid its first egg. Each point represents the data for a single year. (From Perrins, 1965).

may have both a direct and an indirect effect on the timing of birds' breeding seasons. The Pied Flycatcher provides a clear example of such an indirect effect. Like the Great Tit (Fig. 4.6), the Pied Flycatcher breeds earlier when spring temperatures are relatively high. However, unlike the Great Tit (which is resident), the Pied Flycatcher is a migrant, does not arrive in England until late April, and therefore cannot have experienced the variation in weather directly. It seems likely therefore that the timing of breeding in this species occurs in response to the general level of advancement of the season, such as the availability of its food supply (insects).

Relatively high spring temperatures may also affect birds directly. In warmer weather birds need less food to maintain themselves and as a result may come into breeding condition earlier than they would in a cooler spring.

### 4.4.3 *Habitat*

Even within a small geographical area in the same year, the same species in different habitats may breed at slightly different times (Table 4.4). Though the reasons for this are not always clear, it seems likely that the habitat in which breeding starts earlier is usually the one with the richer food supply.

### 4.4.4 *Age*

The factors discussed above (geographical position, temperature and habitat) have all been concerned with the timing of breeding *between* populations of birds. Female age is one factor which affects the timing of breeding *within* populations.

In many species, older individuals breed earlier in the year than those breeding for the first time. Table 4.5 gives some examples of the difference

**Table 4.4** Laying dates in different habitats.

| Species | Habitat and difference in laying date | | Author |
|---------|-----------------------|------------------------|--------|
| Sparrowhawk | River valley forests, 7 May | Poor hillside forests, 16 May | Newton (1976) |
| Common Tern | Good feeding habitat, 25 May | Poor feeding habitat, 28 May | Nisbet (1977) |
| Blackbird | Gardens | Woodland, 1–2 weeks later | Snow (1958) |
| Great Tit | Gardens | Woodland, 3–5 days later | Perrins (1965) |

**Table 4.5** Laying date in relation to age of female.

| Species | Age (yr) | Laying date | Author |
|---|---|---|---|
| Gannet | — | Progressively earlier for first four breeding attempts | Nelson (1978) |
| Sparrowhawk | 1 | May 10 | Newton (1976) |
| | 2 or older | May 4 | |
| Great Tit | 1 | April 31 | Perrins and Moss (1974) |
| | 2 or older | April 29 | |
| Pied Flycatcher | 1 | June 1 | Von Haartman (1967) |
| | 2 or older | May 29 | |

in timing of breeding among birds of different ages. The most likely explanation for this effect is that since older, more experienced birds are more proficient at feeding (e.g. Dunn, 1972) they are able to attain breeding condition earlier than younger birds.

## 4.5 Non-annual cycles

In most parts of the world, seasons are closely linked with the annual solar cycle. Even within the tropics most areas are seasonal to some extent and most birds breeding there have annual cycles. Some of the tropical seas, however, appear to be remarkably aseasonal, and perhaps as a consequence of this a small number of sea-bird species have non-annual breeding cycles (Ashmole, 1971). The Bridled Tern on Cousin Island in the Seychelles (Indian Ocean), and the Sooty Tern on Ascension Island (just south of the equator in the mid-Atlantic) have non-annual breeding cycles. The Bridled Tern breeds every eight months (Diamond, 1976), and the Sooty Tern every 9.6 months (Fig. 4.7). The most reasonable evolutionary explanation for such non-annual cycles is that food availability allows birds to breed and moult and prepare to breed again in less than a year, and that such a pattern is adaptive because birds rear almost four broods every three years, instead of three if they had an annual cycle.

## 4.6 Summary

Birds time their breeding so that they have young in the nest at the time when food is most abundant. The availability of food is the ultimate factor affecting the timing of breeding. To have young in the nest at the peak of food availability, birds must start breeding earlier in the season and use

AVIAN ECOLOGY

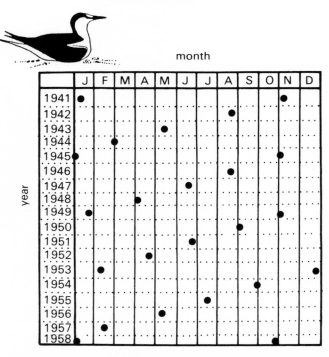

month

**Figure 4.7** The nesting cycle of the Wideawake or Sooty Tern on Ascension Island. The circles denote the early egg stage in each cycle. (From Chapin and Wing, 1959).

cues such as daylength (a proximate factor) to time the onset of breeding. There is evidence that birds do not always time their breeding as well as they might, and an important constraint on the timing of breeding is food availability for the female when forming eggs. The experimental provision of extra food prior to egg-laying confirms that food availability affects the timing of breeding. Birds may overcome this problem to some extent, either by laying down food reserves or by the male providing food for the female. Factors affecting the duration of the breeding season include geographic location, food abundance, duration of parental care, and the cost benefits of rearing young late in the season. The timing of birds' breeding seasons varies geographically (with latitude, longitude and altitude), between years at the same location according to spring temperatures, and in different habitats. Within populations older females breed earlier than young ones. A very few birds (tropical sea-birds) have non-annual breeding cycles.

# CHAPTER FIVE

# REPRODUCTION II: CLUTCH-SIZE

## 5.1 Introduction

All bird species produce a characteristic number of eggs in a clutch. The average size of clutch varies from a single egg in many sea-birds to eight or more eggs in some wildfowl, and fifteen or more in some game birds. The clutch-size of a range of species is shown in Table 5.1. In this chapter we

**Table 5.1** Clutch size in different birds. *Note*: where the clutch-size for a group or family is given, this is the usual range for most of the species; individuals or certain species may fall outside this range. Emphasis is placed on the better-known, north temperate groups; many tropical species have smaller clutches; some hole-nesting passerines e.g. wrens, tits, may have larger ones (up to 11). For further information see text.

| | | | |
|---|---|---|---|
| Penguins | 1–2 | Grouse/ptarmigan | 5–12 |
| Divers (loons) | 2 | Quail | 10–16 |
| Grebes | 3–5 | Pheasants/partridges | 8–18 |
| Albatrosses, | | Cranes | 2 |
| shearwaters and | | Rails, coots etc. | 5–12 |
| petrels | 1 | Waders (shore-birds) | 3–4 |
| Pelicans | 1–4 | Gulls | 2–3 |
| Cormorants | 3–4 | Terns | 2–3 |
| Herons/egrets | 3–5 | Auks | 1–2 |
| Swans | 4–6 | Pigeons/doves | 2 |
| Geese | 3–6 | Owls | 2–7 |
| Ducks | 7–12 | Nightjars | 2 |
| Vultures | 1–2 | Swifts | 1–5 |
| Hawks | 2–5 | Humming-birds | 2 |
| Eagles | 2 | Kingfishers | 4–7 |
| Osprey | 3 | Woodpeckers | 3–6 |
| Falcons | 3–5 | Passerines | 2–5 |

shall examine a number of theories concerning the evolution of clutch-size, and shall consider the factors which influence clutch-size between and within species.

## 5.2 Evolution of clutch-size: theories

The reason that birds should lay clutches of the sizes that they do has aroused considerable interest and controversy. A number of theories have been proposed, including the following:

(1) Birds lay as many eggs as they can incubate properly, i.e. that they can adequately cover and keep warm.

(2) They lay as many eggs as they are physiologically capable of laying.

(3) They lay a clutch whose size is related to the prevalent mortality of that species; in other words, that their clutch-size has evolved to be sufficient to replace the dying adults and so maintain a stable population.

(4) The parents produce a clutch of the size which will result in the greatest number of young surviving to maturity.

The first two theories can be disposed of fairly quickly.

(1) There is no evidence that the clutch-size of many species is adapted to the largest number of eggs that can be incubated. Indeed, birds tend to have the same hatching success with large and average-sized clutches (Lack, 1947).

(2) The clutch-size of many species is not related to the physiological capabilities of the parents (see section 5.6).

(3) The third theory, that birds adjust their clutch-size to match adult mortality, has been proposed by Wynne-Edwards (1955, 1962), and may be stated essentially as follows. If a species becomes too abundant, it will overeat its food supply and suffer a population crash. Wynne-Edwards suggested that birds (and other animals) have evolved ways in which such an over-exploitation of food supplies does not occur, and thought that one of the ways in which birds might do this was by lowering their rate of reproduction. He noted, for example, that many sea-birds produce only a single-egg clutch, and interpreted this as a way of reducing their reproductive rate in order to decrease the risk of over-population. Wynne-Edwards' ideas have provoked a great deal of discussion (e.g. Maynard-Smith, 1964), since the type of system he proposed required the operation of 'group selection'. In Chapter 2 we pointed out the theoretical difficulties with this concept. Specifically, Wynne-Edwards suggested that birds were 'altruistic' and laid a clutch which was smaller than the number of young

they could rear in order to prevent an excessive increase in the local population.

In other words, birds acted, in terms of their clutch-size, for the good of the local population or group. These ideas have not gained general acceptance, because it is difficult to see how such a system could evolve. This can be illustrated with an hypothetical example. The sort of population that Wynne-Edwards envisaged would comprise 'altruistic' birds, all of which produced a single-egg clutch even though they were capable of rearing, say, two young. By laying only one egg, the population is kept in check and the birds do not over-eat their food supply. Now imagine that a 'selfish' mutant arises in the population, which lays a two-egg clutch. The mutant form will reproduce twice as fast as the original type and the frequency of two-egg birds will spread through the population at the expense of the first type. Clearly the genes for a single-egg clutch could not be maintained in the population for long; single-egg individuals would be out-competed by the faster-reproducing two-egg birds.

(4) The fourth idea, that birds lay the number of eggs in a clutch which results in the largest number of surviving young, was originally proposed by Lack (1948, 1954). This is the most commonly accepted theory for the evolution of clutch-size. In the following section, we consider Lack's ideas in more detail and look at how he tested his hypothesis.

## 5.3 Lack's hypothesis

Stated simply, Lack's hypothesis is that the clutch-size which evolves is that which leads to the parents rearing the largest number of young which survive to breed. In other words, natural selection favours those birds which produce clutches which leave the largest numbers of young in succeeding generations. Lack considered the amount of food which the parents could bring to the nest to feed the young to be the most important factor in producing this effect. The situation is shown graphically in Fig. 5.1. First, the more eggs that are laid, the more young will hatch (line $X$ in Fig. 5.1$a$). However, since individual young in larger broods receive less food (because the parents have to share it among more young), the mortality rate of young increases with size of brood (line $Y$ in Fig. 5.1$a$). The optimum clutch-size is then the one giving rise to the most surviving young (Fig. 5.1$b$).

Lack first tested his idea by examining the survival of young Starlings in relation to the size of brood in which they were reared (Table 5.2).

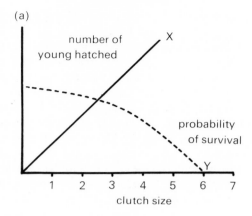

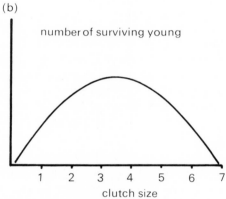

**Figure 5.1** The relationship between clutch-size, the number of young hatched (*X*), the probability of survival for individual young (*Y*) and the number surviving per brood.

**Table 5.2** Family size in the starling; for explanation see text (from Lack, 1948).

| Brood size | No. broods | No. young recovered ≥ 3 months | % | No. recovered/brood |
|---|---|---|---|---|
| 1 | 65 | — | — | — |
| 2 | 164 | 6 | 1.8 | 3.7 |
| 3 | 426 | 26 | 2.0 | 6.1 |
| 4 | 989 | 82 | 2.1 | 8.3 |
| 5 | 1235 | 128 | 2.1 | 10.4 |
| 6 | 526 | 53 | 1.7 | 10.1 |
| 7 | 93 | 10 | 1.8⎫ | 10.2 |
| 8 | 15 | 1 | 0.8⎭ | |
| 9–10 | 3 | 0 | 0 | — |

The average brood-size in Starlings was five, and he found, as predicted, that broods of five young produced the largest number of surviving young. In other words, broods of five were commonest because they were most successful. Note, however, that the success of broods of five was only slightly greater than that of larger broods. We shall return to this in section 5.3.1.

The second species to be examined in detail was the European Swift, which provides a good example of how the amount of food brought to the young affects the number of young reared. The European Swift produces a clutch of either two or three eggs, and feeds its young exclusively on aerial arthropods (insects and spiders). The ease with which it catches these depends upon the weather, since there are many more arthropods available during fine weather than in poor weather. Consequently, in good summers the parents can usually bring sufficient food to feed three young. In poor summers the foraging efficiency of the adults decreases considerably, and they are unable to provide sufficient food for three chicks. As a result some young die (Table 5.3). The important point here is that *fewer* young are raised from broods of three than are raised from broods of two. Hence in poor summers a clutch of two eggs is the most productive, whereas in good summers the birds rear more young from broods of three eggs. The swift is therefore slightly different from the starling, in that either a clutch of two or a clutch of three may be the most productive; which of these is the more productive at any given moment depends upon the weather, which, presumably, the swift cannot forecast (see 5.5) Clutches of both two and three eggs are common in the population, and this is exactly what one would expect if natural selection was operating.

Another species used to test Lack's hypothesis is the Great Tit. The Great Tit nests in holes in trees and has a relatively large clutch of 8–10

**Table 5.3** Feeding rate of swifts in relation to weather (from Lack, 1956).

| Brood size | No. feeds/brood/ 10 hours | No. feeds/chick/ 10 hours | No. fledged/ brood |
|---|---|---|---|
| | Fine weather | | |
| 2 | 14.9 | 7.4 | 2.0 |
| 3 | 19.3 | 6.4 | 2.75 |
| | Poor weather | | |
| 2 | 7.1 | 3.5 | 1.84 |
| 3 | 6.5 | 2.2 | 1.64 |

eggs. Like most hole-nesting birds, almost all the young (even from very large broods) survive to the point of leaving the nest. Just as in the Swift, the parents bring more food to the nest for larger broods, but individual young in large broods get less food than do chicks in smaller broods (Table 5.4). Although almost all the young survive to leave the nest, the difference in feeding rate results in young from large broods being lighter in weight than those from smaller broods (Fig. 5.2). The weight of young at fledging has a

**Table 5.4**  Number of feeds per day to nests of Great Tits in relation to brood size (from Gibb, 1955).

| Brood size | Feeds/brood/day | Feeds/chick/day |
|---|---|---|
| Small (av. 5.5 young) | 428 | 78 |
| Large (av. 11.0 young) | 637 | 58 |

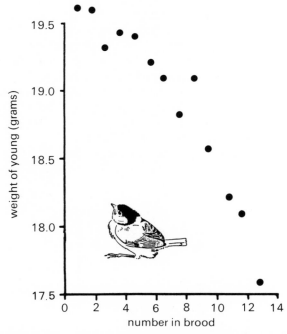

**Figure 5.2**  The relationship between brood-size and weight just before leaving the nest in the Great Tit. (From Perrins, 1965).

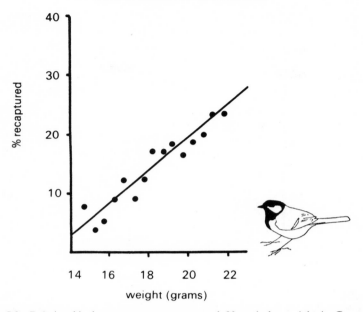

**Figure 5.3** Relationship between recapture rate and fifteenth-day weight in Great Tits. (From Perrins, 1980).

marked effect on their subsequent chances of survival (Fig. 5.3), with heavy young surviving best. Young Great Tits from small broods have the greatest chance of survival, but the greatest *number* of survivors comes from broods of medium size. In other words, the commonest clutch-size appears to be the most productive, as predicted by Lack's hypothesis.

### 5.3.1 Criticisms of Lack's hypothesis

Although Lack's theory is generally accepted (Klomp, 1970; Ricklefs, 1977), there have been some minor criticisms of it, and consequently some modifications. The main criticism of the theory stems from a closer inspection of the examples which have been used to support the hypothesis, such as those in the previous section. This reveals, in some cases, a discrepancy between the most frequent clutch-size found in nature and the clutch-size which produced the largest number of surviving young. In virtually all cases where a discrepancy occurred, the commonest clutch-size was smaller than the most productive one (Klomp, 1970; Perrins and Moss,

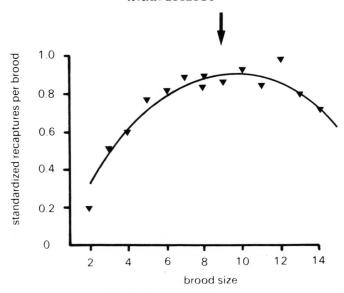

**Figure 5.4**  The numbers of survivors per brood in relation to brood-size in Great Tits. The line shows the fitted curve, the triangles the actual data. Note that the most productive brood-size is around 10 while the average clutch-size is only about 9.0. (From Perrins and Moss, 1974).

1975; Fig. 5.4), which means that birds often lay a clutch which is slightly conservative in relation to the number of young they can raise. There have been several suggestions to explain this apparent anomaly, and more than one may be operating at any time.

(a)  *Analytical faults*. One of the commonest causes for the sort of discrepancy outlined above is faulty analysis. An example is shown in Fig. 5.5, where a species has a decrease in clutch-size with laying date (Fig. 5.5*a*), i.e. clutches laid later in the season are smaller. In many species showing such a trend the earliest hatched broods are the most successful (Fig. 5.5*b*). If the number of survivors per brood is then plotted we find that the largest broods are (apparently) the most successful (Fig. 5.5*c*). This analysis is of course invalid unless the effect of season is taken into account. This type of analytical error could occur in any situation where there are correlations between brood-size and survival and a third factor.

(b)  *Female ability*. If females differ in their ability to raise young (e.g. some may be more efficient at feeding than others), and if each female lays a

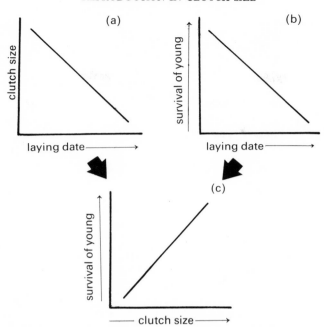

**Figure 5.5** Hypothetical diagrams in which (*a*) clutch-size decreases with season, (*b*) survival of young decreases with season. Using these data, if one plotted survival against clutch-size, one would obtain a result as in (*c*) in which survival was highest from the largest clutches. For further explanation see text.

clutch which is related to its own ability, then this will produce results which indicate that larger clutches are more successful than smaller ones. To examine the possibility that females differ in their ability to rear young, Perrins and Moss (1975) manipulated a number of Great Tit broods so that they were larger or smaller than their original size. The success of these manipulated broods was different from that of natural broods of the same size, and in particular large natural broods were more successful than broods of the same size which had been artificially increased (Figure 5.6). This indicates that females 'knew' the sort of number of young they were able to rear and laid a clutch of the appropriate size.

A similar result was obtained by Hogstedt (1980) with magpies. He was able to show that much of the variation in clutch-size was related to the quality of territory in which the birds bred. Regardless of the initial clutch-size, birds were less successful at raising young if the brood size was artificially increased. As with the Great Tits, females laid the 'right' size of

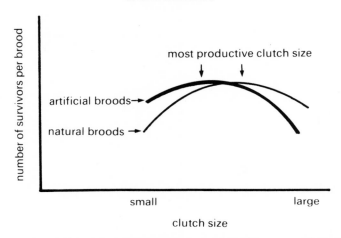

**Figure 5.6** Schematic explanation of the differences in breeding success between natural broods and those that are artificially manipulated. The explanation assumes that the clutch laid by each individual female is adaptive in that it is related to the number of young that the pair can raise. Hence broods that are artificially increased are not as successful as natural large broods, since they are raised by birds which laid a smaller clutch because they did not 'expect' to be able to raise so many young. On the other hand artificial small broods are raised by birds which laid (and therefore 'expected' to be able to raise) larger broods and are therefore more successful than birds which laid small clutches. As a result, the curve for the numbers of young raised by birds whose broods were artificially manipulated produce a peak at a lower level than that for natural broods. (From Perrins and Moss, 1974).

clutch for the particular conditions in which they were breeding. These results indicate that individual females have their own optimum clutch-size and that the clutch-size of a population is in fact composed of a family of individual optima (Fig. 5.7) which gives the appearance of larger clutches being more successful than the average clutch-size.

(c)  *Success within a season compared with life-time success.* Lack's hypothesis states that the most productive clutch-size is the one giving rise to the greatest number of surviving young. All the evidence which Lack had to support his theory used the number of surviving young within a single season. Many birds breed over several seasons, and Williams (1966) pointed out that the only meaningful measure of success is the number of young reared over a parent's lifetime, not within a season, which was the measure Lack had used. In light of William's point, a number of models which examine the relationship between lifetime reproductive success and adult survival have been constructed. As a result of these, Lack's hypothesis has been modified slightly.

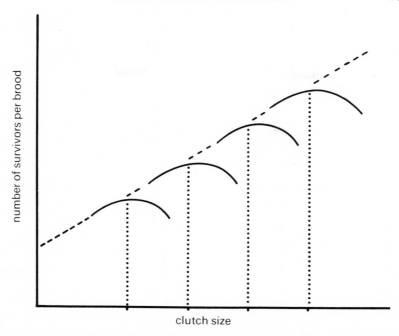

**Figure 5.7**  Optimum clutch-size of different females. It is assumed here that the number of eggs laid by each female is related to her ability to raise that number of young; by laying either fewer or more eggs she will be less successful. Each curve in the figure denotes the situation for a different female; by combining these, one would be led to believe that, since the largest clutches produce the most surviving young, all birds would produce more young if they laid a larger clutch.

### 5.3.2  Modifications of Lack's hypothesis

Natural selection will tend to favour parents which produce the greatest number of young in their lifetime, not from a brood or within a single season. However, if the chance of parents' dying between one season and the next is higher for those rearing large broods, then selection may favour a slightly smaller clutch. In other words, there will be a balance between adult survival and the size of clutch produced. One way in which this could operate is shown in Fig. 5.8, based on a model by Charnov and Krebs (1974). The model is formulated in terms of costs and benefits, where the cost is a reduction in the chances of survival, and the benefit is the production of young which survive to breed. The benefit curve, as already pointed out (see Fig. 5.1) is an inverted 'U' (Fig. 5.8a) with a particular clutch-size being most productive. Lack's hypothesis predicts that the most

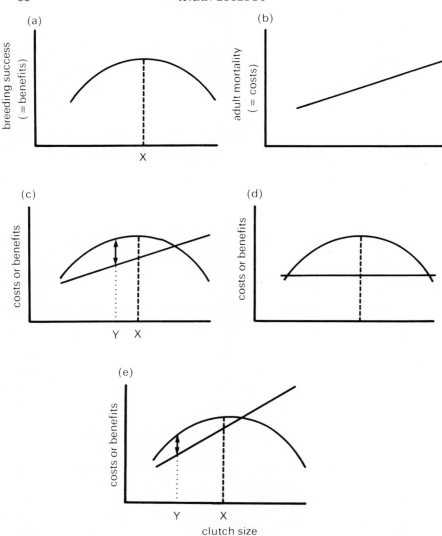

**Figure 5.8** Trade-off between clutch-size and adult survival. (*a*) Relationship between breeding success (benefit) and clutch-size; Lack's hypothesis predicts that the commonest clutch-size (*Y*) is also the most productive. (*b*) The costs of breeding increase with clutch-size. (*c*) Combining the benefit curve and cost function, the greatest net benefit occurs at *X*, a clutch-size less than *Y*. (*d*) If the costs of breeding remain constant with clutch-size *X* and *Y* coincide. (*e*) If the costs increase very steeply, the most productive clutch-size (*X*) is shifted further to the left. (Modified from Charnov and Krebs, 1974).

frequent clutch-size in nature will also be the most productive one (point $Y$ in Fig. 5.8$a$). With an increase in clutch-size, the cost also increases (Fig. 5.8$b$): parents have to work harder to feed a larger brood, and they may also be more vulnerable to predation. If we combine Figs. 5.8$a$ and $b$, as in Fig. 5.8$c$, we find that the point where the cost and benefit curves are most different (i.e. where the net benefits are greatest), lies to the left of Lack's optimum ($Y$). Hence the most productive clutch-size is smaller than Lack's hypothesis would have predicted.

Fig. 5.8 also considers two extreme cases. In Fig. 5.8$d$ the costs of breeding remain constant with clutch-size (i.e. the cost function is horizontal). In this case, the most productive clutch-size is exactly as Lack's hypothesis would have predicted. At the other extreme, Fig. 5.8$e$ shows a situation where the cost of breeding increases very rapidly with increasing clutch-size (i.e. the cost function is very steep; cf. Fig. 5.8$c$). The greater the cost of reproduction the further to the left will the optimum clutch-size be shifted. In conclusion, we can say that since there will usually be a cost associated with breeding, there will often be a discrepancy between the most productive clutch-size and the one most frequently occurring in nature. Charnov and Krebs's 1974 model then predicts that the average clutch-size for a species will often be smaller than that which is most productive.

As yet, this model has not been tested directly, but there is some evidence that increased reproductive effort involves a cost. Bryant (1979) found that House Martins which reared two broods in a year had a significantly lower survival rate (28%, compared with 58% for birds which reared only a single brood). In addition to the energetic cost of reproduction, birds rearing large broods may be more vulnerable to predation, since large broods are more easily found by predators than are small ones (Table 5.5), and so parents of large broods may also be at greater risk than those of small broods.

A second explanation for average clutch-size being smaller than the most productive ones involves the effect of nest predation. All but the largest bird species suffer predation of their eggs or young, and in some passerines as many as 70–80% of all breeding attempts fail because of predation. As mentioned above, the size of brood may influence their chances of being taken by a predator, and as Table 5.5 shows, larger broods may be more vulnerable than small ones. There are three reasons for this. It may occur because large broods are hungrier (see Tables 5.3 and 5.4) and therefore noisier than small ones. As a result predators are able to find them more easily. Secondly, a large brood means that parents have to visit the nest

D

**Table 5.5** Predation in relation to brood-size in Great Tits. The predator is the weasel, *Mustela nivalis* (from Perrins, 1965).

| Brood size | Early season | | | Late season | | |
|---|---|---|---|---|---|---|
| | No. nests | No. lost | % | No. nests | No. lost | % |
| 2–7 | 31 | 1 | 3.3 | 42 | 5 | 11.9 |
| 8–10 | 30 | 3 | 10.0 | 26 | 4 | 15.4 |
| 11–14 | 20 | 3 | 15.0 | 19 | 4 | 21.1 |

more often with food than they do with a smaller brood and the higher visiting rate may draw the attention of predators to the nest. The clutch-size of many tropical passerines is small, comprising only one or two eggs (see later, 5.4.1). Such small clutches may be an adaptation to the need for extreme secrecy in order to avoid the relatively high number of predators in the tropics. With only one or two chicks the nest can be very small and the parents need only visit the nest infrequently to feed the chicks, thereby reducing the chances of a predator finding the nest (Skutch, 1976; Snow, 1976). The third effect which predation has on the evolution of clutch-size concerns the period of time that the nest contents are vulnerable to predators. Since most birds lay one egg each day, the smaller the clutch, the shorter time the clutch and brood are in the nest and vulnerable to predation (Perrins, 1977; Ricklefs, 1977). A reduction in clutch-size may seem to make only a small difference to the vulnerability of a nesting attempt. However, if predation rates are high the reduction in the time eggs and chicks are in the nest may have important effects on their chances of survival.

To summarize this section so far, we have two theories for why the commonest clutch-size is often smaller than the most productive one. The first is concerned with adult survival (Fig. 5.8) and the second with the effect of predation. As we have indicated, both are likely to play a role in the evolution of clutch-size, but at present we know very little about their relative importance. However, for one group of birds, those with precocial young, the effect of predation has probably been the single most important factor in the evolution of clutch size.

In this chapter so far we have considered only nidicolous (= altricial) species, i.e. those whose young hatch blind and helpless and are fed and reared by their parents in the nest. Nidifugous (= precocia¹) species produce young which can feed themselves soon after hatching. In most species of game birds, water-fowl and waders the parents do not feed the young, but take them away from the nest soon after hatching, leading them to feeding areas where they guard them. The clutch-size of these species cannot be related to the amount of food which the parents can bring to the young (see section 5.3), since they do not do this. It seems likely that predation influences the upper limit for clutch-size among precocial birds.

**Table 5.6** Nesting success of Semi-palmated Sandpipers in relation to brood size. Note that the natural clutch is almost always four eggs; the broods of five were artificially increased at hatching (from Safriel, 1975).

| Brood size | N | No. birds raising young | | | No. raised/brood |
| | | All | Some | None | |
| --- | --- | --- | --- | --- | --- |
| 4 | 39 | 2 | 30 | 7 | 1.74 |
| 5 | 27 | 1 | 11 | 15 | 1.00 |

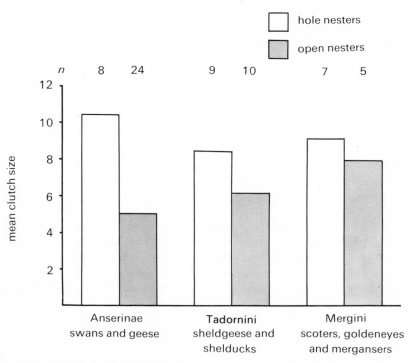

**Figure 5.9** The clutch-size of different species of ducks and geese in relation to whether they nest in the open (shaded) or in holes (unshaded). (From Lack, 1968).

Most of these species nest on the ground and are especially vulnerable to predation. As outlined above, larger clutches will be vulnerable for a longer period of time than smaller ones. In addition, it is likely that predators take more large broods than smaller ones, and in precocial birds this may occur for the following reason. Large groups of birds cover more ground per unit time when foraging, than do small groups (Morse, 1970). This presumably has to happen if each individual is to obtain sufficient food. If the same effect occurs in broods of young precocial birds then large broods will be more likely to encounter a predator than small broods. There is little information on this situation, but the one field experiment conducted has shown that enlarged broods suffer higher predation than normal-sized broods (Table 5.6).

Some of the best evidence for the role of predation in the evolution of clutch-size in precocial birds comes from a comparison of ducks breeding in different situations. Lack (1968) showed that for three families of ducks, those which bred in holes, relatively safe from predators, had larger clutches than those nesting on the ground in the open where they were especially vulnerable to predators (Fig. 5.9).

## 5.4  Variations in clutch-size

In this section we examine some of the factors which affect clutch-size in birds, both between species and within species. The single most important factor producing differences in clutch-size between species is their ecology, mainly food availability and predation. In the previous section we discussed the role of predation in the evolution of clutch-size in precocial birds. Before that, for nidicolous species, we emphasized the importance of how much food the parents could bring to the nest in the evolution of clutch-sizes. The influence of food on clutch-size is clearly demonstrated by a comparison of inshore and offshore-feeding sea-birds. Inshore species such as gulls, terns and cormorants are able to make several feeding visits to their young each day, whereas offshore feeders, such as petrels, albatrosses and large penguins, feed their young less frequently, in some species only once every 3–6 days (Croxall and Prince, 1980). Inshore sea-birds tend to have clutches of two or three eggs, while offshore-feeding species have single-egg clutches (Lack, 1967).

There are two other factors which are related to clutch-size, but are not obviously related to the ecology of birds. One is the taxonomy of the bird and the other is its body size. There is a strong tendency for birds in the same order or family to have clutches of similar size. For example virtually all birds in the order Anseriformes (ducks, geese and swans) produce clutches of four or more eggs, whereas every single species in the order Procellariiformes (albatrosses, shearwaters and petrels) lays only a single egg. To some extent the effect of taxonomy is not unexpected since closely related species will tend to have similar ecologies. Within birds as a whole, small species tend to produce relatively larger eggs (see section 5.3) and larger clutches than large species. The reason for this pattern is not clear.

The ecology of different bird species is affected by a wide range of factors, and in the following sections we examine some which affect the feeding ecology of birds and hence their clutch-size. We consider variables which influence clutch-size both between species, such as latitude and habitat and factors such as population density, time of breeding and age, all of which operate primarily within species.

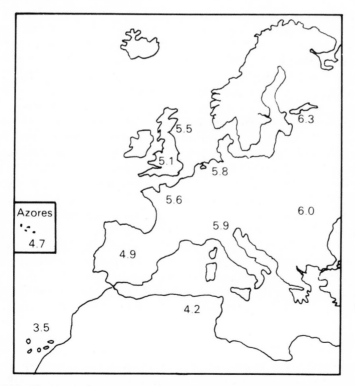

**Figure 5.10**   The clutch-size of the European Robin in relation to latitude. Note general tendency for clutches to be larger as one goes north. (From Lack, 1943).

### 5.4.1   *Latitude*

One of the most striking and well-established variations in clutch-size both between and within species is the increase with latitude (Fig. 5.10). The usual explanation for this trend is that in the northern hemisphere the days in summer get longer as one goes northwards. Parents therefore have a longer day in which to collect food for their young at higher latitudes and so are able to rear more young. There are however, problems with this explanation. First, in most cases clutch-size does not increase proportionately with the change in daylength. This might not matter if it were consistent, since other factors could also be involved, but in fact the increase in clutch-size is not consistent. In some species the change in clutch-size is greater and in other species less than the change in daylength. Two examples will illustrate the problem. In the Snow Bunting those birds which breed far north of the Arctic Circle produce larger clutches than those breeding close to the Arctic Circle, despite the fact that birds in both areas have virtually 24 hours of daylight each day at the time when they are rearing young (Hussell, 1972; Salomonsen, 1972). The second problem concerns owls. These are nocturnal species, so we might expect a reversal of the clutch-size-latitude trend; however, even these species produce larger clutches at higher latitudes (Lack, 1947, 1948).

The most likely explanation for the latitudinal trend in clutch-size is related more to the relative productivity of the area rather than to daylength (Ashmole, 1963; Ricklef, 1980). The differences in seasonal variation in productivity between habitats is enormous, and in general, arctic habitats show greater variation than habitats at lower latitudes (Fig. 5.11). The birds of tropical rain forests, for example, have a relatively stable food supply throughout the year and their numbers are always close to the carrying capacity (see 6.1.2) of the habitat. As a result, even during the breeding season the increase in food is relatively small, and when divided between all the birds present does not provide an enormous excess for breeding. In contrast, spring and summer productivity in the Arctic is dramatic. Food is probably so abundant that competition (see Chapter 7) is of little importance, and most species can find sufficient food to rear large broods.

### 5.4.2   *Habitat*

Within the tropics birds breeding in savannas have larger clutches than those species breeding in rain forest (Lack and Moreau, 1965). This

(a)

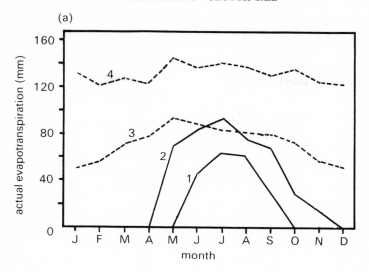

(b)   Arctic

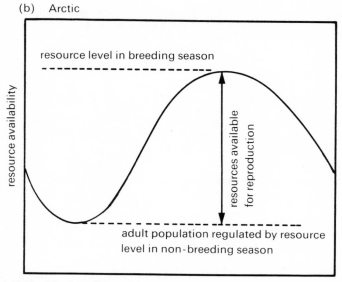

**Figure 5.11**   (For legend see over)

(c)  Tropics

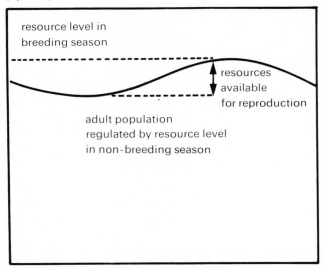

**Figure 5.11** (*a*) Evapotranspiration rates in different areas. (1) Alaska; (2) Southern Finland; (3) Central America (highlands); (4) Borneo. (*b*) Resource availability in the Arctic (a highly seasonal environment) is reflected by evapotranspiration rates (lines 1 and 2 in (*a*)). (*c*) Resource availability in the tropics (a very constant environment) is similarly reflected (lines 3 and 4 in (*a*)). Clutch size is proportional to the ratio of the resource levels in the breeding and non-breeding seasons. (Based on Ricklefs, 1980).

**Table 5.7**  Clutch-size of certain species in different habitats. *Note*: The clutches of Great Tits were corrected for standard density of 8 pairs/10ha.

| Species | Good habitat | Clutch-size | Poor habitat | Clutch-size | Author |
|---------|--------------|-------------|--------------|-------------|--------|
| Sparrowhawk | Woods in valleys | 5.3 | Hill woods | 4.5 | Newton (1976) |
| Common Tern | Colony with good feeding nearby | 2.95 | Colony with less good feeding nearby | 2.78 | Nisbet (1977) |
| Blackbird | Rural sites | 3.92 | Urban sites | 3.78 | Snow (1958) |
| Great Tit | Deciduous woodland | 10.53 | Conifer | 9.77 | van Balen (1973) |
| Blue Tit | Oak woodland | 10.9 | Gardens | 8.8 | Perrins (1965) |

difference in clutch-size between habitats may be explicable in the same way as the latitudinal effect discussed above. Savannas show greater seasonal variation in productivity than rain forests and hence food supplies per bird are greater in the breeding season in savanna than in rain forest. Species breeding in savanna are therefore able to rear larger broods of young than those in rain forests.

Individuals of the same species may produce different-sized clutches in different habitats. For example, many European passerines breeding in gardens produce smaller clutches than those breeding in adjacent wood-land (Table 5.7). This effect may result from differences in the absolute levels of food abundance in the two habitats. Another possibility is that it arises because differences in the density of breeding birds in the two areas in-directly affects food availability. This idea is discussed in the next section.

### 5.4.3 *Population density*

Population density can affect clutch-size both within and between species. Several studies have shown an inverse relationship between the density of conspecifics and clutch-size (Fig. 5.12). This effect is probably related to food availability. At high population densities territories are relatively small (see section 6.3.2) and the competition between birds for food may be more intense.

Exactly the same effect may occur between species, and some of the best evidence comes from studies of birds breeding on islands. On some islands, clutch-sizes are smaller than on the adjacent mainland (Crowell and Rothstein, 1981). For example on the island of Corsica off southern

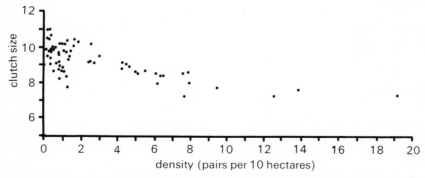

**Figure 5.12** The clutch-size of female Great Tits in relation to breeding density. (From Kluijver, 1951).

France, clutches are 2–5 eggs smaller than in the same species breeding in mainland France (Blondel and Isenmann, 1979). It has been suggested that this difference exists because the population density of the tits breeding on Corsica is much higher than on the mainland. This in turn comes about because there are fewer species on islands and hence reduced interspecific competition (see section 7.3.1).

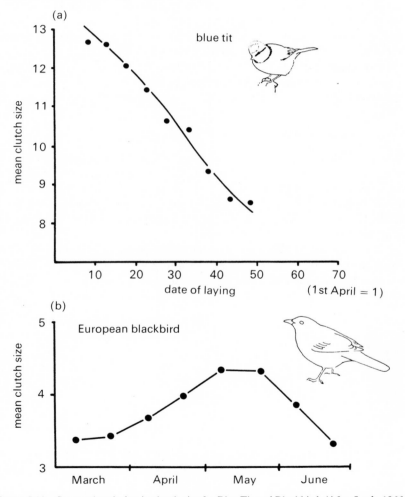

**Figure 5.13**    Seasonal variation in clutch-size for Blue Tit and Blackbird. (After Lack, 1966; Snow, 1958).

### 5.4.4    *Time of season*

In many birds, clutch-size changes through the season, and one of the commonest patterns is for late-breeding individuals to lay smaller clutches than those breeding early (Fig. 5.13). Among single-brooded species, individuals which lay relatively late in the season are usually less successful in rearing young than early breeders. The decline in clutch-size through the season is thought to be associated with the reduced chances of successfully rearing a large brood. The seasonal decline in breeding success occurs because late broods hatch after the peak of food availability has passed. Consequently a reduction in clutch-size among late breeders is an adaptation to a worsening food supply for the young. Under these conditions birds will be more likely to be successful in rearing a small, rather than a large brood (Perrins, 1970).

### 5.4.5    *Age of bird*

In many species of bird, young females lay smaller clutches than older ones. Since young birds also tend to be less successful in rearing young, the smaller clutch-size may be an adaptation to the individual's ability to rear young (Table 5.8). A complicating factor is that young birds also tend to lay later in the season than older birds and this may partly account for the seasonal decline in clutch-size (see Fig. 5.13). However, among different-aged birds breeding on the same dates, young females still tend to produce relatively small clutches, e.g. Snow Geese (Finney and Cooke, 1978). The

**Table 5.8**  Clutch-size in relation to female age. *Note*: (1) for the Kittiwake the mean clutches relate to birds breeding for the 1st, 2nd and 3rd and 4th and 5th times, rather than actual age.
(2) For the Sparrowhawk, Pied Flycatcher and Great Tit the figure at age 2 relates to birds aged 2 or older.
(3) For the Hawaiian Goose, the data refer to a captive collection at the Wildfowl Trust, fed *ad. lib.*

| Species | 1 | 2 | 3 | 4 | 5 | Author |
|---|---|---|---|---|---|---|
| | | *Age/mean clutch* | | | | |
| Hawaiian Goose | — | 3.68 | 4.07 | 4.18 | 4.31 | Kear (1980) |
| Red-billed Gull | — | 1.33 | 1.69 | 1.76 | 2.09 | Mills (1973) |
| Kittiwake | 1.78 | 1.94 | | 2.39 | | Coulson and White (1961) |
| Sparrowhawk | 4.8 | 5.4 | | | | Newton (1976) |
| Pied Flycatcher | 5.65 | 6.33 | | | | Von Haartman (1967) |
| Great Tit | 8.4 | 9.1 | | | | Perrins and Moss (1974) |

later start to breeding among young birds may occur because they are less efficient at feeding and take longer to come into reproductive condition (see section 4.3).

## 5.5   Asynchronous hatching and brood reduction

In general natural selection will tend to favour those individuals in which the number of eggs laid closely matches the number of young they can rear. However, if the food supply at the time of hatching is very variable then it will be impossible for birds to predict, when they are laying eggs, what the food supply for their young will be like. In such cases the match between clutch-size and number of young which can be reared may not be very close. We have already mentioned one species, the European Swift, where the birds appear unable to forecast the feeding conditions; in good weather three young can be reared, but in poor weather birds may have difficulty rearing even two young. The Swift has partly solved the problem of an unpredictable food supply for its young by hatching its eggs asynchronously. It does this by starting incubation before the clutch is complete. Since eggs are laid on alternate days in this species, they will hatch about two days apart. As a result the young are very different in size and if food is scarce the larger chick takes most of it and the smallest one dies. If, however, food is plentiful the largest chick is quickly satiated and there is also sufficient for the smallest chick. Asynchronous hatching and brood reduction are widespread among predatory birds such as herons, owls and eagles (O' Connor, 1978).

Among many small birds and precocial species, asynchronous hatching is relatively rare and there are good reasons why it is important for all the young of a brood to be similar in size. In passerines a single small, hungry chick in the nest may, by calling for food, result in the nest being found by a predator. In precocial birds it is important that the whole brood hatches at the same time so they can be taken away from the nest together, by the parents. Hatching synchrony is achieved partly by delaying incubation until the clutch is complete, and also by the chicks themselves communicating with each other before they hatch (Vince, 1969).

## 5.6   Energetic requirements for breeding

Reproduction is energetically expensive. Table 4.1 provides an indication of these energy requirements by showing clutch weight as a percentage of female body weight for a variety of species. However, these figures do not show the amount of extra energy females need for themselves. Females expend energy in collecting food to form eggs, and in the metabolic conversion of food into eggs. In addition, because several eggs develop simultaneously, females may be relatively heavy at this time, which makes foraging energetically more costly than usual. For example, before the start of laying the female Common Tern may weigh 180 g, compared with a normal weight of about 120 g. Similarly, a female Blue Tit may weigh 15 g just before laying compared with a normal weight of around 10–11 grams. In both species the laying female is about 50% heavier than usual.

How do birds obtain the extra energy they require for reproduction? Obviously if a female has only sufficient food for its daily needs it cannot start breeding. However, if food is more abundant there are two ways a female can obtain sufficient energy to breed. It could either store reserves over a period of time until it had sufficient to breed, or it could collect each day the additional food it needed to produce each egg. These alternatives are not exclusive; birds may store some reserves, but rely on finding a considerable amount of extra food each day. Storing reserves may be disadvantageous because flying with such extra weight over a long period is energetically expensive. To rely on finding sufficient food each day may also be disadvantageous, in that a bird may have to wait until late in the season for food to become sufficiently abundant. So which of the methods do birds use? The answer is that different species use both methods. For convenience we will refer to them as 'reserve users' and 'daily surplus users'.

### 5.6.1 Reserve users

We have already mentioned the best examples of reserve users, the Arctic-nesting geese, which fly from their wintering grounds carrying all the reserves they require for egg-laying and most of those for incubation. The Lesser Snow Goose arrives at its breeding grounds about 20% heavier than

**Table 5.9** Body weight and fat reserves of female Lesser Snow Geese on arrival on their breeding grounds. Clutch-size can be assessed by counting the large ovarian follicles (from Ankney and MacInnes, 1978).

| Clutch-size | 2 | 3 | 4 | 5 | 6 |
|---|---|---|---|---|---|
| Mean total body weight (g) | 2400 | 2710 | 2920 | 3080 | 3300 |
| Mean fat reserves (g) | 349 | 443 | 487 | 544 | 598 |
| N | 3 | 13 | 31 | 25 | 6 |

its normal weight, and the amount of reserves is closely related to the size of clutch produced (Table 5.9).

The importance of the size of reserve in geese is clearly illustrated by another study. Brent Geese were caught, weighed and ringed on their wintering grounds in Holland during May, just before leaving for their Siberian breeding grounds. In the autumn when the birds returned it was found that those birds which had been relatively heavy in the spring had young, while those which had been lighter in weight had none (Drent and Daan, 1980). The lighter birds probably had insufficient energy reserves to complete incubation.

Relatively few passerines are reserve users, but the Red-billed Quelea does store protein in its flight muscle for use in breeding. Just as in the Lesser Snow Goose, females with larger protein reserves produce larger clutches (Jones and Ward 1974, 1976; see also 4.3.2).

### 5.6.2   *Daily surplus users*

In contrast to species like the Lesser Snow Goose and Red-billed Quelea, many species produce clutches whose size is unrelated to the extent of their body reserves. These species are apparently able to find sufficient 'surplus' food each day to produce a clutch of eggs. The Blue Tit, for example, produces a clutch of 10–12 eggs (see Table 4.1). It would be impossible for it to store all the reserves necessary for a clutch. Indeed, there is as much calcium in the 10–12 egg shells as in the female's total skeleton! Further evidence for the availability of sufficient food comes from small birds which lose their clutch to a predator part way through laying. If this occurs, they may build another nest very quickly and continue laying almost without a break. The combined number of eggs in the two nests is often much greater than the normal clutch.

Some of the most striking evidence that birds can obtain sufficient food each day to produce eggs comes from egg-removal experiments. In several species, the daily removal of an egg resulted in birds continuing to lay and producing many more eggs than in a normal clutch. The most frequently quoted (and exceptional) case is of a Yellow-shafted Flicker which laid 71 eggs in 73 days. Clearly the individual was able to obtain sufficient food each day for egg formation.

At the present time we have insufficient information to generalize about which birds are likely to be reserve users and which daily surplus users. It seems likely, though, that larger species and those with small clutches and/or very large eggs may be reserve users, while small species or ones with large clutches and small eggs may be daily surplus users.

### 5.6.3    *The costs and benefits of breeding*

In evolutionary terms the advantage, or benefit, of breeding is the production of young. However, breeding is often dangerous, so there are also some costs. The costs include additional energetic demands, and the risk of predation. Breeding commits parent birds to a way of life which

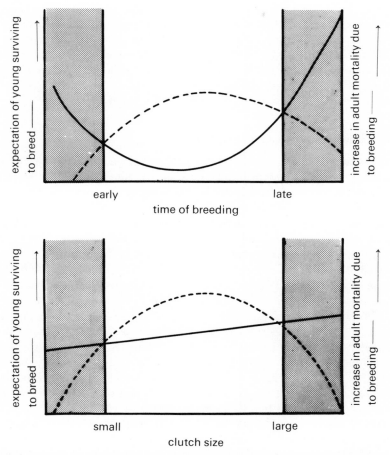

**Figure 5.14** Hypothetical figures showing the costs and benefits of breeding. In both figures it is assumed that there is some risk to the parent in breeding (solid lines and right-hand axes) and in both that the likelihood of raising young will vary (dotted lines, left-hand axes). Birds should breed whenever the probability is that the production of surviving young will exceed the likely increase in adult mortality; this is true in the unshaded central area of each figure where the dotted line is above the solid one.

puts them at greater risk from predators than when they are not breeding.

Natural selection will favour only those individuals in which the benefits exceed the costs. A bird should not breed if the likely number of surviving offspring will on average be less than the increase in mortality to the adult. Two ways in which this might operate in terms of breeding seasons and clutch-size are shown in Fig. 5.14. In evolutionary terms these sort of effects have probably played an important role in shaping the limits to the breeding seasons of birds and the size of clutch they produce. In practice, however, it is difficult to establish what these limits are. This is because (i) parent birds are either conservative and do not run too much risk, or (ii) they allow the brood to suffer rather than themselves. This is adaptive because the chances of the young birds' surviving are much lower than those of the adults (see Chapter 6). Moreover, if the adults were to die raising young, the young birds would perish anyway.

## 5.7 Evolutionary aspects of reproduction

In this chapter and the previous one we have considered reproductive rates and the timing of breeding, implicitly assuming that they are the product of natural selection. For this to be the case it is necessary that these characteristics are heritable. Until recently there has been relatively little evidence for this, because such investigations require detailed records over several generations of birds. Now, however, there is good evidence that characteristics such as egg size, adult body size, laying date and clutch-size are all inherited (van Noordwijk *et al.*, 1980). As yet such effects have been demonstrated for only a few species, but it seems likely they will also hold true for others.

Offspring do not inherit the exact laying date or clutch-size of their parents. As with other heritable traits (such as height in humans) the correlation between parent and offspring traits is far from perfect. The daughter of a mother which lays early is likely to be among the early breeders. Similarly, the daughter of a mother which lays a clutch of above average size is likely to do so herself. In analysing such data one must take into account the fact that average laying dates and clutch-size may differ between years. What this means is that the daughter of an early breeder is likely to lay early in relation to the average laying date for that year, rather than at any precise date. The same is true for clutch-size. Although the size of clutch is inherited, the number of eggs an individual lays may be modified by ecological conditions such as habitat or laying date (see sections 5.4.2, 5.4.4). It seems likely, although it has not been demonstrated, that these short-term modifications of clutch-size are also inherited. In other words, a bird inherits the tendency to lay a clutch similar in size to that of its mother and also the ability to modify its clutch-size in relation to conditions at the time of egg-laying. Since the time at which birds breed and the number of eggs they lay are so closely linked with reproductive success, natural selection has probably operated on them very strongly.

In most areas of the northern part of the northern hemisphere birds are only relatively recent colonists, since most of these areas were uninhabitable during the Ice Age. During the last 8 000 years or so, as the ice receded, birds have been moving in and presumably modifying their clutch-size and laying date according to the local conditions. We would therefore expect there to have been a continual, steady modification of these characteristics as the selective forces in the new environment demanded Only one detailed study has attempted to calculate the rates at which these characteristics could potentially change. Van Noordwijk *et al.* (1980) calculated that in Great Tits clutch size could change by 0.3 eggs, and laying date by 0.5 days, per generation. Since Great Tits are very short-lived birds this could lead, if environmental pressures were strong enough, to changes of as much as 1.5 eggs in the clutch or 5 days in laying-date, within a single decade. This is obviously a very rapid change and birds with smaller clutch sizes and longer life spans might adapt to changes more slowly. There is very little field evidence that changes of this sort actually occur. However, there is some evidence that the clutch size of the Little Owl declined following its introduction into England from Europe at the beginning of this century (Lack 1947, 1948). House Sparrows in the southern part of North America have smaller clutches than in Canada (Murphy, 1978), and in Costa Rica, House Sparrows most commonly lay clutches of two eggs, similar to many other tropical species, but much smaller than House Sparrows in temperate areas (Fleischer, 1982). House Sparrows have only been in these areas for a relatively short time (120–150 years).

Similarly in the Netherlands the date of laying of certain species of waders has advanced by about two weeks during the last 50 years. The reason for this is thought to be that these birds all breed in meadows, and as mechanized mowing of hay has become more common, a greater proportion of late broods have been destroyed, thereby increasing selection for earlier breeding (Beintema, 1978).

## 5.8  Summary

Several theories for the evolution of clutch size are presented, but that proposed by Lack is best supported by the evidence. Lack's hypothesis is that, in nidicolous birds, clutch-size is adapted to the maximum number of young that the parents can adequately feed and raise. Tests of this hypothesis indicate that Lack's idea is correct. However, more detailed studies show that in some cases a discrepancy exists between the theory and facts, since the average clutch-size is often less than the most productive one. There are two explanations for this. First, Lack did not take into account the effect of adult survival. By laying a slightly conservative-size clutch, adult survival may be enhanced. A graphical model by Charnov and Krebs shows how this may occur. Second, predation may affect the evolution of clutch size. As larger clutches take longer to produce and are therefore more vulnerable to predation, selection may favour clutches which are smaller than the most productive ones. Lack's hypothesis has been modified in the light of these factors. In precocial species, the upper limit of clutch-size is thought to be set by the risks of predation.

A range of factors affects clutch-size, both within and between species. These include latitude, habitat and population density. Factors operating within species include time of breeding and age.

For some species, the food supply at the time of hatching is very variable, and so at the time of egg laying they cannot predict food availability for their young. These species show asynchronous hatching and brood reduction: if food is short, the last-hatched chicks starve, whereas, if it is abundant, all the young survive. In the final section, the heritability of characteristics such as laying date and clutch-size are discussed.

# CHAPTER SIX

# LIFE CYCLES AND POPULATION STUDIES

## 6.1 Introduction: the properties of populations

Ecologists have attempted to answer two main questions about animal populations: why do numbers in an area change from year to year, and why are numbers of a particular species higher in some areas than others? There is a clear practical need to know the answers to these questions in order to manage animal populations. For example, we may wish to protect rare species, reduce those which are pests, or harvest those which are edible. In this chapter we shall see how ecologists have attempted to answer these two questions.

First we must define what we mean by a population. A population is the number of animals living within a certain area. The area is usually defined by the ecologist. So we may talk about the blackbird population of a particular island, the Great Tit population of a particular forest, or the Herring Gull population of the North Atlantic. We usually refer to the number of individuals (or pairs) per unit area, hence we talk about *population densities*.

Population density is affected by three primary population parameters: natality, mortality and dispersal (immigration and emigration). *Natality* is the reproductive rate of the population and is expressed as the number of young produced per female per unit time. In birds natality, equivalent to clutch-size, varies markedly from species to species (Chapter 5). The input of young into a population results in an increase in density. *Mortality* is the death rate of the population, and ecologists are especially interested in the ages at which individuals die. Obviously, mortality results in a decrease in population density. The term 'mortality' is the converse of survival, that is survival = 1 − mortality, and can be expressed either as percentages or as proportions from 0 to 1. For example, a species in which 10% of the individuals die each year has a survival rate of 90% or 0.9. *Dispersal* (i.e. immigration and emigration) is only rarely measured in population studies, because it is usually extremely difficult to do so. Consequently, ecologists have to work on populations in areas such as islands where dispersal is not important, or they assume that it is negligible and that the immigration and emigration balance each other.

Population densities for most species are difficult to measure and there are relatively few animal species where it is possible to measure their absolute density. Ecologists have derived a number of techniques for doing this (see C. J. Krebs, 1978). Among birds, species which breed colonially, such as herons and sea-birds, and those which breed in nest-boxes provided by man, are among the easiest to census accurately. Studies of bird population densities made over a number of years have shown that populations have a number of important properties; these are discussed in the following sections.

### 6.1.1 *Stability of numbers*

One of the most striking characteristics of populations is that densities change relatively little from year to year. In other words populations tend to be stable. Clearly annual fluctuations in density do occur, but they usually do so within fairly narrow limits. More importantly, such fluctuations are small compared with what is theoretically possible (see 6.1.2). A second characteristic, which is an important component of the first, is that if the population density is reduced by some natural disaster (e.g. unusually severe weather conditions), numbers usually recover and return to their former level very rapidly.

The Grey Heron provides a clear example of this effect. During hard winters this species suffers particularly high mortality because lakes and rivers freeze over and its food supply becomes inaccessible. However, as Fig. 6.1 shows, after a severe winter the number of herons rapidly increases and within a few years has regained its former level.

### 6.1.2 *Potential rates of increase*

The rapid recovery in Grey Heron numbers following a hard winter (Fig. 6.1) illustrates that the potential for an increase in numbers is high. To show just what this potential is we will use the European Robin as an

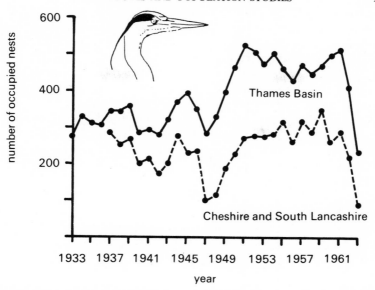

**Figure 6.1** The breeding population of Grey Herons in two areas of Britain. The upper graph is for the Thames drainage area, the lower one for Cheshire and South Lancashire. Unusually hard winters occurred in 1940, 1941, 1942, 1945, 1947, 1962 and 1963. (From data collected by the British Trust for Ornithology).

example. This species often rears two broods of four young in a year (Lack, 1943). Hence, at the end of the breeding season there could be 10 robins where there had been two only to start with. If all these survived to breed there could be 25 pairs at the end of the second year, 125 after three years, 625 after four and over 19 800 000 after ten years! Although this example is an over-simplification since it ignores the fact that robins do not usually live for 10 years, it does illustrate the high potential rate of population growth.

The clearest natural example of the potential rate of increase comes from cases where a species has been introduced into a new area. One of the best documented examples in birds is the introduction of the pheasant to Protection Island, a 160-hectare island off the coast of Washington, U.S.A. No pheasants lived on this island before 1937, when two males and six females were released. The increase in just six breeding seasons from 8 to 1898 individuals is truly remarkable, although it should be noted that even in this case there was appreciable winter mortality (Fig. 6.2). Another interesting feature of the data is that the rate of increase slowed towards the end of the study period. The reason for this is discussed in the next section.

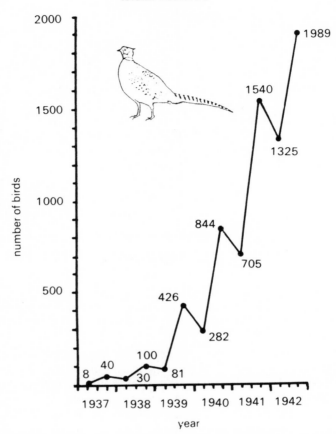

**Figure 6.2**  The numbers of pheasants on Protection Island, Washington. Two cocks and six hens were released in 1937. For further explanation see text. (From Einarsen, 1945).

### 6.1.3.  *Carrying capacity and limiting resources*

In the case of both the Grey Heron and the pheasant discussed in the previous sections, there appears to be some sort of upper limit to the numbers of individuals which can live in a particular area. In the Grey Heron, numbers ceased to increase once they had regained their former level. Similarly, the rate of increase in pheasant numbers started to decline towards the end of the study. Ecologists refer to this limit as the *carrying capacity*. The carrying capacity of an environment is related to the availability of resources, and numbers are controlled because one of the resources is limiting. For many species food is the most important resource but for others resources may include breeding sites or territories.

In the Grey Heron what seems to be happening is this. A hard winter results in the death of many adult herons, through starvation. After the winter, the food is just as abundant as it was before, but there are fewer herons to exploit it. With abundant food the reproductive output is high and mortality low so numbers increase. Eventually, however, the population reaches a point where food is limiting, reproductive output and mortality balance each other and numbers stabilize. At this point the Herons have reached the carrying capacity of the environment.

The carrying capacity for the same species may vary in different habitats. For example, in Great Tits the carrying capacity is higher in deciduous woodland (where population densities are 0.8–2.0 pairs/hectare) than in coniferous woodland (densities are 0.2–0.4 pairs/hectare) (Fig. 6.3). This difference is thought to occur because food availability (the limiting resource) is greater in deciduous than in coniferous woodland (Lack, 1966). Figure 6.3 shows two other ways in which the carrying capacity may change. Population densities varied from year to year, with high

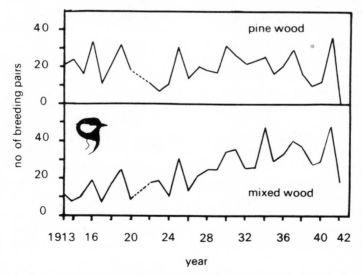

**Figure 6.3** Numbers of breeding pairs of Great Tits in two parts of a wood in Holland, 1913–42. Upper: mature conifer. Lower: maturing deciduous woodland. Note increase in breeding pairs in the latter area. (From Kluijver, 1951).

numbers occurring after winters in which there was a good crop of beech seeds, *Fagus sylvatica*, on which the birds feed. We can thus think of the carrying capacity of the same area changing from year to year, although the term is not usually used in this sense. In addition it can be seen that the population density of Great Tits in the deciduous woodland increased with time. This occurred because as the trees matured over the 30-year study period the carrying capacity also increased.

## 6.2 Survival rates and life tables

The two main population parameters affecting population density are mortality and natality. In this section we will look at ways in which such information is obtained, and how these two parameters interact to affect population density.

### 6.2.1 *Mortality*

The most important aspect of mortality for population studies is the age at which individuals die. The best way to look at the pattern of mortality within a population is to individually mark (by ringing) a group of birds which are born at the same time (called a *cohort*) and follow them through their lives, recording the number which die at each age. The resulting information is usually recorded as a *life-table*, which is simply an age-specific summary of the death rates operating on the population. The information can also be plotted as a *survivorship curve*.

Ecologists have recognized three main types of survivorship curve (Fig. 6.4a); type I, which is typical of man, shows a high mortality initially (of the very young—less marked in civilized man than in other animals), followed by low mortality until old age. Type II shows a constant mortality with respect to age. Type III, typical of many invertebrates, is characterized by very high juvenile mortality. Note that in Fig. 6.4a the number of individuals alive (the vertical axis)·is expressed on a logarithmic scale. This is because ecologists are usually interested in *rates* of mortality rather than absolute numerical changes. The fact that the type II survivorship curve is a straight line means that the rate of mortality with age is constant. For man, however,.(type I), the rate of mortality increases rapidly in old age.

Fig. 6.4b shows a survivorship curve for the Herring Gull, starting with 1000 eggs and continuing until all individuals have died. It can be seen

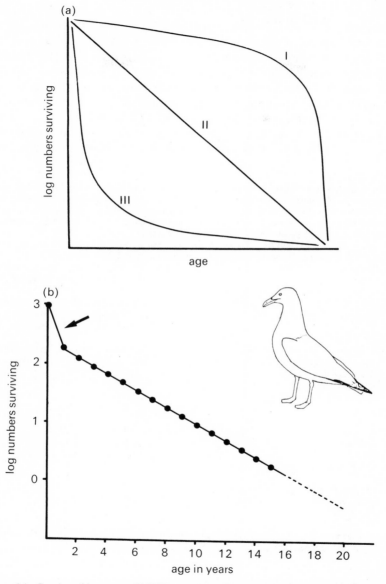

**Figure 6.4** Survivorship curves. (*a*) Different types of survivorship curves; for explanation see text. (*b*) Survivorship curve for the Herring Gull, based on 1000 eggs at start. The arrow marks the high mortality in the first year, primarily as a result of losses of eggs and small chicks (based on Paynter, 1966).

that, except for the earliest part of the curve, where the mortality of eggs and young birds in their first year is high, the rate of mortality remains constant.

The survivorship curve of the Herring Gull is typical of almost all birds, which indicates that death from old age is relatively rare. Data of this type are available for many species of wild bird and for none of them is there any good evidence that many individuals die of old age. There is, however, an analytical problem with detecting such an effect. All studies of this sort have to be based on birds ringed when young (i.e. of known age) and inevitably the number of individuals which reach an advanced age is very

**Table 6.1** Average annual mortality of adult birds and their young. *Note*: This table calculates, on the basis of mortality rates of adult birds, the percentage of eggs which must survive to become breeding adults in a stable population. Figures will vary under different circumstances. In one sense they are an over-estimate; many species (especially the smaller ones) lose many nests to predators and then lay repeat clutches. In such species the percentage of eggs which survive will be markedly lower than shown here. The proportion of fledged young which reaches breeding age will be higher than the figures shown; for example in the Manx Shearwater about 70% of the eggs laid produce fledged young, so about 29% of the fledged young survive to breed $(0.1 \times 2) \times 100$ (100/70). For further information see text.

| Species | Annual adult mortality Survival = 100 − mortality | Clutch-size ( × number of broods) | Proportion of eggs which survive to reach breeding to (%) |
|---|---|---|---|
| Yellow-eyed Penguin | 13 | 2 | 13 |
| Royal Albatross | 3 | 1 | 6 |
| Manx Shearwater | 10 | 1 | 20 |
| Gannet | 10 | 1 | 20 |
| White Stork | 21 | 4 | 10 |
| Mallard | 48 | 11 | 8.7 |
| Brent Goose | 15 | 4 | 7.5 |
| Mute Swan | 18 | 6 | 6 |
| Buzzard | 20 | 3 | 13 |
| African Fish Eagle | 4 | 2 | 4 |
| Osprey | 18 | 3 | 12 |
| European Kestrel | 40 | 5 | 16 |
| American Kestrel | 50 | 5 | 20 |
| Herring Gull | 8 | 3 | 5.3 |
| Puffin | 5 | 1 | 10 |
| Wood Pigeon | 35 | 2( × 3) | 11.7 |
| Black-and-white Manakin | 11 | 2( × 3) | 3.7 |
| European Robin | 50 | 4( × 2) | 12.5 |
| European Blackbird} American Robin } | 35 | 4( × 2) | 8.7 |
| Blue Tit | 70 | 11 | 12.7 |
| House (= English) Sparrow | 50 | 5( × 2) | 10.0 |

small. It is therefore possible that mortality does increase among old individuals, but we do not have adequate data to show it. In fact, an increase in mortality must occur since with a constant mortality rate there is a finite chance of some birds reaching very old ages. For example, if we assume that adult Herring Gulls have an average survival rate of 0.90 per annum and there is no increase in mortality with age, then out of every million birds about 26 would live to be 100 years old, and one would reach 131 years old. Clearly, this is extremely unlikely. However, it is obvious that old age is not an important cause of death in birds; at most it affects only a very small proportion of the population.

Because mortality is constant with respect to age in adult birds, the life tables of birds are relatively simple compared with other animals (see C.J. Krebs, 1978). As Fig. 6.4b indicates, the death rates of eggs and young birds are higher than among adults. Table 6.1 gives some examples of the survival rates of adult and immature birds. Adult survival values vary from as little as 30% in the British Blue Tit, 70% in the American Robin, to 95% in the Royal Albatross. Juvenile survival rates are both lower and more variable than adult rates. Adult survival rates can be used to calculate the mean expectation of further life using the following formula

$$\text{Mean life expectancy} = \frac{2 - m}{2m}$$

where $m$ is the annual mortality expressed as a proportion. For example, a bird with an average annual mortality rate of 48%, such as the mallard (Table 6.1) has an average life expectancy of $(2-0.48)/0.96$ or 1.58 years. In contrast, a species such as the Bald Eagle with a 5% annual mortality can expect to live for $(2-0.05)/0.1 = 19.5$ years on average. It is important to note that these values are averages; some individuals of these species will have shorter or longer life spans. Also, they refer to birds once they have reached sexual maturity. As we discuss in the next section, the survival rates of immature birds are almost always lower than those for adults.

### 6.2.2 *Mortality of immature birds and age at first breeding*

The proportion of young birds which survive to reach maturity will vary from species to species (Table 6.1) and is dependent, to some extent, upon the age at which they first start to breed. The longer the period of immaturity, the greater the chance of a bird dying.

Most small, temperate birds first start to breed when one year old. In the tropics at least some species of small birds do not start to breed until later

**Table 6.2** Age of first breeding of a variety of species. Note that the range shown is the usual age at which birds commence breeding, but the variation may be considerable in some species.

| | |
|---|---|
| Royal Albatross | 10 |
| Fulmar | 7–9 |
| Manx Shearwater | 5–6 |
| Storm petrel | 4 |
| Gannet | 4–5 |
| Small falcons/accipiters | 1–2 |
| Buzzard | 2 |
| Large eagles | 4–9 |
| Condors | 8 + |
| Mallard | 1 |
| Mute Swan | 4 |
| Coot | 1–2 |
| Small gulls | 2–3 |
| Large gulls | 4–5 |
| Puffin | 4–5 |
| Most temperate small passerines | 1 |

than this, although we have this information for relatively few species (Snow and Lill, 1974). In some species there may be differences between the sexes in the age of first breeding. For example, almost all female European Starlings breed when one year old, but most of the males do not breed until they are two years old (Coulson, 1960). In general, larger birds do not breed until they are at least two years old, and some, like the Fulmar, Petrel and Royal Albatross, not until they are nine years old (Table 6.2).

Juvenile birds typically disperse some distance from their nest-site, and as a result, it can be very difficult to measure their survival rate. However, if we have a measure of the adult survival rate and know that the population under study is stable, we can estimate the survival of juveniles between fledging and breeding. In a stable population the adults which die must be replaced by young birds which have survived to breed. For example, if the adult survival rate of Herring Gulls is 90% then 0.2 adults will die per *pair* per year $((1.0-0.9) \times 2)$. Let us suppose that Herring Gulls rear an average of two chicks per year, then the survival of young birds from fledging to breeding age would be 0.2/2 or 10%. Note that this is not an annual survival rate since Herring Gulls take about 4 years to reach sexual maturity (Table 6.2). A 90% mortality ($= 10\%$ survival) over four years is approximately equivalent to an annual mortality of 44%. Even this is something of a simplification since, as Fig. 6.4b shows, the mortality rate of young birds is high soon after fledging and then declines.

6.2.3 *Natality*

Mortality rates provide only part of the information we need to see how populations work. We also need information on natality: the reproductive rate of the population. Just as with mortality, we need to examine reproductive rates in relation to age. In some species of birds it has been found that the youngest breeders are relatively unsuccessful. Table 6.3 gives some examples of the effect of age on breeding success and shows the differences in the number of young reared per pair between species. If breeding success among young birds is very low, then there may be little advantage in breeding. This may be the main reason why many of these species defer breeding until they are several years old. In some cases they may be advantages in starting to breed at an early age, even if the chances of success are small. In the Yellow-eyed Penguin for example, Richdale (1957) found that among birds breeding at three years old, those which had attempted to breed at two were more successful than those breeding for the first time at three. This example indicates that breeding experience may be advantageous.

Although in some species differences in reproductive output may exist between birds of different ages, these differences are generally small and are usually ignored when combining mortality and natality estimates to look at how populations work (see 6.2.5).

6.2.4 *Immigration and emigration*

So far we have emphasized the importance of mortality and natality in affecting populations, but clearly a high rate of immigration could result in an increase in population density, just as emigration could lead to a

**Table 6.3** Breeding success in relation to age of female. The main reason for the large difference between first-year and older blackbirds is that the latter have more nesting attempts per season. Note the decline in success in the Great Tits of age 5–7 years.

| Arctic Tern | Age | 3 | 4–5 | | | 6–8 | Coulson and |
|---|---|---|---|---|---|---|---|
| | No. raised/ pair | 0.24 | 0.39 | | | 0.58 | Horobin (1976) |
| Blackbird | Age | 1 | 2 or older | | | | Snow (1956) |
| | No. raised/ pair | 3.4 | 6.3 | | | | |
| Great Tit | Age | 1 | 2 | 3 | 4 | 5–7 | Perrins and |
| | No. survived/ pair | 0.82 | 1.06 | 1.23 | 1.19 | 0.74 | Moss (1974) |

decrease. Unfortunately in most birds dispersal is difficult to measure. However, rather like the death rate of immature birds (6.2.2) we can sometimes obtain an indirect estimate of immigration or emigration. Imagine a population whose density is increasing at a constant rate, and that we had all the necessary information to construct a complete life-table for the species in question. We could then calculate the potential increase of that population. Assuming that all our estimates were accurate, if we found that the potential rate of increase was less than the observed rate, then the only explanation would be that immigration was occurring.

The Atlantic Puffin provides an example of this type of effect. In this case, however, an extensive colour-ringing study confirmed that immigration was occurring. At the Isle of May, off eastern Scotland, the puffin population has increased at a rate of 22% per annum. However, a detailed life-table (see 6.2.5) indicates that the maximum rate of increase could only be 7%. This suggests that much of the increase in numbers was due to immigration. Ringing showed that the additional birds had emigrated from the Farne Islands, 80 km to the south, where breeding success was high and space for new breeders almost non-existent (Harris, 1983).

### 6.2.5 *Examples of population studies*

The population parameters of different bird species vary markedly (Table 6.1). In general small birds tend to have high reproductive rates (i.e. large clutches and possibly more than one brood in a season), low adult survival, and breeding starting at an early age. The converse tends to be true of large birds. The most notable exception to this generalization concerns tropical passerines, which have life-history features more closely resembling large birds. In this section we present examples of population studies and life-tables for a small temperate passerine, a tropical passerine and a sea-bird. Other examples can be found in Lack (1966).

**Table 6.4** Survival rates of adult Blue Tits in different parts of its range (from Snow, 1956).

| Locality | % Adult survival per year |
|---|---|
| Canary Island, Iberia | 55 |
| North Africa | 42 |
| Northern Europe | 35 |
| Britain | 30 |

It is important to note that the life-tables of a particular species are not wholly immutable. In the Blue Tit, for example, the proportion of one-year-old birds in the breeding population varies markedly with latitude (Table 6.4). From this it follows that adult mortality must also vary if the populations are stable. The reason for the variation in input of young birds to the breeding population is related to the latitudinal variation in clutch size, which we have already discussed (section 5.4.1). A second example of variation in life tables is shown in Table 6.5.

*The Great Tit.* Some of the most comprehensive population studies yet made on birds have been made on the Great Tit. There have been two main studies: one which started in the Netherlands in 1912, under the guidance of H. N. Kluyver, the other in Oxford, England, started in 1947 by D. Lack. We have already used the Great Tit to illustrate a number of points

**Table 6.5** Life-table for Mute Swans in two different areas. *Note*: The Thames population had been increasing up to about the time of this study; the Abbotsbury population has not increased as rapidly as might be thought from these figures, because (not shown in these figures) a proportion of the breeding adults fail to nest in some years, so lowering the reproductive output. Note the much higher adult survival at Abbotsbury compared with the Thames and that survival of the young (though very variable in the first year) tends to be much higher also.

---

(a) *Life-table for Mute Swan (River Thames)* (from Perrins and Reynolds, 1967).

| Each pair of swans lays | 6 eggs |
| ,,   ,,   ,,   ,,   hatches | 4 young (includes total losses). |
| ,,   ,,   ,,   ,,   raises | 2 young to September (survival 50% for 3 months). |
| ,,   ,,   ,,   ,,   ,, | 1.3 young .... to 1 year ( .... 67% for rest of year). |
| ,,   ,,   ,,   ,,   ,, | 0.89 young .... to 2 years ( .... 67% per year). |
| ,,   ,,   ,,   ,,   ,, | 0.67 young .... to 3 years ( .... 75% per year). |
| ,,   ,,   ,,   ,,   ,, | 0.43 young .... to 4 years ( .... 82% per year). |
| Adult survival is | 82%   ,,   ,, |

So $(1 - 0.82) \times 2$ birds die per pair per year = 0.36
and the number of young per pair per year which reach breeding age = 0.43.

(b) *Life-table for Mute Swan at Abbotsbury* (from Perrins and Ogilvie, 1981).

| Each pair of swans lays | 5 eggs |
| ,,   ,,   ,,   ,,   hatches | 4 young |
| ,,   ,,   ,,   ,,   raises | 0.5 to 1.0 young to September. |
| ,,   ,,   ,,   ,,   ,, | 0.19 − 0.375 to 1 year (survival 37.7) |
|  | 92.2% for rest of year) |
| ,,   ,,   ,,   ,,   ,, | 0.17 − 0.34 to 2 years (survival 90%) |
| ,,   ,,   ,,   ,,   ,, | 0.15 − 0.30 ” 3 ” ( ,, ,, ) |
| ,,   ,,   ,,   ,,   ,, | 0.14 − 0.27 ” 2 ” ( ,, ,, ) |
| Adult survival is | 93% |

So $(1 - 0.93) \times 2$ birds die per pair per year = 0.14
and the number of young per pair per year which reach breeding age is 0.14 to 0.27

---

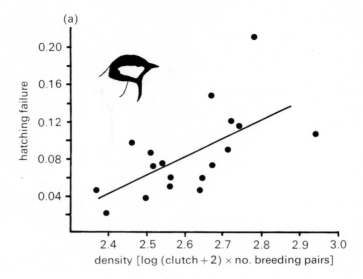

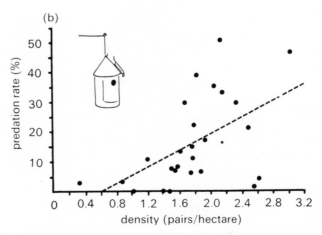

**Figure 6.5** (*a*) The relationship between egg losses and density; 'hatching failure' is mostly due to losses of clutches to predators. (From Krebs, 1970*a*). (*b*) The relationship between the percentage of tits nests (all species) preyed upon by weasels and nesting density. (From Dunn, 1977). In both diagrams each point is the data for a separate year.

**Table 6.6**   Life-table for the British Great Tit (from Bulmer and Perrins, 1973). *Notes*: 1. The number of breeding pairs fluctuates from year to year (see Fig. 6.3.).
2. Because females have a slightly lower survival rate than males, some males (mainly one-year old birds) fail to obtain a mate.
3. In this population second broods are very rare. On the Continent 30–60% of birds may have second broods. The adult survival rate there is similar, so the survival of young birds is lower.

| | | |
|---|---|---|
| Clutch-size | | 8.6 eggs |
| No. of nests lost (mostly to predators) | | 30% |
| Mortality of eggs and chicks (excluding predation) | | 17% |
| No. chicks reared per successful brood | | 7.6 |
| No. of chicks reared per pair including those which fail. | | 5.0 |
| Mortality in first year | | 90% (range 71–99%) |
| No. of young surviving to breeding age per nest | | 1.05 |
| Adult survival | Male | 56% ⎫ 52% (range 40–70%) |
| | Female | 48% ⎭ |

throughout this book, and the main results of the population studies can be summarized briefly. First, numbers fluctuate from year to year, and densities vary between habitats (Fig. 6.3). The reproductive output is determined by clutch-size and the number of broods per season (see section 4.4). Predation on eggs and young is a density-dependent mortality factor (Fig. 6.5). Excluding the 30% of nests destroyed by predators, most young fledge successfully, but then suffer heavy mortality during the first few months of life. A life-table for the Great Tit is shown in Table 6.6.

The differences in population densities which occur between years (Fig. 6.3) must be explained either by reproductive output or mortality. Reproductive output is not found to be closely associated with population changes. However, the mortality rate of young birds following fledging was closely correlated with the observed population changes. The mortality of young birds in late summer was much more variable than the annual mortality of the adults. For example, in the Oxford study the annual survival of the adults was between 40–70%, less than a two-fold difference, in different years. In contrast, the survival of young birds showed more than a ten-fold variation. Not surprisingly, we find that a high survival rate of juvenile Great Tits leads to an increase in the population, and a low survival leads to a decrease (Fig. 6.6). In this species the major cause of year to year changes in numbers is the variation in the number of surviving young. This is a particularly useful observation since it enables us to

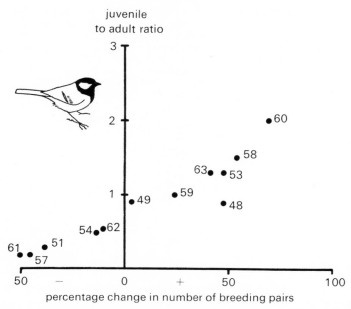

**Figure 6.6** Ratio of juvenile to adult Great Tits in winter in Wytham Wood in relation to change in breeding population in the following year. Numbers refer to year. (From Perrins, 1965).

predict, at least approximately, the level of the next year's breeding population. This is especially useful in the management of certain populations, such as those of game birds, since it enables us to predict how many birds can be taken during the hunting season (see section 6.4).

*The Black-and-White Manakin.* One of the most thorough studies of a tropical passerine yet made is that of the Black-and-White Manakin in Trinidad (Snow, 1962). In this species the male is, as its name suggests, black and white, but the female is a dull green. This small bird lives fairly close to the forest floor, making it suitable for study.

   The males do not start breeding until they are two or more years old. They gather together at leks (see 3.3.2) where they display. There were relatively few leks in the study area and most birds were faithful to a particular lek. By colour-ringing the individual males, it was possible to observe them over a series of years and determine that they had an annual mortality of only 11%, a very low figure for a passerine (though probably fairly typical of a tropical one). Survival rates of females were less easy to

**Table 6.7** Life-table for the Black-and-white Manakin
(from Snow, 1962). *Note*: the figure for survival of
fledgings to reach breeding age is based on a very small
sample and only the survival rate of the breeding males
could easily be measured. It is thought that many tropical
passerines have a similar life history with very low annual
productivity and high adult survival.

| | |
|---|---|
| Clutch-size | 2 eggs |
| No. broods per year | 2–4 |
| % of nests lost | 81 |
| No. young fledged/female/year | 1 |
| Survived from fledging to breeding | 0.33 |
| Adult survival rate | 0.89 |

measure, but since, out of a small sample, most survived the period of the
study, it was assumed that they had a survival rate similar to the males.

The females came to the leks for mating, went away and built the nest,
incubated the eggs and raised the young entirely on their own. Over 90% of
the nests had two eggs. Nestling losses were high; only 44 out of 227 nests
yielded fledged young; and almost all the rest were taken by predators,
usually snakes. On average they made three nesting attempts per year and
raised roughly one chick per female per year or one-third of a chick per
nesting attempt.

On a very small sample, about one-third of the fledglings were known to
have survived to one year old and so each female produced about 0.33
young per year to replace the 0.22 adults which died. In view of the
difficulties in studying these birds these figures seem reasonably good.
A life-table is set out in Table 6.7.

*The Atlantic Puffin.* The Atlantic Puffin, a member of the auk family,
breeds on the eastern sea-board of North America (mainly Canada) and
along the coasts of Britain and Northern Europe. In some parts of its
range its numbers have undoubtedly decreased during the present century,
but the population in Eastern Britain has increased during the last 30
years. In contrast to the Great Tit, accurate assessment of population size
is relatively difficult. The Puffin has a number of life-history features in
common with many other sea-birds, namely low adult mortality, deferred
maturity and a small clutch-size. Harris (1983) has produced a life-table
for this species breeding on the Isle of May, eastern Scotland (Table 6.8).
Puffins produce a single-egg clutch and about 80% of all breeding pairs
rear a chick to fledging. About 30% of the adult population may not
breed in any one year, so taking this into account, breeding success is

**Table 6.8** Population parameters and life table for the Atlantic Puffin at the Isle of May, Scotland (from Harris, 1983). *Note*: (1) a 39% survival rate from fledging to 5 years is equivalent to an annual survival rate of about 83%; it is unlikely that the survival rate is the same each year, more likely that it is lower in the first year than later.
(2) In this population, some 218 young birds per 1 000 pairs are surviving to reach breeding age while only 80 adults per 1 000 pairs are dying per year. Hence the population is increasing rapidly.

| | |
|---|---|
| Clutch-size | 1 egg |
| No. of young reared to fledging per breeding pair | 0.80 chicks |
| Percent adults not breeding | 30 |
| No. young fledged per pair including non-breeders | 0.56 |
| Survival of young to breeding age (5 years) | 0.39 |
| No. young fledged per pair reaching breeding age. | 0.21 |
| Adult survival | 0.96 |

0.56 chicks/pair. Like several other auks, puffins breed for the first time at 5 years old and extensive ringing of young birds has shown that 39% of chicks which fledge survive to this age. This is equivalent to an *average* annual survival rate during this period of 83% (but see section 6.2.2). The mortality rate of adults is very low, with only 4% of birds dying each year; i.e. a 96% annual survival rate. The mean expectation of further life is 24.5 years (see section 6.2.1). We can now draw this information together to examine the life-table for the Atlantic Puffin on the Isle of May.

Assuming for simplicity a population of 1000 pairs, these would produce 560 fledged young, which would be reduced to 218 after five years. With a 96% adult survival rate, 0.08 (2 × 0.04 mortality) birds per pair will die each year. The number of young which need to survive to breeding age to maintain a stable population is therefore 0.08 × 1000 = 80. Since 218 young survive to breed there is a surplus of 138 birds (= 69 pairs). Consequently the population will increase at 69/1000 = 7% per annum. (In fact the population increased at a faster rate than this because of immigration; see 6.2.4).

## 6.3   Natural regulation of population density

There are two fundamental and distinct questions concerning the regulation of animal populations: what factors lead to changes in population density from year to year, and why do the fluctuations in population density occur around the observed mean and not at some different level? This is the same as asking why the abundance of a particular species varies between areas.

There have been a number of theories and much controversy about how animal populations are regulated—see C.J. Krebs (1978), Ricklefs, (1973), for reviews. The main controversy concerns the *type* of factor which regulates populations. Two types of factor are involved: density-dependent and density-independent factors. Density-dependent factors are those which operate more or less severely according to the density of the population. They are stabilizing in nature and cause numbers to return to the average density. In contrast, density-independent factors are those which act at random with respect to the population density. As we shall see, the distinction between density-dependent and density-independent factors is not always clear-cut —see Lack (1966), Andrewartha and Birch (1954), Varley (1963).

### 6.3.1   *Density-independent factors*

A number of density-independent factors have been shown to affect the population densities of birds, and the most obvious ones are climatic. Extreme weather conditions such as severe winters or very wet or dry summers can cause the deaths of many birds (see Fig. 6.1). The food supply may also affect the survival of birds in a density-independent manner, since its abundance may vary markedly from year to year according to whether or not there is a seed crop, for example.

Confusion between density-independent and density-dependent factors may arise when a given environmental variable seems to have components of both types of factor. For example, imagine a species whose chances of survival in bad weather depend upon finding a suitable hole to roost in. The number of such holes is small, so at high population densities more birds will die in bad weather than at low population levels. In this case is the bad weather density-dependent or a density-independent factor? The simplest answer is that the weather acts in a density-independent manner, but the availability of roosting holes has a density-dependent effect on the population. Not all individuals in the population are equally affected by the bad weather, but it is the availability of holes which determines this, not the weather.

There has been considerable discussion about the role of density-independent factors in regulating population size. In the sense that we have used the word 'regulate' (i.e. regulatory factors being compensating or stabilizing) they cannot do so by definition. However, it has been suggested that for organisms like small mammals and insects living in strongly seasonal environments, the overwhelming effect of density-independent factors, compared with density-dependent ones, means that density-dependent factors are rarely important. For birds, as we shall see, the converse is probably true; density-dependent factors are more important than density-independent ones.

### 6.3.2   *Density-dependent factors*

A number of density-dependent effects have been recorded in birds. These include (a) territory size and the proportion of birds holding territories, (b) several aspects of reproductive output, and (c) mortality.

(a)   *Territory*. Territorial behaviour has already been discussed in Chapter 2, and here we are concerned only with those aspects of territoriality which affect population density. In many species birds occupy

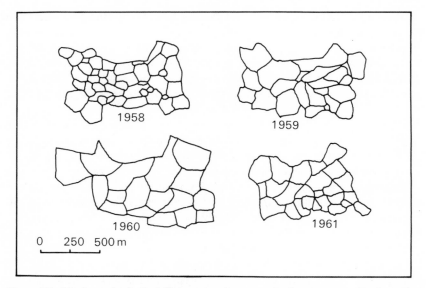

**Figure 6.7**   Territory size in Red Grouse over four years in the same area. Territory size varied with population density. Mean territory size for each year was, 1958: 1.18 hectares; 1959: 2.48 hectares; 1960, 3.92 hectares and 1961: 1.42 hectares. (From Jenkins *et al.*, 1963; Watson and Miller, 1971).

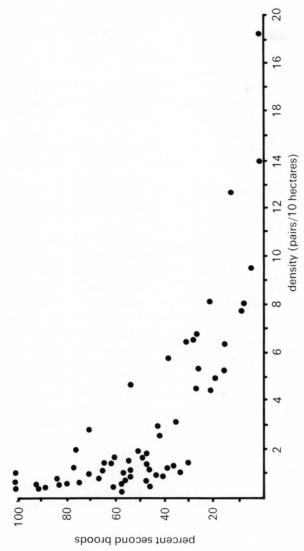

**Figure 6.8**   The proportion of female Great Tits which have a second brood in relation to population density. (From Kluijver, 1951).

all suitable habitats at both high and low population densities. As a result, therefore, individuals have smaller territories in years of high population density than in years of low density. It follows that the territory size varies with the total number of territory holders (Fig. 6.7).

(b) *Reproductive output.* At high densities part of the population may not breed because of territorial behaviour, but other more direct effects have been recorded. First, as we have already shown, clutch-size may be reduced at high population densities (Fig. 5.12). Second, the proportion of birds which have second broods may be reduced at high population levels (Fig. 6.8). Third, at high densities the proportion of young reared may be reduced (Fig. 6.5a). In the Great Tit this occurs because nest-predation by weasels (*Mustela nivalis*) increases with the density of tits (Fig. 6.5b).

(c) *Mortality.* The mortality of young birds following fledging may be positively correlated with population density. This has been demonstrated by two elegant experiments conducted on Great Tits by Kluyver (1966, 1971). In the first experiment, conducted on Vlieland, one of the Friesian Islands, Netherlands, the survival rate of young birds had been measured over a number of years. Then for 4 years the size of all broods was experimentally reduced. The survival of both adults and young increased (Table 6.9) but the total number of individuals surviving remained almost the same. This experiment indicated that juvenile mortality and population density were linked. It also showed that there was an upper limit to the number of birds which could survive at this location, and that young birds competed for these 'places' in the population.

The second experiment was conducted on the mainland of Holland. Kluyver (1971) noted that the young from first broods normally had a higher survival rate than those from second broods. In one year, 1955, bad weather meant that very few of the young from first broods survived, but the young of second broods had a higher survival rate than usual. Kluijver reasoned that young from second broods were normally at a disadvantage in competition with young from first broods. To test this idea, 90% of the

**Table 6.9** Survival of Great Tits on Vlieland (from Kluyver, 1966).

|  | Adult survival (%) | Young survival (%) |
|---|---|---|
| Normal years | 27 | 11 |
| with 60% of young removed | 54 | 20 |

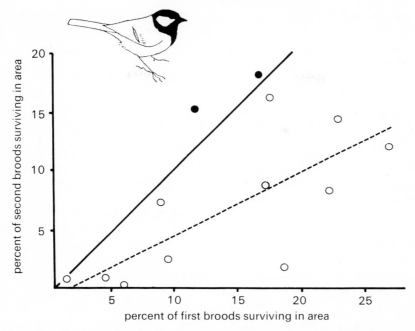

**Figure 6.9** The proportion of young from first and second broods which remained in the study area. In normal years ( o ), higher percentages of first brood young remain than do those from second broods. In years when a high percentage of the first brood young are removed (●), local survival from second broods increases markedly; in normal years it was, on average, 6% while in the two experimental years it was 16% and 18%. The dotted line shows the mean for normal years, the solid line joins points where survival from both first and second broods are equal. (From Kluyver, 1971).

young from first broods were removed just before fledging. The increase in the survival of young from second broods was quite dramatic (Fig. 6.9), showing quite clearly that population density affects the survival rate of young birds.

### 6.3.3 *The importance of density-dependent factors in population regulation*

The existence of strong density-dependent effects on both reproductive output and mortality (see section 6.2) provides strong support for the idea that density-dependent factors play an important role in the population regulation of birds. Not all ecologists agree with this and there

**Table 6.10**  Survival of adults and young in relation to population change: for explanation see text.

| No. pairs | Clutch-size | No. adults + young | No. next year | Change in numbers |
|-----------|-------------|--------------------|---------------|-------------------|
| 10        | 11          | 20 + 110 = 130     | 10 + 11 = 21  | + 5%              |
| 80        | 8           | 160 + 640 = 800    | 80 + 64 = 144 | − 10%             |

have been three main arguments against the importance of density-dependence. These are as follows:

(a)  *The reduction in reproductive output at high densities is not sufficient to compensate for the increase in density.* This argument is based on the observation that if the population density doubles, clutch-size or hatching success are not reduced by half, so the reduction in reproductive output does not lead to a reduction in numbers. The fallacy of this argument is illustrated in Table 6.10. Here two Great Tit populations, one of low and the other of high density, are followed through from one year to the next. In making the calculations we have used the average clutch-size for Great Tits breeding at high and low population densities (see Fig. 5.12), and the same figures for both situations, for survival of eggs (10%) and adults (50%). The large clutch-size in the low-density years leads to a small (5%) increase in numbers, and the small clutch-size in the high-density year leads to a slightly greater (10%) decrease in numbers. Therefore, even without any difference in egg and adult survival rates between years, the difference in clutch-size is sufficient to have a regulatory effect upon the population. This comes about because in the low-density year more young birds survive than adults die, while in the high-density year the reverse is true.

(b) *Density-dependent effects are often masked by subsequent density-independent effects.* For example, if the number of young produced is affected by density, but there is subsequently a high winter mortality as a result of the weather, the latter will completely obscure the density-dependent effect. This argument is also false. If the weather results in the death of a number of birds independent of density, then on average a higher number of birds will survive if there were high summer numbers than if there were low summer numbers. In other words, the pre-winter numbers affect the post-winter numbers. Unless subsequent mortality factors are density-dependent, earlier effects will have an influence on population size.

Hence density-dependent effects in summer will not be cancelled by later density-independent effects.

(c) *The density-dependent effects demonstrated are mostly rather small and therefore are unimportant compared with the often very large effects of density-independent factors.* This is not true. Since density-independent effects are random with regard to population density, they will not tend to cause the population size to alter in any particular direction. Against such large random shifts in numbers, small regulatory alterations will have an effect. The relative sizes of the effects of the two types of factors influence how constant the population size is. If the density-dependent effects are small and the density-independent ones large, then the population will fluctuate more widely than if the reverse is true. The interval between major perturbations in the population also affects its pattern. If the density-independent factors occur only at long intervals (e.g. a very cold winter every 10 or 15 years), then the population will tend to drop sharply from its normal level and then more steadily come back to it. If however, the density-independent factors occur more frequently, the size of the population will fluctuate more erratically. This is because the effects of the density-dependent factors will often not have got the population back to its average size before it is again knocked further away from its mean level.

### 6.3.4 *The social regulation of populations*

Most of the theories for the regulation of animal populations, including those of Lack, have emphasized the importance of *extrinsic* factors such as food, predators, weather, etc. Some ecologists, however, have suggested that *intrinsic* factors involving differences between individuals within the population itself are important in the regulation of numbers—in other words, populations are 'self-regulating'. The idea of self-regulation has been approached from several viewpoints (Christian, 1971; Chitty, 1970), but only the ideas of Wynne-Edwards were directly relevant to birds. He suggested that populations were regulated through social behaviour.

Wynne-Edwards' (1955, 1962) views on the role of social behaviour in regulating animal populations have not gained wide acceptance, mainly because they involve the concept of group selection (see 2.2.4, 5.2). They have, however, caused considerable debate (Lack, 1966; Dawkins, 1976), and we include them here because they can help us focus on the way natural selection can and cannot operate.

Wynne-Edwards suggested that populations of birds, and other animals, would be ultimately limited by food, but never actually reach such a limit because they maintain their numbers at a level at which food resources are used to their fullest extent without depletion, that is optimally for the population as a whole. Wynne-Edwards drew a parallel with man's activities regarding fish and whale stocks, and concluded that bird populations have evolved mechanisms which prevent them 'over-fishing' and lead to optimum use of their food supply. The actual regulation of population density occurs through various social behaviours, such as territoriality (see 2.2.3) and flocking. Wynne-Edwards proposed that aggregations such as flocks, communal roosts and breeding colonies evolved to allow members of the population to assess its density. If the population density was high some individuals would refrain from breeding. He also suggested that groups or populations which contained individuals 'prepared' to do this would survive because they would not over-eat their food supplies. In contrast, groups without such individuals would become extinct. This mechanism involves selection acting at the group or population level, and as already indicated (section 5.2) is not a real possibility for the following reasons. First, group selection is unlikely to be a powerful evolutionary force because it would operate much more slowly than individual selection; that is, it would take many times longer for an entire group or population to die out than it would for one individual to die. Second, individuals which refrained from breeding would be voluntarily reducing their own fitness, that is, they would be behaving 'altruistically'. As we have already stated in Chapter 2, such behaviour raises a number of evolutionary problems, the main one being that if an individual is genetically 'programmed' to cease breeding, how could such behaviour be inherited?

Wynne-Edwards (1978) subsequently accepted the evolutionary problems associated with his ideas. However, his views have been valuable in forcing ecologists to consider the behavioural aspects of population regulation.

### 6.4   Practical applications

We have seen that reproductive rates of birds tend to be higher than is 'necessary' to maintain their populations, since very large numbers of young birds die before they reach breeding age. This 'over-production' is an important component of natural populations in two quite different ways. First, it is the mechanism by which natural selection works. Darwin realised that the large number of animals which die before breeding in each generation formed the basis for evolution: only the fittest survive.

Second, and more relevant to this section, the concept that 'over-production' is normal is important to the management of wild populations. Most management theories depend on this and another concept which we have discussed, density-dependent regulation. In this section we will examine how the management of populations depends on these theories. The concept of density-dependent mortality is particularly important. It is essential to realize that those factors which influence populations in a density-dependent way place an upper limit on the *number* of individuals that can survive. This means that the lower the population density the greater the *proportion* of birds that can survive. Although the number of animals is not rigidly fixed there are resources for only a certain number of individuals and the rest must die (section 6.1.3). The latter are sometimes referred to as the 'doomed surplus'.

The second important aspect of density-dependent mortality is that if one individual (which would otherwise have survived) is removed from the population, another (which would otherwise have died) is likely to survive in its place. In other words, in nature the loss of one individual will tend to be compensated by the survival of another.

The aims of managing wild populations fall into three categories: (1) protecting a species (usually a rare one); (2) reduction or even extermination of a species regarded as a pest; (3) exploitation; hunting a species for sport or food.

### 6.4.1  *Species protection*

Most of the species which fall into this category are rare, often as a result of man's activities. Four main types of animal are rare.

(a)  *Large species*.  Large animals tend to be easy to find and therefore to kill. Even when their numbers are reduced to fairly low levels, there is still a reasonable chance of finding one, so hunting can continue. In addition, large animals tend to have relatively low reproductive rates and long periods of immaturity. Both these factors make it easier to reduce their numbers because their potential rate of increase is lower than for smaller species. Examples include whales (especially the Blue Whale *Balaenoptera musculus*, bears, wolves, and, among birds, eagles. The White-tailed Eagle was hunted to extinction in the British Isles (Witherby *et al.*, 1952).

(b)  *Colonial species*. In the same way that large animals are vulnerable, so are those which breed in colonies. They are easy to find even when numbers are considerably reduced. Examples include Elephant Seals *Mirounga leonina*, fur seals, and the Great Auk.

(c)  *Animals with very specialized niches*. These animals may be sensitive to small changes in their environment. For example, Kirtland's Warbler of North America is confined to young forests at a particular stage of development. Woodland management changes have reduced the area available and as a result, reduced the numbers of this species (Mayfield, 1961). Woodpeckers may find it difficult to survive in woodland devoted to forestry since foresters take out dead and dying trees and this removes their feeding sites. These trees constitute very small proportion of the forest, but are the critical part as far as woodpeckers are concerned.

(d)  *Animals with very restricted ranges*. These are obviously very vulnerable to local changes. There are two reasons why species with restricted ranges are vulnerable. First, their habitat itself may be vulnerable and even a small change (on a global scale) may remove all the available habitat. Second, because their population size is small anyway, extinction is more likely through pure chance. Many species in this category live on islands where their habitat and numbers are very restricted. Of the 78 bird species which are known to have become extinct in the last 300 years, 88% were island forms. An additional factor which has probably contributed to their extinction has been the introduction of other species from continental areas—often such introduced species out-compete the resident island species.

The conservation of rare species is not difficult in theory. Almost all endangered species could, like commoner ones, maintain their numbers quite successfully given an adequate amount of the right habitat. It is in practice that conservation becomes difficult. In birds, habitats are usually being altered or destroyed by man, and if the species is a large one it may also be hunted for food. As we have seen, birds can make good the losses from an occasional natural disaster, but they cannot do this unless their habitat remains suitable.

For many species a single habitat is not sufficient. Migrants require both favourable breeding and winter quarters, and in addition they may need suitable habitats while on migration so that they can stop to rest and feed. The loss of any one of these may make survival impossible.

We have seen that bird populations are very resilient, but there are limitations. Unless birds can produce more young than the number of birds which die in a year, the species will become extinct.

### 6.4.2 *Control of pest species*

Many species of birds come into conflict with man, in particular with his agricultural practices. Some species, particularly seed-eaters, have found man's farming practices much to their benefit. As a result their numbers have increased markedly, and at times they may become serious competitors with man for the crops which he is growing. Man has often attempted to control such species.

The control of pest species is often very difficult. Pest species are ones with high reproductive output and in the normal course of events (i.e. without any attempt at control) very large numbers of individuals will die each year anyway. If man is to be successful in reducing the population of a pest species he must take more individuals than would die naturally. Frequently this has proved impossible to do.

A good example of this is the Wood Pigeon in Britain (Fig. 6.10). In this study the breeding population averaged 72 Wood Pigeons per 100 acres. By

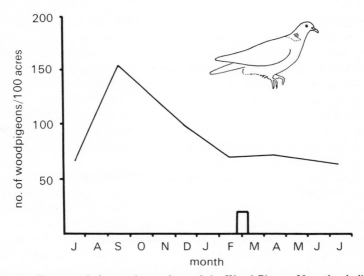

**Figure 6.10** The annual changes in numbers of the Wood Pigeon. Note the decline in numbers through the winter and that shooting (vertical bar) does not lead to a reduction in breeding numbers because of immigration. (From Murton, 1965).

the end of the breeding season the population density had doubled, to 154 birds/100 acres. Since the population was stable, about 90 birds/100 acres died between the autumn and the following spring. Intensive shooting in February and March killed about 20 birds/100 acres. However, this was $3\frac{1}{2}$ times fewer than those that died of natural causes, so the shooting had no effect on the overall numbers. It might have helped to reduce numbers if the shooting had killed breeding birds after their natural winter mortality had occurred. However, the shooting did not even do this and pigeon numbers continued to decline after shooting had ceased. Clearly, there were still 'too many' pigeons and natural mortality continued. There is no doubt that numbers would have fallen to the same level without shooting.

There is another difficulty about attempts to control a pest species. If man is successful in reducing the numbers of an individual pest species, it is natural to relax control efforts, because when there are fewer birds it is much harder to shoot many of them and it seems less worth the effort. However, as soon as control efforts are relaxed at all, the numbers of a species will recover rapidly. Consequently, any success from the earlier control efforts will be lost.

### 6.4.3　*Game birds*

Man's interest in wildfowl, pheasants and their allies is the reverse of his attitude to pest species. In these cases, man wants to be able to harvest ( = shoot) as many as possible without reducing the breeding stock. In other words, the aim is to take as high a proportion as possible of the 'doomed surplus', leaving as little density-dependent mortality as possible. Game biologists call this the 'maximum sustainable yield'. Both the pheasant family and wildfowl have relatively large clutches and so in natural conditions there must be high mortality. This means that man can take a large number of birds from these populations without reducing the breeding numbers.

The calculation of the actual proportion which can be taken depends on a number of factors. It almost goes without saying that these details should be accurately known if the maximum sustainable yield is to be achieved. However, the level of hunting pressure that a species can withstand has often been determined in a trial-and-error way. For only a few species is sufficient accurate information obtained year by year for man to be able to estimate the harvest in *advance* of the shooting season, that is, in response to changes in numbers from the previous year. Often the harvest can be predicted from the proportion of juveniles in the population. One such species is the Mallard in North America (Geis *et al.*, 1969), where the total mortality is 50–55% and hunting accounts for 30–40%.

From what has been said earlier in this chapter, it will be apparent that a number of factors affect the proportion of a population which can be taken without affecting its numbers. Compared with other species, one can take a relatively high proportion of species which have large clutches, short periods of immaturity and low adult survival rates. All these features are common to species which have a high natural turnover rate and a large 'doomed surplus'.

In all the above cases hunters are not selecting any particular age class of birds (usually they cannot do so). As a result adults and juveniles are shot indiscriminately. In practice, however, adults (being experienced) are often a little better at avoiding hunters than are young birds.

Since adults have higher survival rates than young birds (Table 6.1) they are more 'important' to the population because they are more likely to be members of next year's breeding population. Hence, theoretically at least, it would be better to take a higher proportion of the young and leave the adults. This is seldom easy to do, but there is one extreme case of such a situation. This is where eggs rather than young are harvested. For example, many northern temperate peoples have harvested sea-bird eggs for many centuries. An egg has only a rather small chance of becoming a surviving adult, so that a much higher proportion of eggs than of breeding adults can be taken without affecting the overall breeding numbers.

Another factor which affects the proportion of the population which can be harvested is the time at which the harvesting is done. Clearly it is important to do this as early as possible after the young have fledged; at this time the population is at its largest. This is the essential difference between managing a game population and controlling pest species. In the former man attempts to take as much as possible of the surplus while leaving a high breeding population. In the control situation it is pointless to kill only part of the surplus; what is needed is to kill potential breeders, preferably after the most density-dependent mortality has taken place. This was what was planned for the Wood Pigeon, mentioned above. However, it was not effective since birds continued to die after shooting and no reduction in the size of the breeding population was achieved. In actual practice, this 'control' was indistinguishable from the cropping of a game bird population, except that were one trying to maximize the harvest, one would start shooting in the autumn and not in late winter.

## 6.5 Summary

Bird populations have several characteristics: (a) numbers are usually stable and fluctuate only within certain limits; (b) the potential rate of increase is high, but is rarely realized; (c) the number of individuals a particular area can support is determined by limiting resources. The two main factors affecting population density are natality (reproductive output) and mortality. Mortality is examined by means of life-tables or survivorship curves. Unlike that of many other animals the mortality rate of birds is constant with respect to age. Immigration and emigration can also affect population density, but they are often difficult to measure. Some examples of population studies are presented, using species with very different life-history patterns. Controversy exists over the way in which populations are regulated, in particular the types of factors involved. These factors can be density-dependent or density-independent. Most ecologists consider density-dependent factors (especially food) to be the most important in regulating bird populations. The practical application of population dynamics involves the protection of rare species, the reduction of pest species and the exploitation of edible species.

# CHAPTER SEVEN

# BIRD COMMUNITIES

## 7.1 Introduction

In the last chapter we looked at the ways in which numbers of a single species are regulated. In some ways the view we presented there is an over-simplification. The main simplification was that we considered population regulation only in terms of intraspecific interactions, and ignored any interactions which might occur *between* species. For example we did not consider what would happen to the numbers of species A if species B or C was absent. Almost all animals live in environments also occupied by other species, and within any area a great many species may interact in some way. Examples of complex 'food webs' can be found in most ecology textbooks. In the present chapter we will examine the types of interactions which occur between populations of different bird species living in the same environments. Populations of interacting species are called *communities*.

## 7.2 Differences between species

Even the most naive observer knows that different species have different life-styles. A hawk may eat small mammals, a pelican eats fish and a swallow insects so that it seems unlikely that they would ever compete for food. However, the situation becomes more complex when one asks whether two species of hawk, living in the same area, compete for food.

The subject of interspecific competition was originally examined theoretically by Lotka (1925) and Volterra (1926) who discussed in some detail what one would expect to find in terms of interaction between two individual species. One of the first ecologists to consider these interactions in relation to birds was Gause (1934) who concluded that 'as a result of competition, two similar species scarcely ever occupy similar niches, but displace each other in such a manner that each takes possession of certain peculiar types of food and modes of life in which it has an advantage over its competitor'.

This was an important concept and become known as Gause's principle. In fact, as so often happens, others had said something similar before, but not so explicitly. Gause's principle, often also known as the competitive exclusion principle (Hardin, 1960), has had an important effect on the way ecologists have tackled the problem of community ecology, and in this chapter we shall examine how well this principle is supported by the facts.

### 7.2.1   *Ecological niche: theory*

The position which each species occupies within a community is called its *niche*. A niche is not an easy concept since one cannot see it, nor can one always go out in the field and measure it (or at least not more than a few features of it). Elton (1927) said 'the niche of an animal means its place in the biotic environment, *its relation to food and enemies*'. Imagine a bird which feeds on insects in grassland: such insects might be absent from very short turf and difficult to catch in very long grass. In this case the bird might live in areas of medium-length grass. We could say that grass of medium length was one dimension of its niche. The bird might also need to pounce on these insects from a perch, so the presence of small shrubs might be a second dimension of its niche. Similarly, it might need trees for nesting in, holes for roosting in, berries at the time of year when insects were scarce and so on. Indeed, there is likely to be a long list of factors which define the niche of any particular species. As a result, Hutchinson (1957, 1959) defined a niche as an '*n*-dimensional hyperspace'.

Competition between any two species may occur in one or more of the dimensions. The chances of competition occurring are, intuitively, more likely between species which are similar than those that are very different, i.e. between two species of swallow or between two species of eagle rather than between a swallow and an eagle. This was why Gause used the words 'similar species' in his statement. Most work has therefore been conducted on closely related (usually con-generic) species. For practical purposes this is entirely reasonable, but one should not ignore the possibility that less closely related species may also compete (see 7.2.5). For example in the United States, Winter Wrens, Bluebirds and Tree Swallows all nest in holes and competition for suitable sites may be intense. The Starling, which has been introduced into the U.S.A., also nests in holes and, being larger, may out-compete these species in certain areas. It has been suggested that competition for nest-sites between Starlings and Blue birds may be partly responsible for the decline in Bluebirds that has occurred in parts of the eastern states.

Holes suitable for nesting in often seem to be in short supply and there can be strong competition for them. Slagsvold (1978) showed that Pied Flycatchers, kept out of nesting boxes by Great Tits, would compete aggressively for them. Balat (1977) showed that when he removed Tree Sparrows occupying nest boxes, the Great Tit population increased, strongly suggesting that the numbers of Tree Sparrows prevented some Great Tits from obtaining breeding sites.

### 7.2.2 *Competition*

Let us now consider what might happen if two species with *identical* niches arrived in the same place. For simplicity we shall consider a niche of only one dimension. The following might happen.

(1) They might *co-exist* without deleterious effects. This is only a possibility if the resource is temporarily unlimited. For example, if the numbers of both species were limited by their food supply in winter, they might be able to co-exist on a summer diet of insects. It is perhaps worth stressing here that all discussions of competition between species carry the implication (not always spelled out) that the resource is limited. If the resource is limited, co-existence is impossible by definition. In that case a number of other possibilities arise.

(2) One or other species may be more efficient at harvesting the resource. In this case, either (a) the less efficient species will go extinct, or (b) it will change its niche (Fig. 7.1).

In cases where co-existence occurs it is unlikely that one species would change its niche completely and that the other would not change at all. It is more likely that each will be slightly more efficient than the other in a part of the niche; if so, what will happen is

(3) Both species will alter their niche (Fig. 7.2).

Up to now we have discussed the simplest possible situation, that of just two species, A and B. However, in many habitats there are many more species than that. If we now look at what happens when we add an additional species to a habitat where there are already two or three similar ones, we find a different situation. In this case the additional species has to 'squeeze' in between the others. It is not so easy for all the species to shift their niches away from the adjacent ones if the niches on either side are

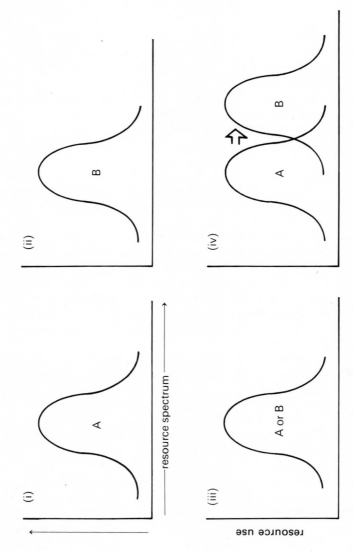

**Figure 7.1** Outcome of competition between two species with identical resource requirements (i) and (ii). Either one species will become extinct (iii) or it will shift its niche to reduce competition, shown here (iv) by species *B* shifting its niche.

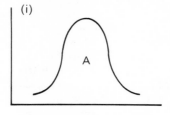

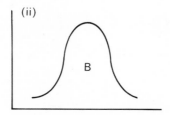

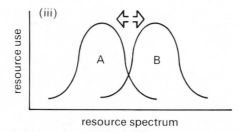

**Figure 7.2** The more likely outcome of competition between two species with identical resource requirements (i and ii). Here (iii) both species *A* and *B* shift their niches.

occupied. As MacArthur (1972) has pointed out, it is far easier for two similar species to co-exist than for three or more. This is because in the former situation each species always has the chance of shifting its niche away from that of its competitor. With three or more species, this may not be possible for the species using the middle part of the resource. If three or more species co-exist, either each species maintains its niche and there is considerable overlap between adjacent species, or each species narrows its niche (Fig. 7.3). In either case the *numbers* of each species will have to decrease. This is because the resource is limiting and there must be fewer

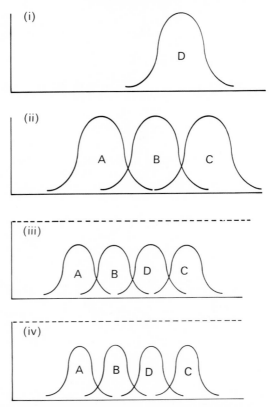

**Figure 7.3**   The outcome of adding an extra species (*D*) to a community (*A, B, C*). Either the species have wider overlaps (iii) or they will have to develop narrower niches (iv); in either case, since their "share" of the resource is reduced, fewer individuals can be supported. Note that, because of the presence of species *A*, species *B* cannot easily shift its niche away from that of species *D*, though species *C* could do so.

individuals of each species if there are more species altogether (see also 7.3.2).

This leads us to another question. How does one know if a species is using all the resource it can or whether its niche is restricted by competition with another species? Hutchinson (1957) distinguished between these two sorts of niche. The *fundamental niche* is that which the species would occupy in the absence of competitors, the *realized niche* is that which they actually occupy in the presence of competitors. In practice it is not easy to distinguish between these two types of niche (see 7.3.3).

In this section we have covered the basic ideas about interspecific competition, but we have done so in an over-simplified form: nature is far more complex. We should also stress that in order to make our discussion simple, we have used an 'evolutionary shorthand' in considering the shifting of niches. A species occupies a particular niche because of a large series of intricate adaptations which have evolved over a long period of time. It does not therefore 'get up' and 'move' to a different niche just on the whim of the moment. A niche shift is shorthand for saying that during the course of evolution those individuals of species B which can most efficiently use that part of the resource spectrum least occupied (or not used at all) by species A will flourish and leave many survivors, whereas those individuals whose resource use most overlaps that of species A will fare less well. As a result of this, the average resource use of species B will gradually move away from that of species A.

There is also likely to be some form of interaction between intra-and interspecific competition. As we have already discussed (Chapter 6) the individuals of the same species compete for resources. We are saying here that individuals of different species also compete for resources. There is no inconsistency here; both can happen simultaneously. Intra-specific competition results in a species having a wide niche. Species can occupy a wide niche by consisting of either generalist individuals, or a range of specialized phenotypes covering the same resource spectrum (see 7.3.2). In contrast, interspecific competition will result in species having relatively narrow niches. This is because individuals whose niche was farthest from the species' average would be those most likely to suffer in competition with adjacent species.

## 7.2.3   *Ecological niches: evidence in birds*

Having outlined the theoretical aspects of ecological niches, we shall now consider some of the evidence that such things occur in nature. In fact birds have provided much of the available evidence on this subject (Lack, 1971). Community ecology is a controversial subject area and the findings of many studies are open to a number of interpretations. Difficulties arise because we are observing a situation as it is and trying to infer what caused it. Unfortunately it is seldom possible to perform experiments to test the theoretical ideas about community structure. For example, if two species of birds differ in their resource use, is this (i) because competition occurred in the past, but is no longer happening, or (ii) is the difference between the two species maintained because there is still competition, or (iii) did the difference between the two species arise for some other reason which has nothing whatever to do with interspecific competition? Usually we cannot distinguish between these alternatives.

Virtually every detailed study of closely related birds has shown that they differ in some aspect of their ecology. We shall now look at some of the main ways in which closely related species differ and then discuss the likelihood that the differences are due to competition.

Closely related birds may differ in a number of ways.

(1) *Different ranges.* Two species may not exist in the same place at any time of year. In this case competition is plainly not occurring at present. However, sometimes the two species appear to replace each other (Fig. 7.4); in some of these cases the complementary nature of such distributions seems unlikely to be coincidence.

(2) *Different habitats.* Different species may occur in the same geographical area, but live primarily in different habitats. For example, in Europe Coal Tits and Blue Tits occur in the same general area, and in parts of the western United States the same is true for the Chestnut-backed Chickadee and the Plain Titmouse. In both cases, however, the first species occurs primarily in coniferous woodland and the second in broad-leaved woodland. They occupy the same geographical area but live in different habitats. Divisions such as this are seldom total, and in both these examples we occasionally find individuals in the 'wrong' habitat, but they occur there at much lower density.

Species of tits and chickadees living in coniferous woodland also show morphological differences from those in broad-leaved deciduous woodland. Coniferous woodland species tend to have finer, more sharply-pointed bills than those which live in broad-leaved deciduous woodland which have rather deeper, stubbier beaks. The difference is thought to be related to the need for a particularly fine beak to probe for insects amongst the narrow bases of conifer needles.

(3) *Separation within a habitat.* In many cases species differ in their use of a single habitat. A well-studied example involves the tits of deciduous woodland in Europe (Fig. 7.5). Birds which live in the same habitat may differ in a number of ways. Birds may have different feeding stations, for example, they may feed in different parts of trees; some concentrate on fine twigs at the outermost edges while others forage on the trunks and large branches (Table 7.1). Among forest species the heights of the feeding

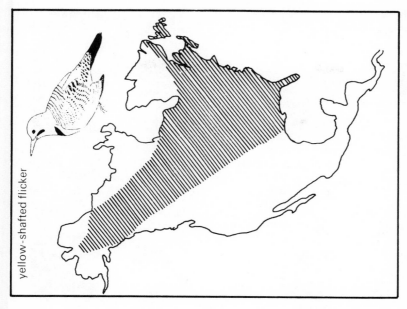

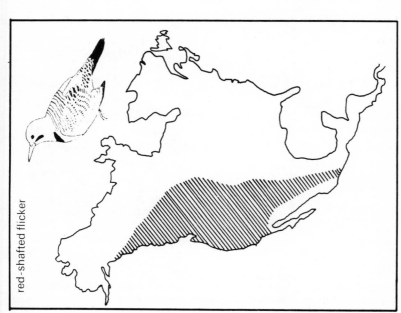

**Figure 7.4** Breeding distribution of **Red-shafted** and **Yellow-shafted** Flickers. The exact boundaries are difficult to determine in some areas where widespread hybridization occurs.

**Figure 7.5** Niches of the three commonest tits in European broad-leaved woodland. The Blue Tit forages high up amongst the leaves and small twigs; the Marsh Tit hunts mainly nearer to the trunk and lower down the tree, often on larger branches, and the Great Tit lowest of all, often on the large branches, and spends more of its time on the ground than the other species. (From Lack, 1971).

**Table 7.1** The main feeding sites of different species of tits in winter. Figures are percentage of time spent in each feeding station. (From Lack, 1971).

|  | Ground | Branches | Twigs and buds | Leaves | Elsewhere |
|---|---|---|---|---|---|
| Blue Tit | 7 | 8 | 34 | 3 | 48 |
| Marsh Tit | 16 | 30 | 19 | 2 | 33 |
| Great Tit | 50 | 16 | 5 | 4 | 25 |

**Table 7.2** Average foraging heights of tits (in feet) when feeding in trees (from Gibb, 1954).

|  | November/December | March/April |
|---|---|---|
| Blue Tit | 34.2 | 31.4 |
| Marsh Tit | 25.5 | 26.0 |
| Great Tit | 29.5 | 19.7 |

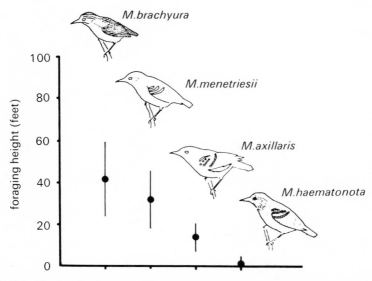

**Figure 7.6** The foraging heights of four species of ant-thrush of the genus *Myrmotherula*. These birds live in rain forest in South America and tend to join mixed flocks of birds travelling through the forest. (From MacArthur, 1972).

stations of different species may be quite distinct (Table 7.2). Vertical separation between species has been reported in a number of cases—an example is shown in Fig. 7.6. Studies of this type which show small differences between species provide some insight into the ecological differences between species. They are, however, very simple in that they examine differences only in one dimension. Actual overlap between species is likely to be much less if differences exist in a number of resource dimensions. For example, if two species take seeds of different sizes mainly in different habitats, the amount of overlap is obviously less than if they were taking them in the same habitats. Although it is not very common, closely related species may sometimes divide up the same habitat by holding interspecific territories. This means that one or both species may be limited by not being able to make use of all the suitable habitats because it is excluded by the territorial behaviour of the other (see 2.2.1).

(4) *Differences in food.* Most bird species differ in the types of food they take. The species of European tits take foods of slightly different sizes (Table 7.3). The two smallest species, Coal and Blue Tits, take food items which are approximately the same size, but since these species usually feed on different species of trees, the ecological overlap between them remains small. In much the same way, closely related species of finch often differ markedly in body size and in the size and shape of their bill. The size of the bill closely matches the size of seeds which they are able to break open as Fig. 7.7 shows.

## 7.2.4  Evidence for competition

Because of the problems of interpretation mentioned earlier, it is difficult to decide whether the four differences listed above indicate the occurrence of competition. Perhaps the best evidence for competition comes from those cases in which the absence of one species results in another changing its

**Table 7.3**  Percentage of prey items of each size taken by tits (from Betts, 1955).

| Prey size (mm) | 0–2 | 3–4 | 5–6 | 7–6 |
|---|---|---|---|---|
| Coal Tit | 74 | 17 | 3 | 7 |
| Blue Tit | 59 | 29 | 3 | 10 |
| Marsh Tit | 22 | 52 | 16 | 11 |
| Great Tit | 27 | 20 | 22 | 32 |

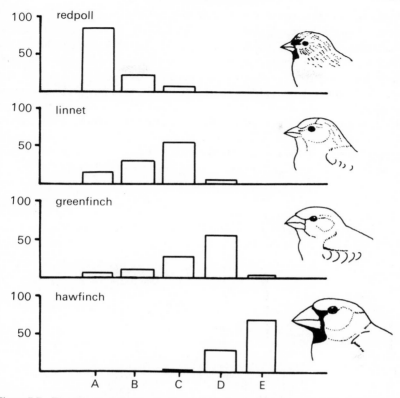

**Figure 7.7** The size of seeds taken by four British finches. Seeds were graded with five sizes from *A* to *E*. (From Newton, 1972).

niche. For example, if species A avoids habitat B in the presence of species B, but uses it when species B is absent, then it seems likely that competition is occurring. We could say that in the presence of species B, species A uses only a realized niche, but in species B's absence it undergoes *competitive release* and occupies something closer to its fundamental niche.

There are a number of examples of this situation. In Sweden Coal and Crested Tits live mainly in coniferous woodland. The two species, however, differ in their feeding stations. Coal Tits spent 84% of their time among twigs and needles and 15% on branches and tree trunks, while Crested Tits spent 74% of their time foraging on the trunks and branches. On the large island of Gotland the Crested Tit is absent, and there the Coal Tit spent 43% of its time on the branches and trunks (Alerstam *et al.*, 1974). These results indicate that the change in behaviour of the Coal Tit on Gotland is related to the absence of the Crested Tit.

Another example of such an ecological shift has been reported by Diamond (1975) in ground-feeding doves in the New Guinea archipelago. There are three similar species on the mainland of New Guinea: the Emerald Dove in the coastal scrub, the Brown-backed Ground Dove in the light forests and the Red-throated Ground Dove in the rain forests. On one island, Bagabag, the Red-throated Ground Dove is absent and the Brown-backed occupies the rain forests there as well as the light forest. On several small islands, both the Emerald Dove and the Red-throated Ground Dove

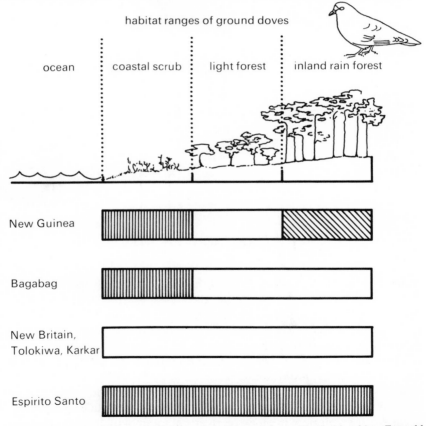

**Figure 7.8** The habitat use by three species of ground doves. Vertical hatching, Emerald Dove; Brown-backed Ground Dove, white; Red-throated Ground Dove, diagonal hatching. For explanation see text (From Diamond, 1975).

are absent; here the Brown-backed occupies all three habitats. However, on Espiritu Santo in the New Hebrides, the only species present is the Emerald Dove and there this species occupies all three habitats (Fig. 7.8). These observations strongly suggest that competition determines the habitat use of the three species.

Blue and Great Tits provide a further example. These species are very different in size, and, as we have shown, exhibit considerable differences in their feeding ecology (Table 7.3). In summer both species feed their nestlings on caterpillars from oak trees, and until recently it had been thought that the caterpillars were so plentiful that competition was unlikely to be very important. It has now been shown that the two species are in fact interacting at this time. Minot (1981) chose three study areas: from one he took all the nestling Blue Tits as they hatched, adding them to nests at a similar stage in the second area: a third area he left as a control. One area therefore had adult Blue Tits with no young to raise, the second one had adult Blue Tits working unusually hard to raise very large broods and the third area was left normal. Minot studied the growth rates of the Great Tits in these three areas and found that the young birds grew best in the absence of young Blue Tits (Table 7.4), showing clearly that the Great Tits benefited from the absence of competition with the Blue Tits.

A similar case of competition concerns the Jackdaw and the Magpie, two similar-sized crows. Magpies build their own nests in hedged and open woodland; Jackdaws nest in holes in trees. By providing nest-boxes, Högstedt (1980) was able to induce Jackdaws to nest in Magpie habitat and examine the effect of Jackdaws on the breeding success of Magpies. In the presence of Jackdaws, Magpies had a lower success, raising only 0.33 young per pair as opposed to 1.68 young in the absence of Jackdaws.

This study added a species to an area occupied by another species. The opposite, a removal experiment, was performed in California by Davis (1973). In this study two small finch-like species, Golden Crowned Sparrows and Slate-coloured Juncos, were common, the Sparrows mainly

**Table 7.4** Mean fledging weights of Great Tits in relation to abundance of Blue Tits; for further explanation see text (from Minot, 1981).

| *Mean weight of nestling Great Tits (g)* | |
| --- | --- |
| Blue Tit nestlings removed | 19.94 |
| No treatment (control) | 19.03 |
| Blue Tit nestlings added | 18.75 |

F

occupying thick scrub and the Juncos more open habitat. By removing the Sparrows through extensive trapping, Davis found that Juncos would spread into 'sparrow-habitat' and use it successfully, but as soon as the sparrows were released the situation reverted to normal.

### 7.2.5   *Diffuse competition*

The examples in the previous section indicate that *closely related* species may compete with one another. However, there is no reason why more distantly related species should not compete to some extent. We know very little about this, but it seems likely that many species may face competition of this sort, which McArthur (1972) termed *diffuse competition*. Evidence for diffuse competition involves the geographical ranges of species. In only relatively few cases is there a clear-cut habitat change at the edge of a species range and often there is no obvious reason why the species should occur only where it does. The most likely explanation is that a variety of factors make it impossible for the species to spread further and that one of these is likely to be competition with other birds in the area.

It is possible also that much diffuse competition may come not only from other birds, but from other animals as well. In the tropics, for example, lizards and frogs are very much more common than birds and these must provide important competition for insectivorous species. Similarly, in desert areas, ants may compete with rodents and finches for seeds (Pulliam and Brand, 1975).

A bizarre case of interspecific competition concerns the Takahe, a large, rare moorhen-like bird in New Zealand, and the Red Deer. Both species eat the same types of grasses, though the Red Deer takes a wider range of other species than the Takahe. As a result of this competition for its rather specialized diet, the bird is in danger of extinction (Mills and Mark, 1977).

## 7.3   The ecology of island avifaunas

The study of island faunas has often provided valuable insight into ecological and evolutionary subjects. It is no coincidence that two of the first biologists to put forward ideas about evolution were much influenced by observations they had made on islands (Darwin in the Galapagos and Wallace in New Guinea and Micronesia). More recently the study of island faunas has yielded important information about ecological niches and the structure of bird communities.

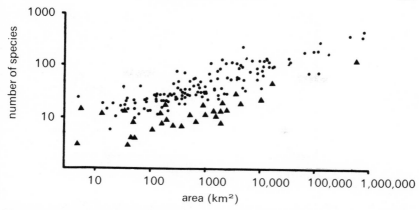

**Figure 7.9** The numbers of land bird species on islands in relation to island size. Note the difference between inshore islands (•) and offshore islands (▲). (From Slud, 1976).

## 7.3.1 *The number of species*

Studies of bird communities on islands show two main trends: the size of island and the number of species found on it are positively correlated, and the further the island is from a large land mass, the smaller the number of species that occur there. Both these features can be seen in Fig. 7.9. Both trends hold remarkably well over a very wide range of island sizes and distances from major land masses. They even hold for islands which are very close to the shores of a large land mass. Some of the inshore islands around New Guinea were connected to the main island at one time and have been cut off only as a result of changes in sea level (Diamond, 1975). It seems likely that at one time these islands held the same assemblage of species as the main island, but have since lost some of them. Similarly, about 40% of the birds that breed in north-western areas of Continental Europe do not breed in the British Isles, and approximately 40% of those that breed in England and Wales do not breed in Ireland. Despite this, almost all those species that do not breed have been recorded in these countries at one time or another, and some of them have bred occasionally (Lack, 1976).

The reasons for the two patterns shown in Fig. 7.9 have been much debated. One explanation, put forward by MacArthur and Wilson (1967), was that the number of species on islands is a balance between the number of new immigrant species arriving and the rate at which other species die out on the islands (Fig. 7.10). There tend to be fewer species on small

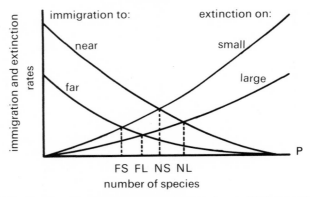

**Figure 7.10** MacArthur and Wilson's (1967) explanation for equilibrium in island populations. Equilibrium occurs where the extinction and immigration curves intersect. *P* is the total pool of species. Note that the intercept is at a higher number of species for near than for far islands and for large compared with small islands. (FS, far small; FL, far large; NS, near small; NL, near large.)

islands because, having smaller populations, these populations tend to die out more frequently than on large islands. Fewer species occur on islands far from large land masses because immigration tends to be less frequent than on islands closer to the large land masses.

Lack (1976) suggested an alternative idea. The number of species on an island could be related to the habitat richness on that island. Smaller islands and more distant islands both tended to have poor ranges of habitats. Thus the number of species which could settle there was reduced accordingly.

In fact, as so often happens, it is unlikely that either of these explanations is wholly true on its own. For example, the range of habitats may be closely linked to the range of plants colonizing an island, which may in turn be determined by factors like those suggested by MacArthur and Wilson. In a recent analysis of the island avifaunas of the islands off the British Isles, Reed (1981) found that distance, size and number of habitats are all contributors to the richness of the avifauna on the island.

Isolated patches of habitat, such as woods, ponds or mountain tops, can be considered as ecological islands. Some of the best information to test MacArthur and Wilson's ideas come from a long-term study of the bird community in a 16-hectare area of oak woodland in southern England. On average, an equilibrium number (see Fig. 7.10) of 32 species bred in the wood each year. Over the 30-year study period a total of 44 different species was recorded breeding, but of these only 16 did so regularly. As MacArthur

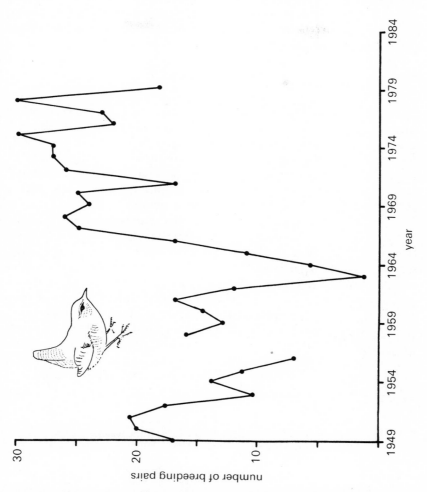

**Figure 7.11**   The number of wrens in a 16-ha. wood. Note how numbers fluctuate between years, and that they nearly became extinct in 1963 (due to cold winter). On an island the birds would have then been absent until a new colonization occurred. (From Beven, 1976).

and Wilson predict, there was a turnover of species, with an average of three new immigrants and three extinctions each year. Figure. 7.11 shows the fluctuations in the number of wrens breeding in the wood. The wren population almost became extinct as a result of the severe 1962–63 winter, and clearly illustrates the risks of extinction on small islands (for further details see Williamson, 1981).

### 7.3.2　The number of individuals

If there are fewer species on an island than on an area of similar size on the adjacent mainland, what happens to the numbers of individuals on islands? There are relatively few studies of this sort and the results are not entirely consistent, but in some cases it has been shown that the density of individuals of a given species is higher on the island than on the mainland (Table 7.5). This effect, called *density compensation*, suggests that a particular habitat is able to support a given number of birds: the smaller the number of species the larger the number of individuals per species.

This type of effect has been recorded for certain islands in a Swedish lake (Nilsson, 1977). Here the density of individuals in groups of closely-related species remained constant regardless of the number of the species on the island. For example, between one and four species of thrush occurred on any particular island, but the total density of thrushes was always around 1.6 pairs per hectare, irrespective of the number of thrush species present. Another example has been recorded for Bermuda where Crowell (1962) found a number of species living at much higher densities than on the adjacent mainland. Nevertheless, in general Williamson (1981) found little convincing evidence for density-compensation in islands.

If there are more individuals per species, but fewer species, this might

**Table 7.5**　Abundance of certain species on the island of Puercos (Pearl Archipelago) compared with the mainland of Panama (from MacArthur *et al.*, 1972).

|  | Pairs per 40 hectares | |
|---|---|---|
|  | Puercos | Panama mainland |
| White-fronted Dove | 24 | 12 |
| Red-crowned Woodpecker | 24 | 4 |
| Barred Ant-shrike | 112 | 8 |
| Streaked Flycatcher | 16 | 4 |
| Yellow-green Vireo | 104 | 35 |
| Red-legged Honeycreeper | 56 | 12 |

indicate reduced interspecific competition but increasing intraspecific competition (as is discussed in section 7.2.2). There has been little work in this area, but one study has shown that island birds have broader niches than their relatives on the mainland and that, accompanying the increase in niche width, there was an increase in the variation in bill width (Van Valen, 1965).

### 7.3.3   How similar can different species be?

There has also been considerable debate about how different species need to be in order to avoid competition. This point is not properly resolved, but there is a tendency for the morphological differences between temperate species to be larger than between tropical ones. The great diversity of species in tropical forests is largely the result of the fact that individual species show smaller differences than those in temperate forests. For example, Klopfer and MacArthur (1961) reported that the average ratio between the bill measurements of closely related temperate birds was in the range of 1.2:1 to 1.4:1; equivalent measurements for tropical species tended to be in the range of 1.0:1 to 1.1:1. They concluded that the 'exclusive portion of the niche of each species has been reduced'. Other workers have also shown higher densities in the tropics than in temperate ones and inferred changes in niche width (Karr, 1971). The reason for this

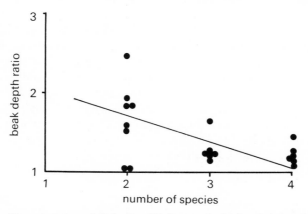

**Figure 7.12**   The ratio between bill-depths of Galapagos finches in relation to the number of species on an island. The measurement is the ratio between the bill depths of the most similar pair of species on the island. Note how the difference becomes smaller as the number of species increases (From Abbot et al., 1977).

reduction in niche width is probably related to the great stability and relatively great age of many of these forests both of which have enabled species to co-exist more easily.

In this respect much attention has been paid to bill size in birds. This is not surprising since it is the main part of a bird's feeding apparatus. Differences in bill size are most likely to be explained by specialization on different diets. Abbot *et al.* (1977) have shown that the difference in beak depth in closely-related species is smaller where there are more species (Fig. 7.12).

## 7.4  Summary

Communities comprise populations of interacting species. The competitive exclusion principle states that species with identical niches cannot co-exist. A 'niche' is defined as an '*n*-dimensional hyperspace'. Competition can occur in any niche dimension. A *realized niche* is one occupied in the presence of a competitor and is part of the *fundamental niche*. which is occupied in the absence of competitors. Closely related bird species differ in one or more niche dimensions, but it is extremely difficult to determine if such differences are the result of competition. Species may differ in (i) geographic range, (ii) habitat, (iii) feeding location or method within a habitat, or (iv) type of food eaten. The best evidence for competition comes from cases where the absence of one species results in another changing its niche: several studies of birds demonstrate this effect.

The study of birds on islands is important to our understanding of avian communities. The number of species on islands declines with decreasing island size and with distance offshore. This effect may be due to the balance between immigration and extinction, or to the range of habitats available. The number of *species* on islands is usually lower than in similar-sized areas of adjacent mainland, but the density of *individuals* may not be reduced; in some cases this means that, for any given species, population density may be higher on islands. This suggests reduced interspecific competition and increased intraspecific competition on islands.

# CHAPTER EIGHT

# FORAGING BEHAVIOUR

## 8.1 Introduction

In Chapter 7 we considered the importance of food from the *species'* point of view, looking at how different bird species occupy particular feeding niches and how the differences in morphology and behaviour between species enables them to utilize different types of food. Here we shall examine feeding behaviour within species, concentrating on the way in which *individual* birds forage.

Although different species of birds exploit an enormous diversity of food types (seeds, fruit, insects, fish or nectar), they all face a similar range of problems whatever they eat. It is these general problems—how to decide where to feed, what food items to select—that concern us here.

We assume that natural selection has favoured individuals which solve these problems in an 'optimal' way, that is, most efficiently in terms of their survival and reproductive success. This is because food is often in short supply, and even when it is plentiful efficient foraging leaves more time for other activities, such as watching for predators or territory defence. Since about 1970, behavioural ecologists have examined feeding behaviour in terms of optimization, a subject known as 'optimal foraging' (Krebs and Davies, 1981). This type of approach to foraging is a functional one rather than a causal one, and is therefore concerned with *why* birds forage in a particular way, i.e. the adaptive significance of particular foraging patterns, rather than with the underlying mechanisms which cause the behaviour (see Chapter 1).

The approach views feeding behaviour in terms of its costs and benefits, and constructs models which predict the 'trade-off' which will maximize the individual's net benefit. Most optimal foraging models, as we shall see, look at how birds might maximize their rate of food intake or more specifically, energy intake per unit time.

All organisms, including birds, face a number of problems when it comes to obtaining food. They have to 'decide' (although obviously not in a conscious way) *where* to forage, because food is rarely evenly distributed; some areas will be more profitable than others. Having selected a particular area a bird is faced with a range of food types, differing in size, quality etc., and it must then 'decide' which of these will prove the most profitable. An additional problem is whether it should feed by itself or as part of a group.

In the following sections we look at a number of optimal foraging models which have been designed to answer these problems, and then consider both the laboratory (aviary) and field tests of the models' predictions.

## 8.2    Where to search for food

### 8.2.1    *Theoretical aspects*

The problem that a bird has of where to forage is rather similar to one we face when picking blackberries. How long should you continue to pick from one bush before moving on to the next? When you first arrive at a bush there are plenty of berries and you can pick at a rapid rate, but as the number of berries left decreases it takes longer and longer to get subsequent berries. At what point should you give up and change bushes? Although if you find another good bush your rate of picking will increase again, you will inevitably lose time (and blackberries) while moving.

Birds have to cope with exactly this type of problem if they are feeding on a food supply which diminishes with time. This may occur because of depletion (e.g. seeds), or because foraging activity makes the food less accessible (e.g. insects hiding in response to the predator foraging nearby). The problem of optimal time allocation in each food patch has been resolved by Charnov (1976), and is summarized in Fig. 8.1. The bird should behave as though it estimates its average rate of food intake over the last few food patches (Fig. 8.1*b*) and compares this average (including the cost of moving between patches) with its current food intake in the present patch. When the rate of food intake within a patch falls to a level equal to the average for the habitat as a whole, it should change feeding patches (Fig. 8.1*c*). Now, to make this type of decision optimally the birds must know rather a lot about their environment, such as the average quality of food patches and the time taken to travel between them. The only way a bird can obtain such information is by sampling different areas and this will

(a)

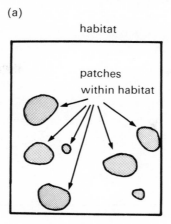

(b)

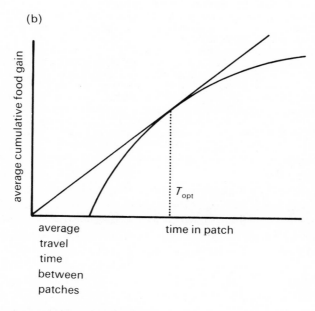

**Figure 8.1** (for legend see over)

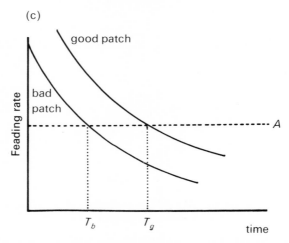

(c)

good patch

bad
patch

Feeding rate

- - - - - - - - - - - - - - - - - - - - - - - - - - - - - - - - -  A

$T_b$          $T_g$

time

**Figure 8.1**  (*a*) Schematic illustration of a hypothetical habitat containing a number of food patches. (*b*) Calculation of the average feeding rate for the habitat as a whole. The bird has to spend some time travelling between patches. Once it has arrived in a patch it feeds at a fast rate initially and so the curve of cumulative food intake rises steeply. As the bird depletes the food supply, however, the curve levels off, until at the asymptote all the food in the patch has been eaten. The bird's problem is at which point on this curve of diminishing returns to leave and fly to the next patch. The optimum 'giving up time' $T_{opt}$, is where the tangent from the origin just touches the gain curve. The ordinate gives the amount of food eaten and the abscissa is time, so the slope of the tangent is the *rate* of food intake (amount of food eaten/time). If the bird left earlier or later than $T_{opt}$, its average rate of food intake would be lower (i.e. a line from the origin to any other point on the curve would be of lower slope). (*c*) Shows when a bird should leave a given patch. Within the habitat there will be good and bad patches. The bird should leave a patch when its feeding rate drops to the average expected rate for the habitat as a whole (line *A* is the average feeding rate for the habitat as a whole (the 'marginal value') calculated from Fig. 8.1*b*, and is equal to the slope of the tangent in that figure. As (*b*) shows it will take longer to reach this critical threshold in a good patch ($T_g$) than it will in a bad patch ($T_b$).

undoubtedly put a constraint on how closely the birds can achieve the optimal solution.

There have been a number of tests of this idea, both with captive birds and in the wild. Aviary experiments have the advantage that the experimenter can control most of the variables, except the one he/she is interested in, but suffer in that the set-up may not be realistic—it is much simpler than the situation in the field.

### 8.2.2  *Laboratory studies*

One of the clearest laboratory tests of Charnov's model (Fig. 8.1) has been made by Cowie (1977), who studied Great Tits foraging in a large aviary for

**Figure 8.2** Great tit on artificial feeder used in optimal foraging experiments described by Krebs and Cowie, 1976 (see text). Photograph by R. Cowie.

pieces of mealworm hidden in sawdust-filled plastic cups on the branches of artificial trees (Fig. 8.2). The experimental set-up ensured that the birds experienced a declining capture rate with time, as shown in Fig. 8.1. Cowie made two predictions from Charnov's model; first, that when the average feeding rate in the habitat was high the birds would spend less time in each patch (i.e. at each cup in this case). This is equivalent to saying that when the curve in Fig. 8.1b is steep the time spent in a patch should be short. The second prediction was that if the travel time between food patches was increased, then birds should spend longer in each patch. If this were true then it would show that the feeding rate determines the length of time spent in a patch, rather than vice versa.

To test prediction 1, six Great Tits were allowed to forage individually in the aviary for two 10-minute trials each. The relationship between the intercatch interval (feeding rate) and the time spent at each cup was positive and significant for each bird as predicted by the model. One example is shown in Fig. 8.3.

To test prediction 2, the travel time was increased by placing a top on each cup, which the Great Tits took about 15 seconds to remove. This increased the time from leaving one patch and starting to forage from five seconds (as in the first experiment) to twenty seconds. Using Charnov's model (Fig. 81b) Cowie was able to make quantitative predictions

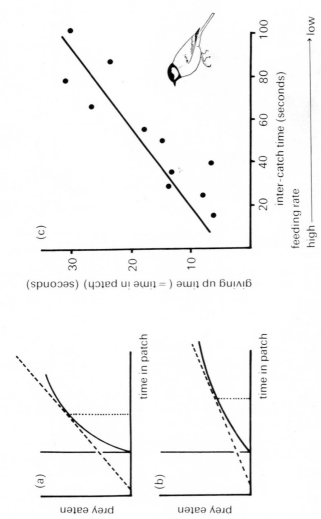

**Figure 8.3** The optimal time allocation model (Fig. 8.1c) predicts a positive relationship between the length of time a bird spends in a patch and its capture rate within a patch. This can be seen by comparing the hypothetical curves in (a) and (b); the optimal time to spend in (a) where the feeding rate is high (steep curve) is shorter than in (b) where the feeding rate is lower (flatter curve). (c) Shows data for one of six Great Tits tested by Cowie (1977)—see text, and shows the predicted positive relationship between the time spent in patch and the inter-catch interval. (From Krebs and Cowie, 1976).

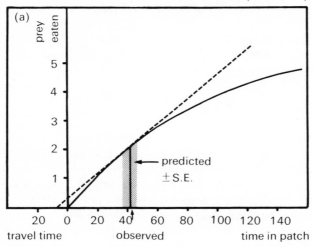

short travel time (5 seconds)

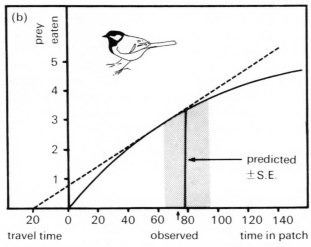

high travel time (20 seconds)

**Figure 8.4** A graphical model which predicts the optimal times that Great Tits should spend in each patch (*a*) where the travel time is 5 seconds, and (*b*) where the travel time is increased experimentally to 20 seconds. The curve of prey eaten *v.* time was determined by observation and is the same in (*a*) and (*b*). The times which the birds should spend in each patch as predicted by the model (see Fig. 8.1) are shown by vertical lines (shaded areas either side of the line indicate standard errors). The observed values (indicated by arrows) are close to the predicted ones and fall within one standard error of the prediction.

regarding the average time spent in patches when the travel time was short (5 seconds) and long (20 seconds). The results (Fig. 8.4) show that behaviour of the Great Tits corresponded quite closely to that predicted, thus confirming that the feeding rate in the first experiment determined the length of time birds spent at each patch, rather than that the time spent in each patch determined the feeding rate.

### 8.2.3   *A field study*

One of the few studies to test the idea of optimal time allocation in patches, under field conditions, has been made by Davies (1977), on wagtails (*Motacilla* species). These birds feed on yellow dungflies (*Scatophaga stercoraria*) on and around cow pats. When a wagtail approached a cow pat the flies flew off into the grass surrounding the pat. In the first 10 seconds the capture rate was high, 0.13 flies/second. In the second and subsequent 10s intervals the rate dropped to 0.07 flies/second, mainly because the flies dispersed farther or hid in the grass. Charnov's model predicts that a wagtail should move to another patch (i.e. cow pat) when its feeding rate drops to the average feeding rate in that habitat, in this case after a time of 10 seconds. In fact the birds changed patches on average every 12.8 seconds, fairly close to the predicted value.

   Most attempts to test Charnov's model in the field, however, have been unsuccessful. This is because for a detailed test, food abundance in a patch must be known. In a laboratory study this presents no problems, because the investigator can determine food abundance himself, but in the field the rapid spatial and temporal changes in food availability can make any measurement extremely difficult (e.g. Orians, 1980).

### 8.3   **What food to eat**

### 8.3.1   *Theory—some basic ideas*

Once it has arrived in a patch a bird has to decide which food items to eat. Optimal foraging predicts that birds will select food types on the basis of their profitability, preferring the most profitable items. 'Profitability' refers to the reward intake per unit time, for example it could be energy or some specific combination of nutrients, but includes the time taken to prepare or 'handle' a food item. The optimal diet model can be outlined as follows (based on MacArthur, 1972; Houston, 1980).

1. *Profitability of food items.* Each type of prey (e.g. insect or seed) has a value to the bird. Let us assume for simplicity that this value is the rate of energy gain. The rate of energy gain from eating prey type 1 will be

$$\frac{E_1}{S_1 + H_1} = \frac{\text{energy content of the prey}}{\text{search time} + \text{handling time}} \tag{1}$$

$S$ is the time it takes to find a food item (search time) and $H$ is the time it takes to handle and consume it. As the abundance of prey type 1 increases the search time will obviously decrease, so the maximum rate of energy gain will be $E_1/H_1$ i.e. when the search time is zero.

2. *The number of food types.* Imagine for the sake of simplicity that there are just two food types in the environment, so that type 1 is more profitable than type 2.

$$\frac{E_1}{H_2} > \frac{E_2}{H_2}$$

Food 1 might be a large seed while food 2 might be a small one, for example. The problem faced by a bird is how to select food so as to maximize its overall rate of energy intake.

3. *Deciding which items to eat.* If we assume that when a bird encounters a food item it has to decide whether to eat it or ignore it, the rule it should use is 'eat this item, if while handling it I could not have found and eaten a better item'. Now if food type 1 is encountered it should always be eaten, because the bird will never do better by rejecting it, even if it encountered a type 2 item immediately. In other words a bird should always eat the most profitable prey it encounters.

What should a bird do when it encounters a type 2 item? The answer is that if it could find a type 1 very soon after rejecting the type 2 item, then it should ignore the type 2 and concentrate on food type 1. If, however, type 1 items are scarce then the bird should eat type 2 items. More precisely, type 2 items should be eaten when encountered if

$$\frac{E_2}{H_2} > \frac{E_1}{S_1 + H_1}$$

$$\tag{2}$$

i.e.

$$\left.\begin{array}{c}\text{energy gain}\\\text{from eating type 2}\end{array}\right\} \geq \begin{array}{c}\text{energy gain from rejecting it and going on}\\\text{to find a type 1 food item}\end{array}$$

(a)

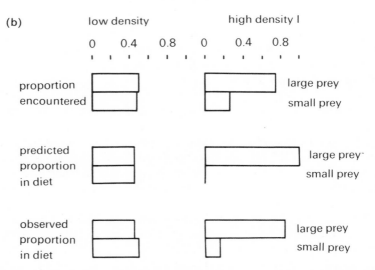

(b)

Figure 8.5 (a) Experimental cage used for testing the optimal diet model. The Great Tit sat in the cage while food types passed by on the conveyor belt. Items were available for only 0.5s as they passed a gap in the cover and the bird had to make its choice in this time. If it took an item it then missed the chance to take subsequent ones while it was eating. (b) Comparison of predicted and observed proportion of large and small prey in the diet when the proportion of large and small prey available were the same (left) and different (right). At low food densities (i.e. $S_1$ and $S_2$ large) Great Tits took equal proportions of large and small prey (left-hand side). At higher densities (right-hand side) (i.e. $S_1$ relatively small—see equation 2) birds switched to eating almost all large prey. (c) Example from one bird switching from generalizing to specializing on more profitable prey. The Great Tit

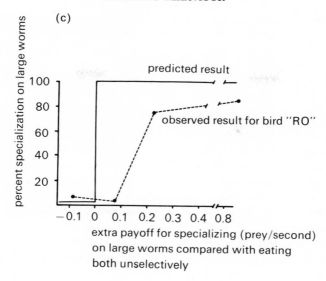

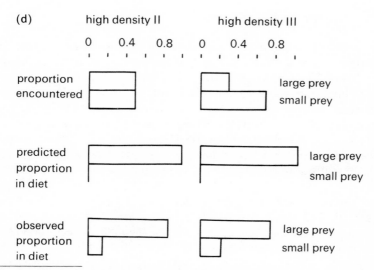

became more selective at about the point predicted by the model, but the switch is not as sudden as predicted. (*d*) When small and large prey are abundant (i.e. $S_2$ and $S_1$ are small) Great Tits concentrated on large prey. Even when the proportion of small prey was increased (right-hand side), i.e. decreasing $S_2$ even further, this did not affect the bird's food selection. (From Krebs and Davies, 1978; 1981).

However, if

$$\frac{E_2}{H_2} < \frac{E_1}{S_1 + H_1} \tag{3}$$

the bird should specialize on food item 1 and ignore any type 2 items it encounters.

The above model makes the following predictions:

(a) A bird should specialize on type 1 items, *or* it should take both type 1 and type 2 (it will never pay to eat only type 2 items).

(b) The switch from specializing to generalizing (i.e. taking type 1 and type 2) should be sudden (the inequalities in equations (1) and (2) must either be true or not true).

(c) The decision to specialize depends only on $S_1$, the abundance of the most profitable food type, not on $S_2$ (note that $S_2$ does not appear in the equations above). Therefore, if equation (2) holds, the bird should ignore type 2 items altogether *irrespective of the value of $S_2$* (i.e. irrespective of how abundant type 2 food items are).

### 8.3.2   *A laboratory test of the optimal diet model*

This model was tested by Krebs *et al.* (1977) in the laboratory, using Great Tits as predators, whole mealworms as type 1 items, and half mealworms as type 2 items. The time to find food types 1 and 2, i.e. $S_1$ and $S_2$, were varied by an ingenious experimental technique in which the predator was stationary and the prey moved past it on a conveyor belt (Fig. 8.5a). The search time ($S$) for each prey type could then be varied by changing the number of prey which moved past the Great Tit in a given time. (Note that in the wild, the prey will tend to be stationary and the predator mobile, but in this case it was difficult to control the predator's encounter rate with its prey).

All three predictions of the model (see (a) (b) and (c) above) were supported. The Great Tit switched from taking both small and large mealworms to taking only large ones as the inequality in equation (2) was reached—in other words, when $S_1$ was such that a tit while handling a type 2 prey, missed the chance of eating a type 1 that came past in the meantime (Fig. 8.5b). However, the switch was not as sudden as predicted. One possibility is that the Great Tits took time to determine the relative reward rates from feeding selectively (i.e. specializing on large prey) *v.* taking both large and small items indiscriminately (i.e. generalizing)

(Fig. 8.5*c*). When $S_1$ was such that the inequality in equation (2) was true, then changing $S_2$ (i.e. increasing the encounter rate with type 2 food items) had no effect on the bird's choice of prey. No matter at what rate prey 2 came past on the conveyor belt, the tits still specialized on prey 1 (Fig. 8.5*d*).

### 8.3.3 *Food selection in the field*

Davies (1977) showed that when wagtails fed on yellow dungflies, they selectively captured flies of a specific size rather than simply taking flies at random. Figure 8.6 shows that dungflies vary in size from 5–10 mm in

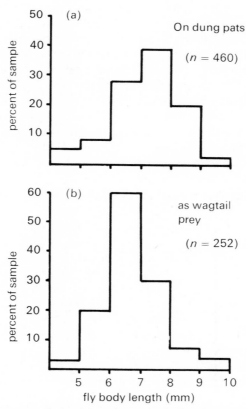

**Figure 8.6** Frequency of different size classes of *Scatophaga* on dung pats (*a*) = prey available, and (*b*) in wagtail diet. The difference between (*a*) and (*b*) is significant (*P* < 0.001). From Davies, 1977.

length, with 8 mm individuals being the most common. In a detailed study of wagtail prey, Davies found that the birds took a disproportionate number of 7 mm dungflies, indicating prey selection by the birds. Davies went on to examine the calorific value of different-sized flies and the time it took for a wagtail to handle flies of various sizes. As dungfly size increases its calorific value increases, but the time it took the wagtail to handle the prey increased more steeply. Thus small flies are quick to handle but they are not worth very much in energetic terms, whereas large flies, although worth considerably more calories, take a disproportionately long time to handle. The flies which gave the highest rate of energy intake were the 7 mm size class—exactly as we would predict if the birds were selecting the most profitable prey (Fig. 8.7).

While these results demonstrate efficient prey selection, they also raise some additional questions. For example, why did the wagtails bother at all with 5, 6 and 10 mm-sized flies? As we saw in the simple model above, the answer to this may be that optimal food selection depends upon food availability and the time it takes to find the most profitable items. Birds feeding in an unselective manner will spend relatively little time searching for food, but will have a relatively low rate of energy intake. At the other extreme, a highly selective feeder will have a high rate of energy intake per unit handling time, but will spend longer searching for profitable prey. So once again we can see that there will be a trade-off, this time between the degree of selection and time spent searching.

Another example in which the optimal diet was tested in the field is that

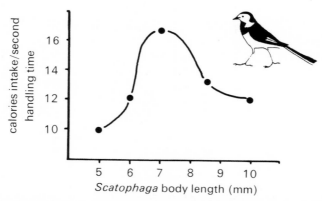

**Figure 8.7**  Energy intake (calories) per unit handling time (seconds) for different sized *Scatophaga*, taken by a captive wagtail. (From Davies, 1977).

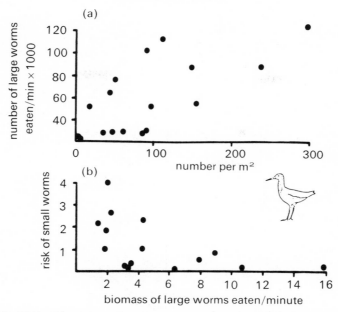

**Figure 8.8** Field evidence for optimal choice of diet in Redshanks feeding on polychaete worms. The positive relationship in (*a*) shows that large worms are eaten in proportion to their abundance. The negative relationship in (*b*) shows that small worms are eaten less often when large worms are abundant. (From Goss-Custard, 1977).

of Goss-Custard (1977), who studied Redshanks feeding on worms (*Nereis* and *Nephthys*) on tidal mudflats. He found that in the areas where the density of large (profitable) worms was high a greater number were taken, but the rate at which small (unprofitable) worms were taken was inversely proportional to the density of large worms. This means that as the density of large worms increased the Redshanks became more and more selective, ignoring small prey as long as the large profitable worms were common (Fig. 8.8). The Redshanks' decision on whether to specialize depended only on the abundance of large worms, not that of small worms, as predicted by the model.

## 8.4 Central place foraging

So far we have considered birds foraging for themselves. However, when foraging for their young in the nest, they are faced with an additional

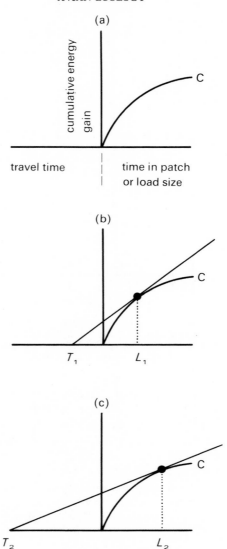

**Figure 8.9**  Central place foraging model. (*a*) The curve *C* represents the diminishing cumulative energy gain with increasing load size or time spent in a patch. (*b*) A hypothetical example in which the travel time ($T_1$) is relatively short. A tangent from $T_1$ which just touches the curve *C*, is the optimal load size ($L_1$) for that travel time. (*c*) Another hypothetical example, this time with a greater travel time ($T_2$) and correspondingly greater optimal load size ($L_2$). (From Orians, 1980).

problem, the energetic cost of a *round trip* between the nest-site and feeding area. Because in this situation the bird has to return to a central place (i.e. the nest), this aspect of optimal foraging is referred to as central place foraging (CPF). The optimal amount of food carried back to the young will depend on how far the parent has to go to collect it. Intuitively we would predict that the most efficient thing to do would be to bring a larger load back to the nest the further the parent has to travel for it. The *precise* relationship between optimal load size and foraging distance (i.e. travel time) can be determined from a graphical model proposed by Orians and Pearson (1979), similar to the model we used to predict how long a bird should forage in a particular patch before moving on (section 8.2). In the patch model (section 8.2) the curve of diminishing returns is due to food depletion in the patch. In the CPF model the curve is due to the increasing inefficiency of foraging by a parent as its load increases. The effect is the same in both cases, i.e. cumulative energy gain levels off with time (Fig. 8.9*a*).

The model is presented in Fig. 8.9. We can start by assuming a diminishing energy gain with increasing load size, or with increasing time spent in the feeding area (curve *C* in Fig. 8.9*a*). Imagine a small bird such as a flycatcher collecting a beakful of insects for its young. As it collects more and more insects, subsequent ones become progressively more difficult to capture and handle because the bird's beak is becoming fuller and fuller. The optimal load size in terms of energy delivered to the young per unit time is determined by the time it takes the bird to travel between the nest and the feeding area, and is calculated by plotting a tangent to the loading curve (*C*) from the *x* axis at a point corresponding to the travel time. Two hypothetical examples are shown in Fig. 8.9*b* and *c*. In Fig. 8.9*b* the travel time is short ($T_1$) and a tangent from $T_1$ to the curve *C* gives us the optimal load size ($L_1$) for that particular travel time. In this case the load size is quite small. However, if the travel time is longer ($T_2$) as in Fig. 8.9*c*, then the predicted load size ($L_2$) is larger.

The most detailed field study of the CPF model to date has been made by Bryant and Turner (1982) with House Martins. As indicated above the main feature of the CPF model is the shape of the loading curve (*C* in Fig. 8.9*a*), that is, there must be a decrease in efficiency of capturing or holding prey as the load size increases. House Martins collect food for their young in a throat pouch and with increasing numbers of insects in the pouch the rate of food gain diminishes (Fig. 8.10). The travel time and the size of each load were known for each feeding trip so it was possible to calculate the predicted (i.e. optimal) load size and compare it with the actual

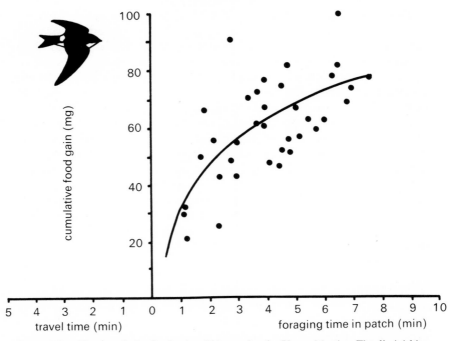

**Figure 8.10** The cumulative food gain within patches for House Martins. The diminishing curve of food gain is an integral part of the central place foraging model (see Fig. 8.9a) (From Bryant and Turner, 1982).

results (Table 8.1). These data provide some support for the CPF model in a qualitative way, in as much as the load size increased with increasing travel time. However, the agreement between the predicted and observed values was not particularly close. Bryant and Turner (1982) suggest that the discrepancy may have arisen because of the inevitable difficulties of making accurate measurements of certain factors, such as travel time, under field conditions.

**Table 8.1** Comparison of optimal load sizes predicted from the central place foraging model, with observed load sizes for the House Martin (from Bryant and Turner, 1982).

| Foraging distance (km) | Travel time (min) | Optimal load size (mg) | Observed load size (mg) |
|---|---|---|---|
| 0.1 | 0.32 | 32 | 52.6 |
| 0.45 | 1.43 | 43 | 55.2 |
| 1.0 | 3.18 | 52 | 65.6 |

## 8.5. Solitary v. group foraging

The third major aspect of feeding behaviour is concerned with the advantages and disadvantages of flock feeding. The decision of whether to forage alone or with other members of your species depends to some extent upon the nature of the food. About half of all bird species feed in flocks exploiting spatially clumped food such as seeds or fruit, whereas solitary feeders exploit animal prey (Lack, 1968). It is important to note that many of the factors which favour the evolution of flock feeding are the same as those favouring colonial breeding (see Chapter 2), and that 99% of all bird species which feed solitarily breed alone, while of those species which feed in flocks 26% breed colonially (Lack,1968). For convenience we will refer to flock feeding and colonial breeding together as 'sociality'.

Just as in earlier sections of this chapter we looked at the costs and benefits of certain aspects of feeding behaviour, we can also think about sociality in this way. The main advantages and disadvantages of sociality are summarized in Table 8.2.

**Table 8.2**   Main advantages of sociality in birds.

| Form of advantage | Type of group which benefits |
| --- | --- |
| Feeding efficiency | |
| 1. Capturing difficult prey | Flocks, e.g. pelicans (see text) |
| 2. Flushing prey | Flocks (e.g. Cattle Egrets among cattle) |
| 3. Efficient exploitation of indefensible food supplies; optimal return times | Flocks, Barnacle Geese (see text) |
| 4. Imitative foraging | Flocks, e.g. Pigeons, Great Tits (see text) |
| 5. Information transfer | Colonies and communal roosts (see chapter 2) |
| | |
| Anti-predator | |
| 1. 'Selfish herd effect'—remaining in the centre of a group reduces risk of predation | Flocks, roosts and colonies (see chapter 2) |
| 2. Increased vigilance, early warning of predator's approach | Flocks, roosts and colonies (see text) |
| 3. Synchronous reproduction swamps predators | Colonies (see chapter 2) |
| 4. Communal mobbing drives predator off | Colonies (see chapter 2) |
| 5. 'Dilution' effect; the more individuals the lower the chances of any one being captured | Flocks, roosts and colonies |
| 6. 'Confusion' effect: a predator may be confused by a large number of prey which may reduce chances of one being captured | Flocks |

Many of the birds which are solitary feeders prey on animals, e.g. insects or vertebrates, which are often more difficult to catch or find once disturbed and which tend to occur at low densities and to be evenly distributed. In contrast, many flock feeders utilize locally clumped food, which is not disturbed by their presence. Some species may even switch from solitary to social foraging depending on the type of food they are using at the time. For example, it was found that when wagtails fed on dungflies they defended (temporary) territories containing fresh cow pats from other wagtails, to keep disturbances to a minimum (once disturbed, dungflies scatter into the surrounding grass and are difficult to find and capture.) However, dungflies are present on cow pats only during the middle part of the day and spend the rest of their time roosting out of sight of predatory wagtails. Both early and late in the day, the wagtails have to feed on some other prey, and they take tiny midges, often at the edge of

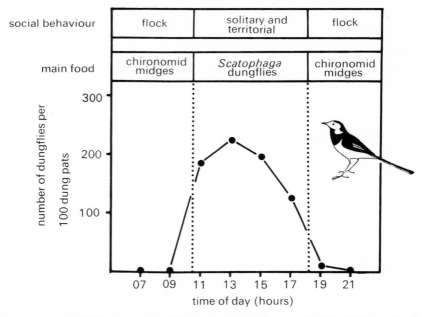

**Figure 8.11** Flexibility in wagtail social behaviour in relation to availability of different food types. The graph shows the diurnal availability of dungflies, *Scatophaga*, the most profitable prey. The horizontal bars at the top indicate the time of day spent feeding on *Scatophaga*, and on midges, and the time spent defending temporary territories and flock feeding. Midges are available all day, but are utilized only when *Scatophaga* are not available (see text). (Modified from Davies, 1977).

pools. Midges are easy to catch and are not as disturbed by the presence of wagtails as are dungflies. They also tend to be clumped along the windward side of pools, so the wagtails feed in flocks (see Fig. 8.11). Such behavioural flexibility appears to be relatively rare, or has not been studied in detail, although it also occurs in certain mammals, (e.g. Spotted Hyenas, *Crocuta crocuta*—Kruuk, 1972).

In this section we consider the ways in which flock feeding enhances foraging success.

(a) *Capturing difficult prey.* Co-operative foraging is well known among social carnivores like lions, *Panthera leo*, and hunting dogs, *Lycaon pictus* (Schaller, 1972; Frame *et. al.*, 1979), but is relatively unusual among birds. One of the best examples is the White Pelican which, when feeding communally, swims in groups of one to four rows of birds. When fish are detected the birds form a semicircle around them, then *synchronously* dip their heads below the surface to catch them (Din and Eltringham, 1974). It is presumed that such a technique improves fishing success. Similar behaviour has also been recorded, although less frequently, for cormorants and mergansers (Bartholomew, 1942; Emlen and Ambrose, 1970).

Several species of booby, the North Atlantic Gannet, and some terns, feed in flocks, plunge-diving on to fish, and it is possible that the confusion thus caused among the fish makes them easier to catch. Alternatively, as with some herons (Krebs, 1974) these flocks may simply be passive aggregations of individuals at a rich food supply (i.e. there is no foraging advantage *per se* to flocking).

(b) *Flushing prey.* It has been suggested that one advantage of flocking among small insectivorous birds is that the activity of the flock flushes insects out of cover, thereby rendering them more vulnerable to capture (Swynnerton, 1915). Swallows and Cattle Egrets regularly forage around cows to exploit the insects disturbed by the cows' movements.

(c) *Renewable food resources and optimal return times.* Cody (1971) suggested that one function of flocking may be that it enables birds to minimize the chances of visiting areas which they have recently depleted. Working in the Mohave Desert in California, Cody found the movement patterns of finch flocks were such that they tended to minimize the frequency at which previous paths were crossed or retraced. However, in those parts of the desert where seed supplies were renewed more rapidly, finch flocks moved faster and turned more often and consequently made successive visits to the same places at shorter intervals than in other areas where food abundance was lower.

The idea of optimal return times for species with renewable food supplies has since been examined in more detail. Obviously, though, such a system will work only if other individuals do not interfere. The most common way that birds avoid such interference is by excluding all other individuals by territoriality (see Chapter 2). However, in some species such as the finches which Cody studied, and Brent Geese, the food supply is not defendable. Brent Geese wintering on salt marshes in Holland feed mainly on sea plantain, *Plantago maritima*, an undefendable food supply because it is covered at high tide. Detailed observations show that the geese return to the same areas of sea plantain at about four-day intervals. This time period was found to be sufficient for the plants to recover, and moreover, the grazing by geese stimulated the growth of young leaves which were particularly nutritious. Even more remarkably, the geese probably maximized their feeding efficiency by having a return time of four days, as Prins *et al.* (1980) showed when they cut the plantain with scissors at varying intervals.

(d) *Other advantages of flock feeding.* As Table 8.2 indicates, the other main benefit from flocking is the avoidance of predators, and this may be achieved in a number of different ways. One advantage, now well documented, is increased vigilance, and studies have shown that flocks of birds are more likely to detect an approaching predator sooner than solitary birds. Some of the first experimental tests of this involved 'flying' a model hawk over different-sized feeding flocks of European Starlings in an aviary. Groups of ten birds responded more rapidly than groups of six or one (Powell, 1974). More realistically, Kenward (1978) flew trained Goshawks at flocks of foraging Wood Pigeons in the wild; larger flocks detected the predator at a greater distance, and if an attack occurred the hawks' success rates were lower for larger flocks.

Bertram (1980) looked at the amount of time which ostriches in groups of different size spent looking for predators, and found that individuals in groups spent less time on vigilance than did solitary individuals (Figure. 8.12). Clearly then, vigilance can affect a bird's time and energy budget; the more time it spends looking round for predators the less time it can spend feeding. Hence, it may be difficult to disentangle the factors favouring flocking; birds may feed together because it renders them safer from predators and they can then devote more time to foraging.

Flock feeding is not without its disadvantages, the main one being

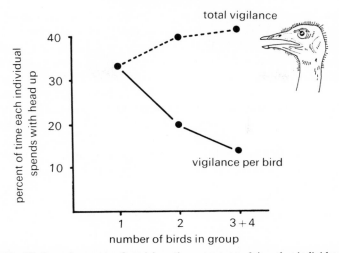

**Figure 8.12**  Vigilance in groups of ostriches; the percentage of time that individuals spend with their head up decreases with increasing group size, but the total vigilance increases. In other words ostriches get two advantages from flocking (*a*) more *total* vigilance (i.e. increased safety from predators and (*b*) less vigilance per individual (i.e. more time spent foraging). (From Bertram, 1980).

competition for food. This can take several forms (Table 8.3), for example birds may interfere with each other's prey capture, or they may fight over particular food items. In some species dominant individuals may join flocks simply to steal food from subordinates!

Because there are both advantages and disadvantages associated with flocking we might expect a trade-off between the various factors involved.

**Table 8.3**  Different forms of interference which depress the feeding rates of birds in flocks (based on Goss-Custard, 1980).

| Form of interference | Examples |
|---|---|
| 1. Intraspecific fighting and food stealing | Oystercatchers which have food stolen have reduced rate of food intake |
| 2. Interspecific food stealing (= kleptoparasitism) | Lapwings suffer from kleptoparasitism by Black-headed Gulls |
| 3. Disturbance of prey | Search paths may be disrupted or birds distracted by others, e.g. Redshank |
| 4. Depletion of prey | Bar-tailed Godwits feeding on lugworms (*Arenicola*) may deplete prey for other godwits |
| 5. Depression of prey availability | Redshanks walking over and causing *Corophium* (amphipod prey) to disappear from the surface for several minutes |

This could manifest itself in a number of different ways, for example there may be an optimum flock density—a compromise between the anti-predator advantages of flocking and the costs of intra- and interspecific feeding interference (e.g. Goss-Custard, 1976). Second, there may be optimum amounts of time spent as part of a flock and alone, as suggested by the wagtail example in Fig. 8.11. Third, there may be an optimum flock size, an idea which has been developed by Pulliam (1976) and Caraco

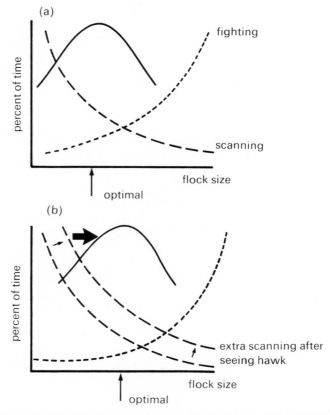

**Figure 8.13**   A model of optimal flock size. (*a*) shows that as flock size increases birds spend less time on vigilance (scanning for predators)– – –, but the rate of fighting increases- - -. In terms of time spent feeding (time remaining after vigilance and fighting) the intermediate flock size is optimal. In (*b*) the time individuals spend scanning is experimentally increased (by flying a trained hawk over the flock). The effect of increased scanning is to push the optimal flock size to the right. i.e. to be increased. (Based on Caraco *et al.*, 1980, redrawn from Krebs and Davies, 1981, see text).

*et al.* (1980). Figure 8.13 shows a model devised by Caraco *et al.* (1980) which makes precise quantitative predictions.

## 8.6 Conclusions on the optimization approach

Not all ecologists are convinced about the usefulness of the optimization approach, and there are at least three main criticisms.

The first is that models based on maximizing energy intake are not always very successful in predicting the foraging behaviour of birds under natural conditions (e.g. Orians, 1980). One reason why this might be so is that at certain times at least, it will be important for birds to eat a certain combination of specific nutrients (e.g. calcium for egg shell formation—Schifferli, 1977), rather than simply maximizing energy value. Another possibility is that the models are too simple and do not incorporate the numerous constraints which in the wild are imposed by competitors, predators and fluctuations in the environment. Proponents of the optimal foraging approach accept that it is often difficult to determine why there should be differences between predicted and observed results.

**Table 8.4** Possible explanation for differences between observed and predicted results in optimal foraging studies (from Krebs and Davies, 1981).

| Explanation | Examples |
| --- | --- |
| 1. Incorrect assumptions about constraints | (a) Birds may need to sample their environment and sampling will increase variability in results |
| | (b) Many studies ignore the role of nutrients; maximizing food intake per unit time may not always be important. Similarly, birds may ignore toxic prey (e.g. Pulliam, 1980). |
| 2. Inappropriate choice of goal | Birds may forage in a way so that they minimize the variation in the rate of food intake, or minimize the risks of predation, rather than maximizing the rate of food intake, which most models assume. |
| 3. Some components of the trade-off not measured | For example, the *time* taken to handle prey may not be directly proportional to the *energy* needed to handle prey. |
| 4. Animals are poorly adapted | An explanation of last resort. The assumption that natural selection has produced an efficient organism may be incorrect. If environmental conditions change rapidly (i.e. due to man's activity) then organisms may not be adapted to current conditions. |

Possible explanations for such discrepancies are presented in Table 8.4.

The second main criticism is that optimal foraging says nothing about the *way* that birds make their decisions. Obviously birds cannot work out the answers to equations and must therefore use use some rule of thumb, just as we might when picking blackberries (section 8.2.1). The optimality approach is concerned with the functional aspect of behaviour and not with the mechanisms involved in foraging.

Third, it has been suggested that optimal foraging theory is a circular argument; natural selection is an optimizing process and the experiments and observations show that birds sometimes behave in an optimal way when foraging. Krebs (1978) has pointed out however that although the argument appears to be circular it is not, because in formulating optimal foraging models the goal which is being maximized must be specified.

On the more positive side, one of the main advantages of optimization models is that they generate testable hypotheses and make quantitative predictions. They also force ecologists to make the underlying assumptions of the model quite explicit. Finally, and perhaps most importantly, these models emphasize the general nature of the problems faced by all organisms, birds as well as other animals, while foraging.

## 8.7 Summary

In this chapter we have considered a number of very general problems which foraging birds face: where to forage, what to eat, and whether to forage alone or as part of a group. These problems are important because they *are* general and faced by all animals when feeding. We have examined foraging from an 'optimal foraging' standpoint, which assumes that natural selection has favoured individuals which forage efficiently. For some of the problems which we have discussed, models have been constructed (8.2., 8.3), which enable us to make precise quantitative predictions about foraging behaviour. Both laboratory and field studies have demonstrated that, in some cases, the models have been reasonably successful in predicting how birds should forage. Most success has been attained in those situations where it has been possible to measure the costs and benefits of particular feeding strategies in terms of energy (i.e. calories) expended and gained. In the final section we pointed out that the optimization approach to foraging (and indeed to other biological problems) is relatively new, and while it has clearly produced some exciting results, it is still somewhat controversial.

# CHAPTER NINE

# MIGRATION

## 9.1 Introduction

Many animals shows some form of seasonal, diurnal or tidal movement (see Baker, 1977, for review), but the migration of birds has been of particular interest since biblical times (e.g. Jeremiah 8:7). Most of the information we now have on destinations of migrating birds has been gained from studies of ringed birds made over the last 50–60 years. Details of migration routes, navigation and the underlying mechanisms of migration have come from radar tracking, homing studies and laboratory experiments. Migration is a rapidly developing area of avian biology, and our aim in this chapter is to provide an ecological and evolutionary view of the subject rather than a description of how birds achieve such journeys. Other aspects of migration are discussed in Keeton (1980) and Emlen (1967).

The carrying capacity (section 6.1.3) of many habitats exhibits very marked seasonal changes. Arctic regions provide an extreme example: they can support large numbers of individuals in the summer, because of the high levels of productivity at that time (see 5.4.2) but, in the winter, conditions are too harsh to support many individuals. Animals using food resources during the arctic summer have three alternatives when conditions deteriorate: they can move out of the area, hibernate or die. Very few birds hibernate (Bartholomew et al., 1957), but many migrate.

Many areas of the world alternate between highly productive and extremely barren (Fig. 5.11). The ability to move into such areas when they are productive, to tap their resources and then move out again before conditions deteriorate, will be advantageous. Because of their great mobility, birds are better able to do this than are most other animal groups.

In this chapter we shall concentrate on those species which perform regular movements from one area to another. Usually these are from a breeding area to a wintering area and back again, but, as we shall see, there are other forms of movement. Because migration of the type exhibited by the Barn Swallow intergrades with other types of movements, it is virtually impossible to produce a perfect definition of migration. Perhaps the most satisfactory one is that provided by Lack (1945): 'a regular, large-scale shift of the population between a restricted breeding area and a restricted wintering area'.

### 9.1.1 *The species which migrate*

The most familiar type of migration involves swallows and warblers which (in the northern hemisphere) migrate northwards to breed in the summer and then, as the insect supply fails, migrate back towards the tropics for the winter. Another type of migration is shown by many waders and wildfowl in the northern hemisphere. Many of these species breed at high latitudes, but migrate only to middle latitudes for the winter. By moving to mainly maritime areas they avoid the harsh conditions at the centres of large continents. For example, many Siberian birds move to western Europe, and many birds from the Canadian Arctic move to the coasts of the United States (Fig. 9.1). Presumably the reason these birds do not migrate farther south is that, usually at least, the wintering areas they use enable them to have a good survival rate; migrating farther south would require greater energy resources and yet not lead to greater survival. Migration is not confined to birds of high latitudes, and many species which spend their lives within Africa undertake long migrations; some, like the Red-billed Quelea for example, follow the rains (see section 4.3.2).

The scale of migration is difficult to comprehend. Moreau (1972) has reviewed the situation for the Palearctic. He estimated that of the 589 species of breeding land birds, 40% left the area completely for the winter. This does not include species like ducks, geese and waders which migrate within the Palearctic region. Detailed calculations have not been made for North America, but the situation is probably similar. Of the 160 species of passerines which breed in Canada, about 120 (75%) species leave for the winter; the majority of the individuals of about 15 of the remaining 40 species also leave.

The effect of competition between these migrants and the resident birds in the wintering areas is not known. Moreau (1972) thought that Palearctic migrants probably had a serious effect on the resident birds in Africa. In

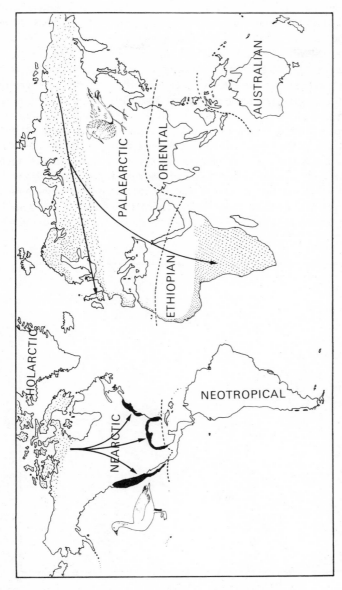

**Figure 9.1**   Breeding and winter grounds of a Nearctic and Palaearctic bird. The Snow Goose migrates from northern Canada to winter on western, southern and eastern shores of the U.S.A., while the Ruff, which breeds over wide areas of the Old World, winters in a range of habitats from the marshes of Africa to those of south and western Europe. Although the majority of the birds winter in Africa, many from Eastern Siberia migrate westwards into Europe and some spend the winter in mild maritime areas there. The figure also shows the main zoogeographical zones.

addition since Central America is a small area relative to North America, he thought that competition between migrants and residents might be even greater there than in Africa. However, Brown *et al.* (1982) calculated that there may be 70 000–75 000 million birds resident in Africa, many more than Moreau thought. Since only about one bird in 15 is a migrant, the effect of the migrants on resident species is probably much less than Moreau had supposed. Nonetheless, there still may be competition between resident and migrant species. There may also be local effects, since migrants do not use all areas or habitats of Africa equally (see below).

Compared with the northern hemisphere there is less land at high latitudes in the southern hemisphere so land bird migration is less extensive there. An example of a southern hemisphere species which migrates north in the southern winter, and migrates south to breeding areas, is shown in Fig. 9.2. For sea-birds the converse is true, in that the southern hemisphere contains larger areas of sea than the northern hemisphere (Fig. 9.3). In both hemispheres large numbers of sea-bird species migrate to warmer

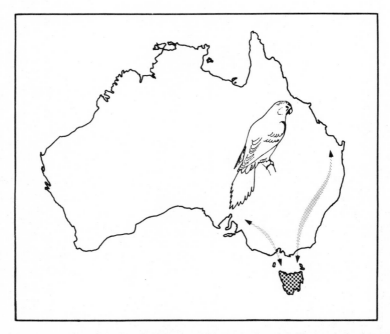

**Figure 9.2**   The migration of the Swift Parrot. This species breeds in Tasmania (and some of the islands of the Bass Strait); almost all migrate northwards during the southern summer.

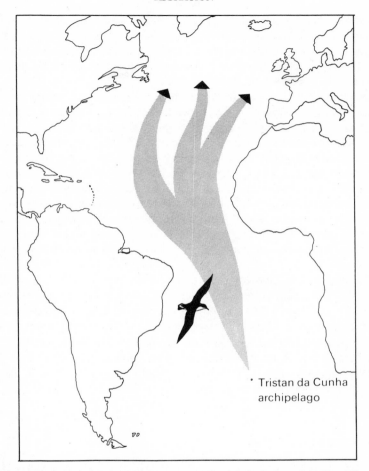

**Figure 9.3** The migration of the Great Shearwater. This species is almost wholly confined as a breeding bird to three islands, Nightingale, Inaccessible and Gough, on all of which it breeds abundantly. It undertakes a transequatorial migration, spending the southern summer in the north Atlantic, as far north as Southern Greenland.

climates for the winter. As with the landbirds, a number of species cross the equator to spend the non-breeding season in the other hemisphere.

## 9.1.2  *The habitats*

The habitats which migrant species occupy in their breeding and wintering grounds may be very different. For example, many waders (shore birds) spend the summer on arctic tundra and the winter on estuaries. North American warblers move from tall, boreal coniferous forest in the summer, to open, scrubby woodlands of Central America in the winter. Obviously food, weather conditions and types of predators will vary markedly between the summer and winter habitats.

One habitat which appears to be under-used by migrants is the tropical forest of Africa. Most Palearctic species which breed in forests avoid the extensive and apparently very rich tropical forest habitat in winter, and instead utilize open scrub and savannah woodland. A possible explanation is that because tropical forests show little seasonality, they are already fully occupied (see Fig. 5.11). However, in the New World the situation is somewhat different, since there a number of northern species do use tropical forests in the northern winter. Many of these have niches different both from each other's and from the resident species', which may enable them to coexist without competition. Migrant species also tend to have broader, less specialized niches than resident species (Keast and Morton, 1980).

Another explanation for the difference between Old and New World migrants in their use of tropical forests concerns the geography of the two areas. In relation to Europe, Africa provides a large wintering area for migrants, whereas Central America provides a relatively small area for North American migrants. We do not know whether this affects the numbers of breeding individuals of these species, but since more New World migrants appear to winter in forests than is the case in the Old World, possibly the pressure for space is one of the reasons for this difference.

## 9.2 Evolution of migration

Migration almost certainly first evolved among birds which lived at low latitudes and spread out into areas to the north and south into habitats which were tenable only for part of the year. One way of visualizing this is to imagine a situation in which there are many birds living in the tropics and very few in temperate regions. Individuals which moved into areas with lower bird density would experience little competition and hence have greater reproductive success. The energetic cost of flying to such areas may have been offset by the advantages in terms of the number of young reared. Indeed, Lack (1954) suggested that 'birds migrate from their winter quarters when breeding is, on the average, more successful elsewhere'.

Our knowledge of the development of migration routes is largely conjectural. Some routes appear rather odd at first sight and are best explained in terms of gradual extension of routes from ancestral wintering grounds. Species breeding in the Old World provide the best examples of this. Most migratory species which breed in Europe fly southwards and winter in Africa. Similarly, most species which breed in central Asia fly south to winter in south-eastern Asia (Moreau, 1952). However, a few species show different patterns. For example the Red-breasted Flycatcher breeds across most of the Palearctic extending into western Europe. All birds winter in Asia (from India to south-west Asia), which means that individuals breeding at the western edge of their range migrate very long distances. Why do they not simply fly south to Africa?

The Wheatear provides another example. It too breeds across the entire Palaearctic, but some birds also cross the Bering Straits in to Alaska and Western Canada, while others breed in Iceland, Greenland and eastern Canada. However, as far as is known all Wheatears migrate to Africa in the winter. Those in western Canada migrate westwards across Asia. Those breeding in eastern Canada untertake long sea crossings as they migrate south-east to Africa via Europe. Both these journeys appear to be long and hazardous compared with flying south to winter in South America. The journey which Alaskan Wheatears undertake is more than twice as far as it is to South America. Thus in both Wheatears and Red-breasted Flycatchers some individuals migrate what appear to be unnecessarily long distances. The simplest explanation is that as the breeding ranges expanded birds continued to return to ancestral wintering grounds. It is possible that a break with tradition may occur at some stage, but the risks for such 'pioneers' would be very great. Such a break may have been made by the Red-backed Shrike. This species also breeds across the entire Palaearctic, but birds in the west migrate to Africa, whereas those in the east migrate to south-east Asia.

## 9.3 Other forms of movement

### 9.3.1 *Partial migrants*

We have already suggested that birds obtain considerable benefits from the ability to migrate. However, there may also be disadvantages, such as the energetic cost, together with the risks of predation, as well as the entirely different ecological conditions in the wintering and breeding areas. For many species the relative advantages and disadvantages are clear-cut, and such species are either migrants or residents. For others, the costs and benefits of migration may depend upon where the individual lives. Almost all Scandinavian robins, for example, migrate southwards for the winter, whereas most robins in southern Britain are resident. Between these areas, e.g. in Denmark, some robins migrate, others are resident. Such species are referred to as partial migrants.

In some species the proportion of migrants within species may vary from year to year, according to environmental conditions. Among Chaffinches breeding in Scandinavia, more birds over-winter there after a series of mild winters than after harsh ones. This is just as one might expect; it will be advantageous to be resident if the winter is mild, but advantageous to be migratory if winter conditions are harsh. The tendency for the local population to migrate will reflect the relative success of these two activities in the recent past.

The relative advantage of migration versus over-wintering applies, not only to different populations of the same species, but also to different individuals within a population. In most species, males are dominant to females and old birds dominant to younger ones (Wilson, 1975), and these differences in status may affect a bird's chances of survival. Among species which are partial migrants, the individuals which move are predominantly females and young individuals. In other words it is advantageous for dominant birds to remain on the breeding grounds since they are more likely to be able to survive there. For subordinate individuals the cost of migration is offset by a survival rate which is higher than if they remained on the breeding grounds.

### 9.3.2  *Irruptive species*

Some species 'migrate' only in some years. These species are mainly predators or birds which feed on the seeds of forest trees. They show one feature in common: their food supply varies markedly from year to year. For the seed-eaters, their food trees produce large quantities of seed every other year or less frequently, and in some years the trees produce no seeds at all. When this happens the birds move, sometimes in enormous numbers; at such times they are found in areas outside their normal habitat and geographic range. These birds have been called irruptive species.

Svärdson (1957) has suggested that these birds behave like normal migrants, except that they cease migration once they have reached an area

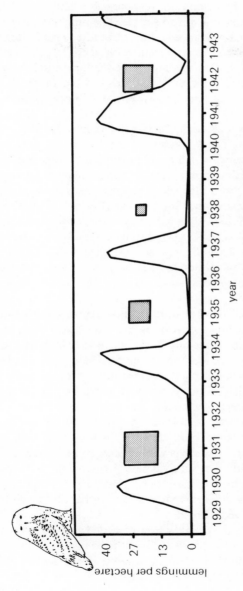

**Figure 9.4** Irruptions of the Snowy Owl (hatched squares) in relation to the abundance of the lemming (line), one of its main prey. Note tendency for Snowy Owls to move out when the lemmings become scarce. (From Shefford, 1945).

with abundant food. Some authors (Lack, 1954) have suggested that such irruptive behaviour occurs in response to high population density. However, the situation is not so simple. The numbers of birds increase in years of good seed abundance and decrease after seed failures. Since years of good seed crops tend to alternate with years of poor seed crops, bird numbers tend to be highest in years of seed failures and lowest during years with abundant seed. Hence it is difficult to distinguish between the importance of the food supply and effects of population density on the birds' behaviour.

Irruptive species include the Crossbill, Evening Grosbeak and several of the European tits. These species all eat the seeds of forest trees. The (Bohemian) Waxwing, which feeds mainly on berries, is also an irruptive species. Several birds of prey which feed on small mammals (e.g. lemmings) on the northern tundra also show irruptive behaviour; these include the Rough-legged Buzzard and Snowy Owl (Fig. 9.4). Pallas' Sandgrouse is unusual in that unlike all other irruptive species which breed at high latitudes, it occurs on the Central Asian steppes. It migrates westward into Europe when its main food (grass seeds) fails. It used to irrupt into Europe in large numbers, but during the last 50 years or so, irruptions have been rare, partly perhaps because changes to its habitat have reduced its population size.

Several species of Australian bird show irruptive movement. These are mainly species that breed in arid regions after heavy rains and then move elsewhere as the area dries out. Some of these species have unpredictable patterns of movement, stopping in areas where there has been rain and passing over areas where there has been no rain (Serventy, 1971).

Irruptions usually result in very high mortality, because the birds are already short of food when moving into new areas. At first sight, then, such behaviour may appear non-adaptive. However, the alternatives are to remain on the breeding grounds with no food and with no chance of survival, or move to new areas with at least some chance of finding food. Under such conditions a survival rate greater than zero may be advantageous for irrupting species. Indeed, ringing recoveries show that some individuals return to their breeding areas, so that at least some individuals which irrupt survive to breed.

Irruptive species are perhaps best regarded as a special type of partial migrant. In years when there is sufficient food in or near the breeding areas the advantage lies in being resident, whereas in years when the food supply fails the advantage is in being migratory.

## 9.4  Fat reserves for migration

In order to make long migratory flights, birds need substantial energy reserves, and these are formed by laying down fat. This is the most economic way of storing energy, since fat provides more energy per gram than either protein or carbohydrate. In addition, water is produced as fat is metabolized, thus preventing birds from becoming dehydrated.

The fat reserves that have to be laid down are considerable, and the problem is greatest for small birds. They need more food per gram of body weight than large birds simply to stay alive, because of their surface to volume ratio (and hence their rate of energy loss) is higher than in large birds. In addition, they have lower flight speeds and therefore need to fly for longer. Their fat reserves immediately before migration can double their body weight. For example, the Blackpoll Warbler of North America and the Sedge Warbler of Europe weigh about 11 g at most times of the year, but as much as 20–22 g just before migration. Nisbet *et al.* (1963) calculated that these reserves would enable them to fly for 105–115 hours (see 9.4.1). Similarly, the Sanderling, which migrates from arctic areas to temperate shores, weighs about 50 g normally and up to 110 g prior to migration. Such a fat reserve enables it to fly for about 2000 miles.

Not all migrants lay down large fat reserves. Many species migrate shorter distances and need smaller reserves. Others, such as finches, stop to feed each day, migrating only short distances at a time.

Relatively little is known about reserves laid down by larger migratory species. Among sea-birds, some young shearwaters leave their nesting grounds with large fat reserves. Manx Shearwaters, for example, leave their British nesting grounds weighing over 600 g, 50% more than their parents' normal weight. Many of these young shearwaters migrate to the coasts of Brazil and Argentina, 8 000 km away. One ringed bird made this trip in just 14 days, averaging 570 km/day. The greater the size of their fat reserves, the higher their chances of survival (Perrins *et al.*, 1973).

## 9.5  Variation on a theme

Not all species have simple migration patterns to and from breeding or wintering areas. In some species the basic pattern is altered, usually for some good ecological reason. In this section some variations on the basic pattern are examined.

In several species of wildfowl and wader, the spring and autumn migration routes differ. For example, the White-fronted Goose, which breeds in north Russia, migrates to western Europe for the winter. The geese do this by flying westwards at high latitudes, then heading south across the Baltic to Denmark, the Netherlands and Britain. If they were to return by the same route in the spring they would encounter inhospitable conditions soon after starting. To avoid this they fly eastwards at low latitudes and only when they reach the longitude of their breeding area do they fly north. The route keeps them out of the arctic area for as long as possible. The patterns of migration in old and young geese differ in one respect. All the birds fly to the breeding grounds together. Once there, the adults settle down to breed, but the young birds continue to move northwards during the summer. By following the thaw as it moves northwards the young birds can exploit a fresh food supply in the absence of competing adults. The adults cannot move while breeding, nor can they breed in the more northerly regions since the season is too short there (Owen, 1980).

Not all birds migrate from breeding grounds to 'winter' quarters. Some species have other reasons for moving from one place to another. One such species is the Shelduck, which in Europe breeds mainly along sandy coastlines. As with other wildfowl, Shelduck moult by dropping all their flight feathers simultaneously, and have a period of flightlessness. Most of the adult birds undertake a 'moult' migration, moving from their breeding areas to the islands off northern Holland and in the mouth of the Baltic where they undergo their moult. The migration commences in July, but by October the first birds are beginning to arrive back at their breeding areas, where they remain all winter (Patterson, 1982).

A similar situation exists in some auks. In guillemots (murres) and Razorbills the young leave the colony when only three weeks old and still flightless, but accompanied by their male parent. After leaving the colony the adults moult, dropping all their flight feathers simultaneously and becoming flightless. In boreal regions the moult occurs during August and September and by October the birds can fly again. Common Guillemots then return to their breeding colonies, which they continue to visit intermittently throughout the winter.

### 9.6  Timing of migration

Natural selection will favour those individuals which time their migration correctly and have high survival rates. Selection will also favour individuals with high reproductive rates, and sometimes migration and breeding requirements will conflict. For example, in order to obtain a good territory and rear a large number of young, selection may favour individuals which arrive at breeding areas relatively early, but the safest time for migration may be later.

Migrants heading towards their breeding grounds may start off from different areas and have different distances to travel. The optimal time for breeding will be similar for all of them, yet those in different areas will have to start their migration at different times in order to arrive at the breeding grounds at the same time. How do birds time their departure from their winter quarters? In many species, birds from quite different breeding areas winter together in the same place. They need to set out for their breeding grounds at different times. Therefore, the food supply in the wintering area cannot be the proximate factor controlling the time of departure. It seems likely that birds from different areas have evolved different responses to time their migration.

After breeding, most birds spend some time on the breeding grounds before departing and many of them moult before setting off on migration. Most waders (shore birds) that breed in the Arctic migrate southwards without moulting, but then pause and moult somewhere on the migration route. Some species of warbler and flycatcher migrate southwards from their breeding grounds to other areas where they stop to feed and lay down fat reserves. The Blackpoll Warbler breeds mainly in coniferous forests in Canada, but migrates southwards to the northern United States where it stops to feed before setting off for Venezuela.

The European Swift spends as little time as possible in its breeding quarters. It arrives in Britain later than most other migrants, in late April or early May, and if conditions are good starts to breed immediately. It then migrates south to Africa as soon as the young leave the nest. The autumn departure of the Swift thus depends upon the time at which it starts breeding and on how quickly it can raise its young.

The timing of migration varies markedly between species, depending on the ecology of the particular species. It is important to realize that the timing is a product of natural selection, those individuals that migrate at the best time being those most likely to survive. This is the ultimate factor influencing the timing of migration, though the actual time of departure may be controlled by proximate cues as in the case with breeding.

## 9.7 Natural selection and migration

Migration routes and habits are generally thought to have evolved slowly over very long periods of time. However, there are two sorts of evidence which indicate that this is not necessarily true.

The first concerns the great change in habitats which occurred during the

Ice Ages. At the peak of the last glaciation, 15000 years ago, most of the North Temperate areas were covered with ice. The descendants of those species which had lived in temperate areas in the previous interglacial were confined to areas far to the south of their ancestral breeding areas. They probably continued to migrate north in the summer and south in the winter, but the distances would have been much shorter than they had been previously. As the ice receded, however, huge areas of the Palaearctic and Nearctic became habitable again, and birds probably exploited these areas as they became available. For most species this probably meant only a small expansion of their range initially, and only later, as the ice receded far to the north, did the long migration routes we see today develop. It is important to note that all the present routes are relatively recent and probably evolved during the last 5000–8000 years. Migration routes have probably changed markedly several times within the last million years, since during that time there have been four glaciations.

The Serin provides a clear example of recent evolution of migratory behaviour. This is a Mediterranean species which has spread over most of Europe during the last century. The areas it has colonized are much colder in winter than the Mediterranean, and the northern colonists have become migratory. Undoubtedly, those individuals which did not migrate suffered heavy winter mortality (Dorst, 1952).

We now know that many nocturnal migrants use some aspects of the star patterns to find their way (Emlen, 1967). However, the star patterns we see today are quite different from those of 1000–2000 years ago (Agron, 1962); species using these patterns must have had to adapt to changes in their navigational cues as well as in their habitats.

The second type of evidence concerning the evolution of migratory behaviour comes from experimental studies. These have shown that the timing of aspects such as migratory restlessness (Berthold and Querner, 1981) and the laying down of fat for migration, varies between different populations of the same species (Berthold and Querner, 1982). Studies of a European warbler, the Blackcap, using 'hybrids' between birds from Germany and the Cape Verde Islands, show migratory behaviours which are intermediate between those of the parent stocks. These studies have demonstrated that the timing of moult, the amount and pattern of migratory restlessness and the seasonal pattern of fat deposition are all under genetic control and therefore are readily influenced by natural selection. There is also evidence, from studies of Garden Warblers, that innate migratory directions vary between different populations, indicating that this aspect of migration is also under genetic control (Gwinner, 1981).

Studies of partial migrants such as the European Blackbird have shown that the young of parents which tend to migrate are much more likely to migrate themselves than are the offspring of parents which are resident. Indeed, this characteristic is so strongly inherited that a population could become almost entirely migratory or resident within just a few generations if conditions were such that the other form was very unsuccessful.

Successful migration is obviously a very important part of a birds' life so it is not surprising to find that many aspects of migratory behaviour are under strict genetic control. However, it is only in the past few years that painstaking research has confirmed what we expected.

## 9.8  Summary

This chapter examines some ecological and evolutionary aspects of migration. Migration encompasses a wide range of movements, but the best definition is 'a regular large-scale shift of the population between a restricted breeding area and a restricted winter area'. The scale of migration is dramatic—in the Palaearctic, 40% of bird species, comprising 5 000 million individuals, leave the Palaearctic for the winter. In wintering areas, the influx of migrants may result in competition with resident local populations. Migrants also face another ecological problem, in that their breeding and wintering areas may be very different.

Some species are partial migrants. In these, only some populations, or some individuals within a population, migrate. Irruptive species are a special type of partial migrant.

Migratory distances vary from a few km to 15000 km in the Arctic Tern. Birds flying from Europe to Africa, or from North America to Central America, fly about 6 000–10 000 km. The maximum distance covered in a single non-stop flight is about 3 000 km. Flight speeds range from 40–65 k.p.h., resulting in single flights lasting 46–75 hours. To make such journeys, birds lay down energy (fat) reserves; such reserves may double a bird's weight. Ten grams of fat on a 12 g warbler enable it to fly for 105–115 hours.

Evidence of recent changes in habitat due to glaciation and in astronomical patterns suggest that migration routes may not be as ancient as had formerly been thought—they may be only 5 000–8 000 years old. Many aspects of migratory behaviour, as demonstrated by recent experiments, are under strict genetic control and hence are readily influenced by natural selection. This is not surprising considering the importance of migration in bird life.

# REFERENCES

Abbott, I., Abbott, L. K. and Grant, P. R. (1977) Comparative ecology of Galapagos ground finches, *Geospiza*. Evaluation of the importance of floristic diversity and interspecific competition. *Ecol. Monogr.* **47**, 151–184.

Agron, S. L. (1962) Evolution of bird navigation and the earth's axial procession. *Evolution* **16**, 524–527.

Ainley, D. G. and De Master, D. P. (1980) Survival and mortality of Adélie Penguins. *Ecology* **61**, 522–530.

Alerstam, T., Nilsson, S. G. and Ulfstrand, S. (1974) Niche differentiation during winter in woodland in birds in southern Sweden and the island of Götland. *Oikos* **25**, 321–330.

Andersson, M. (1982) Female choice selects for extreme tail length in a widowbird. *Nature* **299**, 818–820.

Andrewartha, H. G. and Birch, L. C. (1960) *The Distribution and Abundance of Animals*, Chicago.

Ankey, C. D. and McInnes, C. D. (1978) Nutrient reserves and reproductive performance of female Lesser Snow Geese. *Auk* **95**, 459–471.

Ashmole, N. P. (1963*a*) The biology of the wideawake or Sooty Tern *Sterna fuscata* on Ascension Island. *Ibis* **103**, 297–364.

Ashmole, N. P. (1963*b*) The regulation of numbers of tropical oceanic birds. *Ibis* **103**, 458–473.

Ashmole, N. P. (1971) 'Seabird ecology and the marine environment', in *Avian Biology*, vol. 1, Farner, D. S. and King, J. R. (eds.) Academic Press, New York and London.

Baker, J. R. (1938) The relation between latitude and breeding season in birds. *Proc. Zool. Soc. Lond.* Series A **108**, 557–582.

Baker, R. R. (1978) *The Evolutionary Ecology of Animal Migration*, Hodder and Stoughton, London.

Balat, F. (1977) The effect of local suppression of nesting competition of *Passer montanus* on the utilisation of nest boxes by other bird species. *Folia Zool.* **26**, 341–353.

Balda, R. R. and Bateman, G. C. (1971) Flocking and annual cycle of the Pinon Jay *Gymnorhinus cyanocephalus*. *Condor* **73**, 287–302.

Balen, J. H. van, (1973) A comparative study of the breeding ecology of the Great Tit *Parus major* in different habitats. *Ardea* **61**, 1–93.

Bartholomew, G. A. (1942) The fishing activities of Double-Crested Cormorants on San Francisco Bay. *Condor* **44**, 13–21.

Bartholomew, G. A., Howell, T. R. and Cade, T. J. (1957) Torpidity in the White-throated Swift, Anna Hummingbird and the Poorwill. *Condor* **59**, 145–155.

Beintema, A. J. (1978) Eierzoeken en Vogelbescherming. *Vogeljaar* **25**, 21–27.

Berthold, P. and Querner, W. (1981) Genetic basis of migratory behaviour in European warblers. *Science* **212**, 77–79.

Berthold, P. (1982) Partial migration in birds: experimental proof of polymorphism as a controlling system. *Experientia* **38**, 805–806.

Berthold, P. and Querner, U. (1982) Genetic basis of moult, wing-length and body weight in a migratory bird species, *Sylvia atricapilla. Experientia* **38**, 801–802.

Bertram, B. C. R. (1980) Vigilance and group size in ostriches. *Anim. Behav.* **28**, 278–286.

Betts, M. M. (1955) The food of titmice in oak woodland. *J. Anim. Ecol.* **24**, 282–323.

Beven, G. (1976) Changes in breeding bird populations of an oak-wood on Bookham Common. Survey over twenty-seven years. *London Naturalist* **55**, 23–42 (plus annual results in subsequent volumes).

Bibby, C. J. and Green, R. E. (1980) Foraging behaviour of migrant Pied Flycatchers *Ficedula hypoleuca* on temporary territories. *J. Anim. Ecol.* **49**, 507–521.

Biebach, H. (1978) Regelungsmechanismus zur Reduktion der Warmeverluste bei Anseln. *Verh. Dt. Zool. Ges.* **203,**

Birkhead, M. E. (1981) The social behaviour of the Dunnock *Prunella modularis. Ibis* **123**, 75–84.

Birkhead, T. R. (1977) The effect of habitat and density on breeding success in Common Guillemots *(Uria aalge). J. Anim. Ecol.* **46**, 751–764.

Birkhead, T. R. (1979) Mate guarding in the Magpie *Pica pica. Anim. Behav.* **27**, 866–874.

Birkhead, T. R. (1982) Timing and duration of mate-guarding in Magpies *Pica pica. Anim. Behav.* **30**, 277–283.

Blondel, J. and Isenmann, P. (1979) Insularité et demographie des Mesanges du genre *Parus* (Aves). *Comptes. r. hebd. Séanc. Acad. Sci. Paris* **289**, 161–164.

Bossema, I. (1979) Jays and oaks: and eco-ethological study of symbiosis. *Behaviour* **70**, 1–17.

Boyden, T. C. (1978) Territorial defense against Hummingbirds and insects by tropical Hummingbirds. *Condor* **80**, 216–221.

Bromssen, A. von and Jansson, C. (1980) Effects of food addition to Willow Tit, *Parus montannus* and Crested Tit *P. cristatus* at the time of breeding. *Ornis Scand.* **11**, 173–178.

Brooke, M. de L. (1979) Differences in the quality of territories held by Wheatears (*Oenanthe oenanthe). J. Anim. Ecol.* **48**, 21–32.

Brown, J. L. (1963) Social organisation and behavior of the Mexican Jay. *Condor* **65**, 126–153.

Brown, J. L. (1964) The evolution of diversity in avian territorial systems. *Wilson Bull.* **76**, 160–169.

Brown, J. L. (1969) The buffer effect and productivity in Tit populations. *Amer. Nat.* **103**, 347–354.

Brown, J. L. (1978) Avian communal breeding systems. *Ann. Rev. Ecol. Syst.* **9**, 123–155.

Brown, J. L. and Brown, E. R. (1981) 'Kin selection and individual selection in Babblers', in *Natural Selection and Social Behaviour: Recent Research and New Theory,* Alexander, R.D. and Tinkle, D.W. (eds.). Chiron Press, New York.

Brown, L. H., Urban, E. K. and Newman, K. (1982) *The Birds of Africa,* Vol. 1, Academic Press, London.

Bruning, D. F. (1974) Social structure and reproductive behaviour in the Greater Rhea. *The Living Bird* **13**, 251–294.

Bryant, D. M. (1979) Reproductive costs in the House Martin. *J. Anim. Ecol.* **48**, 655–675.

Bryant, D. M. and Turner, A. K. (1982) Central place foraging by swallows (Hirundinidae): the question of load size. *Anim. Behav.* **30**, 845–856.

Buckley, P. A. and Buckley, F. G. (1977) Hexagonal packing of Royal Tern nests. *Auk* **94**, 36–43.

Bulmer, M. G. and Perrins, C. M. (1973) Mortality in the Great Tit, *Parus major. Ibis* **115**, 277–281.

Bunn, D. S., Warburton, A. B. and Wilson, R. D. S. (1982) *The Barn Owl*. Poyser, Calton.

Camin, J. H. and Moss, W. W. (1970) Nest parasitism, productivity, and clutch-size in Purple Martins. *Science* **1968**, 1000–1002.

Caraco, T., Martindale, S. and Whitham, T. S. (1980) An empirical demonstration of risk-sensitive foraging preferences. *Anim. Behav.* **28**, 820–830.

Chance, E. P. (1940) The truth about the Cuckoo. *Country Life*, London.

Chapin, J. P. and Wing, L. W. (1959) The Wideawake Calendar, 1953 to 1958. *Auk* **76**, 153–158.

Charnov, E. L. (1976) Optimal foraging: the marginal value theorem. *Theor. Popul. Biol.* **9**, 129–136.

Charnov, E. L. and Krebs, J. R. (1974) On clutch-size and fitness. *Ibis* **116**, 217–219.

Chitty, D. (1970) Variation and population density. *Symp. Zool. Soc. Lond.* **26**, 327–333.

Christian, J. J. (1971) Population density and reproductive efficiency. *Biol. Reprod.* **4**, 248–294.

Clapham, C. S. (1964) The birds of the Dahlac archipelago. *Ibis* **106**, 376–388.

Cody, M. L. (1971) Finch flocks in the Mohave desert. *Theor. Popul. Biol.* **2**, 142–148.

Comfort, A. (1956). *The Biology of Senescence*. Routledge and Kegan Paul, London.

Coulson, J. C. (1956) Mortality and egg production of the Meadow Pipit with special reference to altitude. *Bird Study* **3**, 119–132.

Coulson, J. C. (1960) A study of the mortality of the Starling based on ringing recoveries. *J. Anim. Ecol.* **29**, 251–271.

Coulson, J. C. and White, E. (1961) An analysis of the factors influencing the clutch-size of the Kittiwake. *Proc. Zool. Soc. (Lond.)* **136**, 207–217.

Coulson, J. C. (1968) Differences in the quality of birds nesting in the centre and on the edges of a colony. *Nature* **217**, 478–479.

Coulson, J. C. and Horobin, J. (1976) The influence of age on the breeding biology and survival of the Arctic Tern *Sterna paradisaea. J. Zool. Lond.* **178**, 247–260.

Cowie, R. J. (1977) Optimal foraging in Great Tits (*Parus major*). *Nature* **268**, 137–139.

Crook, J. H. (1965) The adaptive significance of avian.social organisation. *Symp. Zool. Soc. Lond.* **14**, 181–218.

Crowell, K. L. (1962) Reduced interspecific competition among birds of Bermuda. *Ecology* **43**, 79–88.

Crowell, K. L. and Rothstein, S. I. (1981) Clutch-sizes and breeding strategies among Bermudan and North American passerines. *Ibis* **123**, 42–50.

Davies, N. B. (1977) Prey selection and social behaviour in Wagtails (Aves: Motacillidae). *J. Anim. Ecol.* **46**, 37–57.

Davies, N. B. (1978) 'Ecological questions about territorial behaviour', in *Behavioural Ecology: An Evolutionary Approach*, Krebs, J. R. and Davies, N. B. (eds.) Blackwell Scientific Publications, Oxford, pp. 317–350.

Davies, N. B. (1980) The economics of territorial behaviour in birds. *Ardea* **68**, 63–74.

Davis, J. (1973) Habitat preferences and competition of wintering juncos and golden crowned sparrows. *Ecology* **54**, 174–180.

Dawkins, R. (1976) *The Selfish Gene*. Oxford University Press, Oxford.

De Groot, P. (1980) A study of the acquisition of information concerning resources by individuals in small groups of Red-Billed Weaver Birds *Quelea quelea*. Ph.D. Thesis, University of Bristol.

Diamond, A. W., (1976) Subannual breeding and moult cycles in the Bridled Tern *Sterna anaethetus* in the Seychelles. *Ibis* **118**, 414–419.

Diamond, J. M. (1975) 'Assembly of species communities', in *Ecology and Evolution of Communities*, Cody, M. L. and Diamond, J. M. (eds.). Harvard University Press.

Din, N. A. and Eltringham, S. K. (1974) Breeding of the Pink-Backed Pelican *Pelecanus rufescens* in Ruwenzori National Park, Uganda; with notes on a colony of Marabou Storks *Leptoptilos crumeniferus. Ibis* **116**, 477–493.

Dorst, J. (1951) *The Migrations of Birds*. Heinemann, London.

Drent, R. H. and Daan, S. (1980) The prudent parent: energetic adjustments in avian breeding. *Ardea* **68**, 225–252.

Duffy, D. C. (1983) The ecology of tick parasitism on densely nesting Peruvian seabirds. *Ecology* **64**, 110–119.

Duncker, H. R. (1978) 'General morphological principles of amniotic lungs', in *Respiratory Function in Birds, Adult and Embryonic*, Piiper, J. (ed.). Springer-Verlag, Berlin.

Dunn, E. K. (1972) Effect of age on the fishing ability of Sandwich Terns, *Sterna sandvicensis*. *Ibis* **114**, 360–366.

Dunn, E. K. (1977) Predation by weasels (*Mustela nivalis*) on breeding tits (*Parus* spp.) in relation to the density of tits and rodents. *J. Anim. Ecol.* **46**, 633–652.

Dymond, J. R. (1947) Fluctuations in animal populations with special reference to those of Canada. *Trans. Roy. Soc. Canada* **41**, 1–34.

Einarsen, A. S. (1945) Some factors affecting Ring-necked Pheasant population density. *Murrelet* **26**, 3–9, 39–44.

Elton, C. S. (1927) *The Ecology of Animals*. Methuen, London.

Emlen, S. T. (1967) Migratory orientation in the Indigo Bunting, *Passerina cyanea*. Part II, Mechanism of celestial orientation. *Auk* **84**, 463–489.

Emlen, S. T. (1978) 'The evolution of co-operative breeding in birds', in *Behavioural Ecology: An Evolutionary Approach*, Krebs, J. R. and Davies, N. B. (eds.). Blackwell Scientific Publications, Oxford, pp. 245–281.

Emlen, S. T. and Ambrose, H. W. (1970) Feeding interactions of Snowy Egrets and Red-breasted Mergansers. *Auk* **87**, 164–165.

Emlen, S. T. and Oring, L. W. (1977) Ecology, sexual selection, and the evolution of mating systems. *Science* **197**, 215–223.

Ewald, P. W. and Rohwer, S. (1982) Effects of supplemental feeding on timing of breeding, clutch-size and polygyny in Red-Winged Blackbirds *Agelaius phoeniceus. J. Anim. Ecol.* **51**, 429–450.

Feare, C. J. (1976) The breeding of the Sooty Tern *Sterna fuscata* in the Seychelles and the effects of experimental removal of eggs. *J. Zool.* **179**, 317–360.

Finney, G. and Cooke, F. (1978) Reproductive habits in the Snow Goose: the influence of female age. *Condor* **80**, 147–158.

Fleischer, R. C. (1982) Clutch size in Costa Rican House Sparrow. *J. Field Ornithol.* **53**, 280–281.

Frame, L. H., Malcolm, J. R., Frame, G. W. and Lawick, H. van. (1979) Social organisation of African wild dogs (*Lycaon pictus*) on the Serengeti plains, Tanzania, 1967–1978. *Z. Tierpsychol.* **50**, 225–249.

Fretwell, S. D. (1972) *Populations in a Seasonal Environment*. Princeton University Press, Princeton.

Frith, H. J. (1962) *The Mallee Fowl*. Angus and Robertson, Sydney.

Garson, P. J., Pleszczynska, W. K. and Holm, G. H. (1981) The "polygyny threshold" model: a reassessment. *Can. J. Zool.* **59**(6), 902–910.

Gaston, A. J. (1978) The evolution of group territorial behaviour and cooperative breeding. *Amer. Natur.* **112**, 1091–1100.

Gaston, A. J. (in press) 'Development of the young', in *The Atlantic Alcidae*, Nettleship D. N. and Birkhead, T. R. (eds.). Academic Press, London.

Gaston, A. J., Chapdelaine, and D. G. Noble (in prep). The growth of thick-billed Murre chicks at colonies in Hudson Strait: inter and intracolony variation.

Geis, A. D., Martinson, R. K. and Anderson, D. R. (1969) Establishing hunting regulations and allowable harvest of Mallards in the United States. *J. Wildl. Manag.* **33**, 848–859.

Gibb, J. A. (1950) The breeding biology of Great and Blue Titmice. *Ibis* **92**, 507–539.

Gibb, J. A. (1954) The feeding ecology of tits, with notes on the Treecreeper and Goldcrest, *Ibis* **96**, 513–543.

Gibb, J. A. (1955) Feeding rates of Great Tits. *Brit. Birds* **48**, 49–58.

Gill, F. B. and Wolf, L. L. (1975) Economics of feeding territoriality in the Golden-Winged Sunbird. *Ecology* **56**, 333–345.

Goss-Custard, J. D. (1970) 'Feeding dispersion in some overwintering wading birds', in *Social Behaviour in Birds and Mammals*, Crook J. M. (ed.). Academic Press, London, pp. 3–34.

Goss-Custard, J. D. (1976) Variation in the dispersion of Redshank (*Tringa totanus*) on their winter feeding grounds. *Ibis* **118**, 257–263.

Goss-Custard, J. D. (1977) Optimal foraging and the size selection of worms by Redshank *Tringa totanus*. *Anim. Behav.* **25**, 10–29.

Goss-Custard, J. D. (1980) Competition for food and interference among Waders. *Ardea* **68**, 31–52.

Gwinner, E. (1981) Ein endogenes Flug-program der Zugvogel. *Umschau* **81**, 248–249.

Haartman, L. von (1967) Clutch-size in the pied flycatcher. *Proc. XIV Intern. Orn. Congr.*, 155–164.

Haartman, L. von (1973) Talgmespopulationen Lemsjoholm. *Lintumeis* **8**, 7–9.

Hardin, G. (1960) The competitive exclusion principle. *Science* **131**, 1292–1297.

Harris, M. P. (1970) Territory limiting the size of the breeding population of the Oystercatcher (*Haematopus ostralegus*)—a removal experiment. *J. Anim. Ecol.* **39**, 707–713.

Harris, M. P. (1983) Biology and survival of the immature Puffin, *Fratercula arctica*. *Ibis* **125**, 56–73.

Hays, H. (1972) Polyandry in the Spotted Sandpiper. *Living Bird* **11**, 43–57.

Hinde, R. A. (1956) The biological significance of the territories of birds. *Ibis* **98**, 340–369.

Hogstedt, G. (1980) Prediction and test of the effects of interspecfic competition. *Nature* **283**, 64–66.

Hogstedt, G. (1980) Evolution of clutch-size in birds: adaptive variation in relation to territory quality. *Science* **210**, 1148–1150.

Hoogland, J. L. and Sherman, P. W. (1976) Advantages and disadvantages of Bank Swallow (*Riparia riparia*) coloniality. *Ecol. Monogr.* **46**, 33–58.

Hopkins, A. D. (1938) Bioclimatics, a science of life and climate relations. *U.S. Dept. Agr., Misc. Publ.* **280**.

Houston, A. I. (1980) 'Godzilla versus the creature from the black lagoon', in *The Analysis of Motivational Processes*, Toates, F. M. and Halliday, T. R. (eds.). Academic Press, London and New York, pp. 297–318.

Houston, D. C. (1976) Breeding of the White-Backed and Ruppell's Griffon Vultures, *Gyps africanus* and *G. rueppellii*. *Ibis* **118**, 14–40.

Hunt, G. L. and Hunt, M. W. (1976) Gull chick survival: the significance of growth rates, timing of breeding and territory size. *Ecology* **57**, 62–75.

Hussell, D. T. (1972) Factors affecting clutch-size in Arctic passerines. *Ecol. Monogr.* **42**, 317–364.

Hutchinson, G. E. (1957) Concluding remarks, *Cold Spring Harbor Symposia on Quantitative Biology* **22**, 415–427.

Hutchinson, G. E. (1959) Homage to Santa Rosalia, or, Why are there so many species of animals? *Amer. Nat.* **193**, 145–159.

Huxley, J. S. (1934) A natural experiment on the territorial instinct. *Brit. Birds* **27**, 270–277.

Immelmann, K. (1971) 'Ecological aspects of periodic reproduction', in *Avian Biology*, Vol. I, Farner D. S. and King, J. R. (eds.). Academic Press, New York and London, pp. 341–389.

Jarvis, M. J. F. (1974) The ecological significance of clutch-size in the South African Gannet (*Sula capensis* Lichtenstein). *J. Anim. Ecol.* **43**, 1–17.

Jenkins, D. J., Watson, A. and Miller, G. R. (1963) Population studies on Red Grouse, *Lagopus lagopus scoticus* (L) in northeast Scotland. *J. Anim. Ecol.* **32**, 317–376.

Jenni, D. A. (1974) Evolution of polyandry in birds. *Amer. Zool.* **14**, 129–144.

Jones, P. J. (1976) The ulitization of calcareous grit by laying *Quelea quelea*. *Ibis* **118**, 575–576.

Jones, P. J. and Ward, P. (1976) The level of reserve protein as the proximate factor controlling the timing of breeding and clutchsize in the Red-Billed Quelea, *Quelea quelea. Ibis* **118**, 547–574.

Kallander, H. (1974) Advancement of laying of Great Tits by the provision of food. *Ibis* **116**, 365–367.

Karr, J. (1971) A comparative study of the structure of avian communities in selected Panama and Illinois habitats. *Ecol. Monogr.* **41**, 207–233.

Kear, J. and Berger, A. J. (1980) *The Hawaiian Goose.* Poyser, Calton.

Keast, A. and Morton, E. S. (Eds.) (1980) *Migrant Birds in the Neotropics.* Smithsonian Inst., Washington.

Keeton, W. T. (1980) Avian orientation and navigation: new developments in an old mystery. *Proc. XVII Intern. Orn. Cong., Berlin* 137–157.

Kenward, R. E. (1978) Hawks and doves: attack success and selection in Goshawk flights at Woodpigeons. *J. Anim Ecol.* **47**, 449–460.

Klomp, H. (1970) The determination of clutch-size in birds. *Ardea* **58**, 1–124.

Klopfer, P. H. and MacArthur, R. H. (1961) On the causes of tropical species diversity: niche overlap. *Amer. Nat.* **95**, 223–226.

Kluijver, H. N. (1935) Waarnemingen over de levenswijze van den Spreeuw (*Sturnus v. vulgaris*) met behulp van geringde individuen. *Ardea* **24**, 133–136.

Kluijver, H. N. (1951) The population ecology of the Great Tit *Parus m. major* L. *Ardea* **39**, 1–135.

Kluijver, H. N. and Tinbergen, L. (1953) Territory and the regulation of density in Titmice. *Arch. Neerl. Zool.* **10**, 265–289.

Kluyver, H. N. (1966) Regulation of a bird population. *Ostrich* Suppl. **6**, 389–396.

Kluyver, H. N. (1971) Regulation of numbers in populations of Great Tit *(Parus m. major). Proc. Adv. Study Inst. Dynamics Numbers Popul.* (Oosterbeek 1970), 507–523.

Koenig, W. D. (1981) Reproductive success, group size, and the evolution of cooperative breeding in the Acorn Woodpecker. *Am. Nat.* **117**, 421–443.

Koenig, W. D. and Pitelka, F. A. (1981) 'Ecological factors and kin selection in the evolution of cooperative breeding in birds', in *Natural Selection and Social Behaviour: Recent Research and New Theory*, Alexander, R. D. Tinkle, D. W. (eds.). Chiron Press, New York.

Krebs, C. J. (1978) *Ecology: The Experimental Analysis of Distribution and Abundance*, 2nd edition. Harper and Row, New York.

Krebs, J. R. (1970a) Regulation of numbers in the Great Tit (Aves: Passeriformes). *J. Zool. Lond,* **162**, 317–333.

Krebs, J. R. (1970b) The efficiency of courtship feeding in the Blue Tit, *Parus caeruleus. Ibis* **112**, 108–110.

Krebs, J. R. (1971) Territory and breeding density in the Great Tit *Parus major* L. *Ecology* **52**, 2–22.

Krebs, J. R. (1974) Colonial nesting and social feeding as strategies for exploiting food resources in the Great Blue Heron (*Ardea herodias*). *Behaviour* **51**, 99–134.

Krebs, J. R. (1977) 'Song and territory in the Great Tit', in *Evolutionary Ecology*, Stonehouse B. and Perrins, C.M. (eds.). Macmillan, London, pp. 47–62.

Krebs, J. R. (1978) 'Optimal foraging: decision rules for predators', in *Behavioural Ecology: An Evolutionary Approach*, Krebs, J. R. and Davies, N. B. (eds.). Blackwell Scientific Publications, Oxford, pp. 23–63.

Krebs, J. R. and Cowie, R. J. (1976) Foraging strategies in birds. *Ardea* **64**, 98–116.

Krebs, J. R., Erichsen, J. T., Webber, M. I. and Charnov, E. L. (1977) Optimal prey selection in the Great Tit *(Parus major). Anim. Behav.* **25**, 30–38.

Krebs, J. R. and Davies, N. B. (eds.) (1978) *Behavioural Ecology: An Evolutionary Approach.* Blackwell Scientific Publications, Oxford.

Krebs, J. R. and Davies, N. B. (eds.) (1981) *An Introduction to Behavioural Ecology.* Blackwell Scientific Publications, Oxford.

Kruuk, H. (1964) Predators and anti-predator behaviour of the Black-Headed Gull *Larus ridibundus*. *Behaviour Suppl.* **11**, 1–129.

Kruuk, H. (1972) *The Spotted Hyena*. University of Chicago Press, Chicago and London.

Lack, D. (1943) *The Life of the Robin*. Witherby, London.

Lack, D. (1947) The significance of clutch-size in the Partridge *(Perdix perdix)*. *J. Anim. Ecol.* **16**, 19–25.

Lack, D. (1947–48) The significance of clutch-size. *Ibis* **89**, 302–352, **90**, 25–45.

Lack, D. (1948) Natural selection and family size in the Starling. *Evolution* **2**, 95–110.

Lack, D. (1948) The significance of litter-size. *J. Anim. Ecol.* **17**, 45–50.

Lack, D. (1954) *The Natural Regulation of Animal Numbers*. Clarendon Press, Oxford.

Lack, D. (1956) *Swifts in a Tower*. Methuen, London.

Lack, D. (1966) *Population Studies of Birds*. Clarendon Press, Oxford.

Lack, D. (1967) Interrelationships in breeding adaptations as shown by marine birds. *Proc XIV Intern. Orn. Congr. Oxford*, 3–31.

Lack, D. (1968) *Ecological Adaptations for Breeding in Birds*. Methuen, London.

Lack, D. (1969) The numbers of bird species on islands. *Bird Study* **16**, 193–209.

Lack, D. (1971) *Ecological Isolation in Birds*. Blackwell, Oxford.

Lack, D. (1976) *Island Biology*. Blackwell, Oxford and London.

Lack, D. and Moreau, R. E. (1965) Clutch-size in tropical passerine birds of forest and savanna. *Oiseau* **35**, No. Special, 76–89.

Lill, A. (1974) Sexual behavior of the lek-forming White-Bearded Manakin (*Manacus manacus trinitatis* Hartert). *Z. Tierpsychol.* **36**, 1–36.

Lill, A. (1976) Lek behavior in the Golden-Headed Manakin *Pipra erythrocephala* in Trinidad (West Indies). *Z. Tierpsychol. Suppl.* **18**.

Lotka, A. J. (1925) *Elements of Physical Biology*. Baltimore.

MacArthur, R. H. (1957) On the relative abundance of bird species. *Proc. Nat. Acad. Sci.* **43**, 293–295.

MacArthur, R. H. (1958) Population ecology of some warblers of northeastern coniferous forests. *Ecology* **39**, 599–619.

MacArthur, R. H. (1972) *Geographical Ecology*. Harper and Row, New York.

MacArthur, R. H. and Wilson, E. O. (1967) *The Theory of Island Biogeography*. Princeton University Press.

MacArthur, R. H., Diamond, J. M. and Karr, J. R. (1972) Density compensation in island faunas. *Ecology* **53**, 330–342.

MacLean, S. F. (1974) Lemming bones as a source of calcium for Arctic Sandpipers. *Ibis* **116**, 552–557.

Martin, S. G. (1974) Adaptations for polygynous breeding in the Bobolink *Dolichonyx oryzivorus*. *Am. Zool.* **14**, 109–119.

Mayfield, H. (1961) Cowbird parasitism and the population of Kirtland's Warbler. *Evolution* **15**, 174–179.

Maynard Smith, J. (1964) Group selection and kin selection. *Nature* **201**, 1145–1147.

Miller, A. H. (1955) Breeding cycles in a constant equatorial environment in Colombia, South America. *Proc. XI Intern. Orn. Congr. Basel* 495–503.

Mills, J. A. (1973) The influence of age and pair-bond on the breeding biology of the Red-billed Gull *Larus novaehollandiae scopulinus*. *J. Anim. Ecol.* **42**, 147–162.

Mills, J. A. and Mark, A. F. (1977) Food preferences of Takahe in Fiordland National Park, New Zealand, and the effect of competition from introduced red deer. *J. Anim. Ecol.* **46**, 939–958.

Mineau, P. and Cooke, F. (1979) Rape in the Lesser Snow Goose. *Behaviour* **70**, 280–291.

Minot, E. O. (1981) Effects of interspecific competition for food in breeding Blue and Great Tits. *J. Anim. Ecol.* **50**, 375–385.

Moreau, R. E. (1947) Relations between number in brood, feeding rate and nestling period in nine species of birds in Tanganyika Territory. *J. Anim. Ecol.* **16**, 205–209.

Moreau, R. E. (1952) The place of Africa in the palaearctic migration system. *J. Anim. Ecol.* **21**, 250–271.

Moreau, R. E. (1972) *The Palaearctic-African Migration Systems.* Academic Press, London.

Morse, D. H. (1970) Ecological aspects of some mixed species of foraging flocks of birds. *Ecol. Monogr.* **40**, 119–168.

Murphy, E. C. (1978) Breeding ecology of House Sparrows: spatial variation. *Condor* **80**, 180–193.

Murton, R. K. (1965) *The Wood-Pigeon.* Collins, London.

Murton, R. K. and Westwood, N. J. (1977) *Avian Breeding Cycles.* Clarendon Press, Oxford.

Nelson, J. B. (1964) Factors influencing clutch-size and chick growth in the North Atlantic Gannet *Sula bassana. Ibis* **106**, 63–77.

Nelson, J. B. (1978) *The Sulidae: Gannets and Boobies.* Oxford University Press.

Newton, I. (1972) *Finches.* Collins, London.

Newton, I. (1976) Breeding of Sparrowhawks (*Accipiter nisus*) in different environments. *J. Anim. Ecol.* **45**, 830–849.

Newton, I. (1979) *Population Ecology of Raptors.* Poyser, Berkhampstead.

Newton, I., Marquiss, M., Weir, D. N. and Moss, D. (1977) Spacing of Sparrowhawk nesting territories. *J. Anim. Ecol.* **46**, 425–441.

Nicolai, J. (1974) Mimicry in parasitic birds. *Scientific Amer.* **231**, 93–98.

Nilsson, S. G. (1977) Density compensation among birds breeding on small islands in a south Swedish lake. *Oikos* **28**, 170–176.

Nisbet, I. C. T., Drury, W. H. and Baird, J. (1963) Weight loss during migration. Part 1: Deposition and consumption of fat by the Blackpoll Warbler, *Dendroica striata. Bird-Banding* **34**, 107–138.

Nisbet, I. C. T. (1973) Courtship feeding, egg-size and breeding success in Common Terns. *Nature* **241**, 141–142.

Nisbet, I. C. T. (1975) Selective effects of predation in a Tern colony. *Condor* **77**, 221–226.

Nisbet, I. C. T. (1977) 'Courtship feeding and clutch-size in Common Terns *Sterna hirundo*', in *Evolutionary Ecology*, Stonehouse, B. and Perrins, C. M. (eds.). Macmillan, London.

Noble, G. K. (1939) The role of dominance in the social life of birds. *Auk* **56**, 263–273.

Noordwijk, A. J. van, Balen, J. H. van and Scharloo, W. (1980) Heritability of ecologically important traits in the Great Tit. *Ardea* **68**, 193–203.

O'Connor, R. J. (1978) Growth strategies in nestling passerines. *The Living Bird* **16**, 209–238.

Ogilvie, M. A. and St. Joseph, A. K. M. (1976) The Dark-bellied Brent Goose in Britain and Europe, 1955–76. *Brit. Birds* **69**, 422–439.

Orians, G. H. (1961) The ecology of Blackbird (*Agelaius*) social systems. *Ecol. Monogr.* **31**, 285–312.

Orians, G. H. (1969) On the evolution of mating systems in birds and mammals. *Amer. Natur.* **103**, 589–603.

Orians, G. H. (1980) *Some Adaptations of Marsh-Nesting Blackbirds.* Princeton University Press, Princeton.

Orians, G. H. and Pearson, N. E. (1979) 'On the theory of central place foraging', in *Analysis of Ecological Systems*, Horn, D. I. Mitchell, R. D. and Stairs, G. R. (eds.). Ohio State University Press, Ohio, pp. 155–177.

Owen, D. F. (1977) 'Latitudinal gradients in clutch size: an extension of Lack's theory', in *Evolutionary Ecology*, Stonehouse B. and Perrins, C.M. (eds.). Macmillan, London.

Owen, M. (1980) *Wild Geese of the World.* Batsford, London.

Parsons, J. (1971) Cannibalism in Herring Gulls. *Brit. Birds* **64**, 528–537.

Patterson, I. J. (1965) Timing and spacing of broods in the Black-Headed Gull *Larus ridibundus. Ibis.* **107**, 433–459.

Patterson, I. (1982) *The Shelduck: a Study in Behavioural Ecology.* Cambridge University Press.

Payne, R. B. (1974) The evolution of clutch size and reproductive rates in parasitic Cuckoos. *Evolution* **28**, 169–181.

Payne, R. B. (1977) The ecology of brood parasitism in birds. *Ann. Rev. Ecol. Syst.* **8**, 1–28.

Payne, R. B. and Payne, K. (1977) Social organization and mating success in local song populations of Village Indigobirds. *Vidua chalybeata. Z. Tierpsychol.* **45**, 113–173.

Paynter, R. A. (1966) A new attempt to construct lifetables for Kent Island Herring Gulls. *Bull. Harvard Univ. Mus. Comp. Anatomy* **133**, 491–528.

Peek, F. W. (1972) An experimental study of the territorial function of vocal and visual display in the male Red-Winged Blackbird *(Agelaius phoeniceus). Anim. Behav.* **20**, 112–118.

Penney, R. L. (1968) 'Territorial and social behaviour in the Adélie Penguin', in *Antarctic Bird Studies*, Austin, O.L. (ed.). pp. 83–131.

Perrins, C. M. (1965) Population fluctuations and clutch-size in the Great Tit, *Parus major* L. *J. Anim. Ecol.* **34**, 601–647.

Perrins, C. M. and Reynolds, C. M. (1967) A preliminary study of the Mute Swan, *Cygnus olor. Wildfowl Trust Ann. Rep.* **18**, 78–84.

Perrins, C. M. (1970) The timing of birds' breeding seasons. *Ibis* **112**, 242–255.

Perrins, C. M., Harris, M. P. and Britton, C. K. (1973) Survival of Manx Shearwaters *Puffinus puffinus. Ibis.* **115**, 535–548.

Perrins, C. M. and Moss, D. (1974) Survival of young Great Tits in relation to age of female parent. *Ibis* **116**, 220–224.

Perrins, C. M. and Moss, D. (1975) Reproductive rates in the Great Tit. *J. Anim. Ecol.* **44**, 695–706.

Perrins, C. M. (1977) 'The role of predation in the evolution of clutch-size', in *Evolutionary Ecology*, Stonehouse, B. and Perrins, C. M. (eds). Macmillan, London.

Perrins, C. M. (1979) *British Tits.* Collins, London.

Perrins, C. M. (1980) Survival of young Great Tits, *Parus major. Proc XVII Intern. Orn. Congr.*, 159–174.

Perrins, C. M. and Ogilvie, M. A. (1981) A study of the Abbotsbury Mute Swans. *Wildfowl* **32**, 35–47.

Peterson, R. T. (1948). *Birds Over America.* New York.

Pitelka, F. A., Holmes, R. T. and MacLean, S. F. Jr. (1974) Ecology and evolution of social organisation in Arctic Sandpipers. *Amer. Zool.* **14**. 185–204.

Plesczynska, W. K. (1978) Microgeographic prediction of polygyny in the lark bunting. *Science*, **201**, 935–937.

Plesczynska, W. and Hansell, R. I. C. (1980) Polygyny and Decision theory: Testing of a model in lark buntings *(Calamospiza melanocorys) Amer. Natur.* **116**, 821–830.

Potts, G. R., Coulson, J. C. and Deans, I. R. (1980) Population dynamics and breeding success of the Shag, *Phalacrocorax aristotelis*, on the Farne Islands, Northumberland. *J. Anim. Ecol.* **49**, 465–484.

Powell, G. V. N. (1974) Experimental analysis of the social value of flocking by Starlings *(Sturnus vulgaris)* in relation to predation and foraging. *Anim. Behav.* **22**, 501–505.

Primack, R. B. and Howe, H. F. (1975) Interference competition between a Humming Bird *(Amazilia tzacatl)* and Skipper Butterfly (Hesperiidae). *Biotropica* 7(1) 55–58.

Prince, P. A. and Ricketts, C. (1981) Relationships between food supply and growth in albatrosses: an interspecific chick fostering experiment. *Orn. Scand.* **12**, 207–210.

Prins, H. H. Th., Ydenberg, R. C. and Drent, R. H. (1980) The interaction of Brent Geese *Branta bernicla* and sea plantain *Plantago maritima* during spring staging: field observations and experiments. *Acta Bot. Neerl.* **29**, 585–596.

Pulliam, H. R. and Brand, M. R. (1975) The production and utilisation of seeds. *Ecology* **56**, 1158–1166.

Pulliam, H. R. (1976) 'The principle of optimal behavior and the theory of communities', in *Perspectives in Ethology*, P. H. Klopfer and P. P. G. Bateson (eds.), pp. 311–332. Plenum Press, New York.

Pulliam, H. R. (1980) Do chipping sparrows forage optimally? *Ardea* **68**, 75–82.

Pyke, G. H. (1979) The economics of territory size and time budget in the Golden-Winged Sunbird. *Amer. Natur.* **114**, 131–145.

Reed, T. (1981) The number of breeding landbird species on British islands. *J. Anim. Ecol.* **50**, 613–624.

Reed, T. M. (1982) Interspecific territoriality in the Chaffinch and Great Tit on islands and the mainland of Scotland: playback and removal experiments. *Anim. Behav.* **30**, 171–181.

Ricklefs, R. E. (1973) *Ecology.* Nelson, London.

Ricklefs, R. E. (1977) On the evolution of reproductive strategies in birds: reproductive effort. *Amer. Nat.* **111**, 453–478.

Ricklefs, R. E. (1977) 'A note on the evolution of clutch size in altricial birds', in *Evolutionary Ecology*, Stonehouse, B. and Perrins, C. M. (eds.). Macmillan, London.

Ricklefs, R. E. (1980) Geographical variations in clutch-size among passerine birds: Ashmole's hypothesis. *Auk* **97**, 38–49.

Riddle, O. and R. W. Bates. (1939) 'The preparation, assay and action of lactogenic hormone', in *Sex and Internal Secretions*, Allen, E. (ed.), Williams and Wilkins, Baltimore, pp. 1088–1117.

Robertson, R. J. (1973) Optimal niche space of the Red-Winged Blackbird: spatial and temporal patterns of nesting activity and success. *Ecology* **54**, 1085–1093.

Rowan, W. (1926) On photoperiodism, reproductive periodicity and the annual migration of birds and certain fishes. *Proc. Boston Soc. Nat. Hist.* **38**, 147–189.

Rowley, I. (1965) The life history of the Superb Blue Wren, *Malurus cyaneus*. *Emu* **64**, 251–297.

Royama, T. (1966) A re-interpretation of courtship feeding. *Bird Study* **13**, 116–129.

Safriel, U. N. (1975) On the significance of clutch-size in nidifugous birds. *Ecology* **56**, 703–708.

Salomonsen, F. (1972) Zoogeographical and ecological problems in arctic birds. *Proc. XV. Intern. Orn. Congr.*, 25–77.

Schaller, G. B. (1972) *The Serengeti Lion.* Chicago University Press, Chicago.

Schifferli, L. (1977) Bruchstücke von Schneckenhaüschen als calciumquelle für die Bildung der Eischale beim Haussperling *Passer domesticus*. *Ornithol. Beobacht.* **74**, 71–74.

Schmidt-Koenig and Keeton, W. T. (eds.) (1978) *Animal Migration, Navigation and Homing.* Springer-Verlag, Berlin and New York.

Schoener, T. W. (1968) Sizes of feeding territories among birds. *Ecology* **49**, 123–141.

Scott, D. K. (1980) Functional aspects of prolonged parental care in Bewick's Swans. *Anim. Behav.* **28**, 938–952.

Serventy, D. L. (1971) 'Biology of desert birds,' in *Avian Biology*, Vol. 1, Farner, D. S. and King, J. R. (eds.) Academic Press, New York, London.

Shelford, V. E. (1945) The relation of Snowy Owl migration to the abundance of the Collared Lemming. *Auk* **62**, 592–596.

Sherrod, S. K., White, C. M. and Williamson, F. S. L. (1977) Biology of the Bald Eagle on Amchitka Island, Alaska. *Living Bird* **15**, 143–182.

Skutch, A. F. (1949) Do tropical birds raise as many young as they can nourish? *Ibis* **91**, 430–455.

Skutch, A. F. (1976) *Parent Birds and Their Young.* University Press, Texas.

Slagsvold, T. (1978) Competition between the Great Tit, *Parus major* and the Pied Flycatcher, *Ficedula hypoleuca*: an experiment. *Ornis. Scand.* **9**, 46–50.

Slud, P. (1976) Geographic and climatic relationships of avifaunas with special reference to comparative distribution in the Neotropics. *Smithsonian Contr. Zoology* **212**.

Smith, J. M. N., Montgomerie, R. D., Taitt, M. J. and Yom-Tov, Y. (1980) A winter feeding experiment on an island song sparrow population. *Oecologia* **47**, 164–170.

Snow, D. W. (1956) The annual mortality of the Blue Tit in different parts of its range. *Brit. Birds* **49**, 174–177.

Snow, D. W. (1958) *A Study of Blackbirds.* Methuen, London.

Snow, D. W. (1962) A field study of the Black and White Manakin, *Manacus manacus* in Trinidad. *Zoologica* **47**, 65–104.

Snow, D. W., and Lill, A. (1974) Longevity records for neotropical land birds. *Condor* **76**, 262–267.

Snow, D. W. (1976) *The Web of Adaptation: Bird Studies in the American Tropics*. Collins, London.

Southern, H. N. (1954) Tawny Owls and their prey. *Ibis* **96**, 384–410.

Southern, H. N. (1970) The natural control of a population of Tawny Owls (*Strix aluco*). *J. Zool. Lond.* **162**, 197–285.

Stallcup, J. A. and Woolfenden, G. E. (1978) Family status and contributions to breeding by Florida Scrub Jays. *Anim. Behav.* **26**, 1144–1156.

Stenger, J. (1958) Food habits and available food of Ovenbirds in relation to territory size. *Auk* **75**, 335–346.

Svärdson, G. (1957) The "invasion" type of bird migration. *Brit. Birds* **50**, 314–343.

Swynnerton, C. F. M. (1975) Mixed bird parties. *Ibis* **1915**, 346–528.

Tenaza, R. (1971) Behaviour and nesting success relative to nest location in Adelie Penguins (*Pygoscelis adeliae*). *Condor* **73**, 81–92.

Tomback, D. F. (1977) Foraging strategies of the Clark's nutcracker. *The Living Bird* **16**, 123–161.

Trivers, R. L. (1972) 'Parental investment and sexual selection,' in *Sexual Selection and the Descent of Man*, B. Campbell (ed). Aldine, Chicago.

Tschanz, B. (1959) Zur Brutbiologie du Trottellumme (*U. aalge aalge*). *Behaviour* **14**, 1–100.

Tschanz, B. (1968) Trottellummen (*U. aalge aalge*). *Z. Tierpsychol.* Suppl. **4**: 1–103.

Van Valen, L. (1965) Morphological variations and width of ecological niche. *Amer. Natur.* **99**, 377–390.

Varley, G. C. (1959) Density dependent factors in ecology. *Nature* **183**, 911.

Varley, G. C. (1963) The interpretation of change and stability in insect populations. *Proc. Int. Congr. Ent.* **10**, 619–624.

Vaughan, R. (1961) *Falco eleonorae*. Ibis **103**, 114–128.

Veen, J. (1977) *Functional and Causal Aspects of Nest Distribution in Colonies of the Sandwich Tern (Sterna s. sandvicensis* Lath.). Brill, Leiden.

Verner, J. and Willson, M. F. (1966) The influence of habitats on mating systems of North American passerine birds. *Ecology* **47**, 143–147.

Vince, M. A. (1969) 'Embryonic communication, respiration and the synchronization of hatching,' in *Bird Vocalizations*, Hinde, R. A. (ed.) Cambridge University Press.

Voitkevitch, A. A. (1966) *The Feathers and Plumage of Birds*. Sidgwick and Jackson, London.

Volterra, V. (1926) Variazioni e fluttuazioni del numero d'individui in specei animali conviventi. (Reprinted in *Animal Ecology*, R. N. Chapman, 1931, New York).

Ward, P. (1965) Feeding behaviour of the Black-Faced Dioch *Quelea quelea* in Nigeria. *Ibis* **107**, 173–214.

Ward, P. and Zahavi, A. (1973) The importance of certain assemblages of birds as 'information-centres' for food-finding. *Ibis* **115**, 517–534.

Watson, A. (1967) Territory and population regulation in the Red Grouse. *Nature* **215**, 1274–1275.

Watson, A. and Miller, G. R. (1971) Territory size and aggression in a fluctuating red grouse population. *J. Anim. Ecol.* **40**, 367–383.

Wiley, R. H. (1973) Territoriality and non-random mating in the Sage Grouse *Centrocercus urophasianus*. *Anim. Behav. Monogr.* **6**, 87–169.

Williams, G. C. (1966) Natural selection, the costs of reproduction, and a refinement of Lack's principle. *Amer. Nat.* **100**, 687–690.

Williamson, M. (1981) *Island Populations*. Oxford University Press.

Wilson, E. O. (1975) *Sociobiology: the New Synthesis*. Belknap Press, Harvard.

Witherby, H. F., Jourdain, F. C. B., Ticehurst, N. P. and Tucker, B. W. (1952) *The Handbook of British Birds*. Witherby, London.

Wittenberger, J. F. and Hunt, G. L. (in press) 'The adaptive significance of coloniality in birds,' in *Avian Biology*, Vol. 7, D. S. Farner and J. R. King (eds). Academic Press, New York and London.

Wittenberger, J. F. and Tilson, R. L. (1980) The evolution of monogamy: hypotheses and evidence. *Ann. Rev. Ecol. Syst.* **11**, 197–232.

Woolfenden, G. E. (1975) Florida Scrub Jay helpers at the nest. *Auk* **92**, 1–15.

Woolfenden, G. E. (1981) 'Selfish behaviour by Florida Scrub Jay helpers,' in *Natural Selection and Social Behaviour: Recent Research and New Theory*, R. D. Alexander and D. W. Tinkle (eds.), Chiron Press, New York.

Wynne-Edwards, V. C. (1955) Low reproductive rates in birds, especially Seabirds. *Proc. XI Intern. Orn. Congr., Basel* 540–547.

Wynne-Edwards, V. C. (1962) *Animal Dispersion in Relation to Social Behaviour*. Oliver and Boyd, Edinburgh.

Wynne-Edwards, V. C. (1978) 'Intrinsic population control: an introduction,' in *Population Control by Social Behaviour*, Ebling, F. J. and Stoddart, D. M. (eds.), Inst. of Biology, London.

Yom-Tov, Y. (1974) The effect of food and predation on breeding density and success, clutch-size and laying of the Crow (*Corvus corone* L.) *J. Anim. Ecol.* **43**, 479–498.

Yom-Tov, Y. (1980) Intraspecific nest parasitism in birds. *Biol. Rev.* **55**, 93–108.

Zimmerman, J. L. (1966) Polygyny in the Dickcissel. *Auk* **83**, 534–546.

# Index

The scientific names of the birds mentioned in the text are entered beside the English name, and *vice versa*.

213